ACEQUIA CULTURE

Water, Land, and Community

in the Southwest

JOSÉ A. RIVERA

Acequia Culture

WATER, LAND, AND COMMUNITY

IN THE SOUTHWEST

✢ ✢ ✢

University of New Mexico Press
Albuquerque

FIRST EDITION
Printed and bound in the United States of America

ISBN-13: 978-0-8263-1859-6

11 10 09 08 07 06 05   2 3 4 5 6 7 8

Library of Congress Cataloging-in-Publication Data
Rivera, José A., 1944–
Acequia culture: water, land, and community in the Southwest / José A. Rivera.
p. cm.
Includes index.
ISBN 0-8263-1858-4 (cloth). ISBN 0-8263-1859-2 (pbk.)
1. Water resources development—Economic aspects—Rio Grande Watershed—
History.
2. Watershed management—Rio Grande Watershed—History.
3. Land use—Rio Grande Watershed—History.
4. Rio Grande Watershed—Economic conditions.
5. Rio Grande Watershed—Social conditions.
6. Rio Grande Watershed—Environmental conditions—History.
1. Title.
HD1694.A3   1998
333.91'15'097644–dc21   98-23877
CIP

Contents

Documents

Illustrations

Maps

Documents

Photos

Preface

Water-resources planning is attracting unparalleled attention around the globe from local, national, and international bodies aware that a sustainable supply of water is crucial to meet growing demands today as well as the projected needs of future generations. Concern over water-management policies and practices is especially critical in arid and semiarid territories, which comprise approximately one-third of the earth's land surface. In the western United States, municipal, industrial, commercial agricultural, and other users increasingly look to new technologies and improved management practices as the means to recycle wastewater or to reduce consumption altogether.

At the same time, the era of large-scale water development, meant to harvest and channel water destined for urbanizing regions or to reclaim desert lands for agricultural production, is rapidly ending. In its place, a new conservation ethic is taking root across the spectrum of users and advocates, from computer-chip manufacturers to mayors of sunbelt cities. Conservation programs extol new water-conserving techniques and urge facilities managers, contractors, farmers, residential consumers, agency employees, and schoolchildren to modify wasteful behaviors. There is growing appreciation that while water is crucial to the survival of communities, it is also renewable, if managed conservatively.

In the long run, however, sustainability of water quantity and quality may depend more on democratic and social processes than on technological or regulatory fixes, particularly when incorporating regions of the world with diverse cultures and equally different, often conflictive, views of water. Past efforts by public officials to impose mandatory conservation and other agricultural practices show that forced or contrived interventions seldom work. The new thinking in development administration is to reach out to indigenous people and to accommodate sources of traditional or otherwise local knowledge where value systems perceive the resource base as an integrative system of community livelihood. Planners and other development officials now propose that cultural diversity itself is a global resource that should be preserved along with the need to maintain biodiversity. Advocates of this new perspective argue that indigenous peoples possess valuable information about community-based conservation methods that work.[1] Who better to conserve life-sustaining resources than land-based peoples and their communal institutions that depend on renewable natural resources?

Around the world, however, the traditional and political rights of land-based peoples are increasingly threatened by demands placed on the limited resource base and life support systems critical to continued survival. From region to region, sectors of the dominant economic and political order encroach on the grazing lands, river and irrigation-canal systems, forests, wildlife areas, fisheries, and other "common-pool resources" that have sustained local cultures over many generations.[2] For the most part, these resources have been renewable precisely because of human adaptation strategies that evolved at the time of initial appropriation, coupled with a strong conservation ethic to manage the resources not only for present needs, but for the livelihoods of heirs already born as well as those yet to come. Many of these traditional communities continue to eke out an existence in rather harsh environments where human life had not previously existed, such as the arid and semiarid climatic zones found throughout the world.

The 1992 Río de Janeiro Declaration and subsequent studies of environment and development have created renewed interest in traditional management systems that have withstood the test of time, regardless of differences in climate, topography, physiographic barriers, or other limitations on human survival.[3] Though diverse from one geographic setting to another, these practices are highly participatory, requiring stewardship of the community properties by the very cultures that depend on the resource base. In regimes of this type, decisions are made that ensure the continuation of regional peoples who control and manage communal resource properties for themselves and future generations. Repeatedly, development programs fail to utilize this reservoir of indigenous knowledge, "mistakenly relying instead on privatization or state ownership to solve development and natural resource problems."[4] There is growing evidence, however, that countries in both the Third World and the West are giving serious attention to alternative models of resources use that emphasize responsibility to the community and emanate from ancestral technologies and institutions embedded in the culture.[5]

Numerous field-research and case studies have documented that sustainability of earth's resources means more than the preservation of biodiversity. In the Southern Hemisphere of the Americas, for example, Redclift and Sage found that rural people who live closest to or in the midst of a valuable natural resource have the least to gain from practices that would exploit and consume the environment around them.[6] People residing in the outlying regions of many countries, while they may be economically poor, have a very large stake in acting as custodians of the resourse base on which their cultures depend. From Ghana to Mexico and the Philippines, according to Redclift and Sage, many development projects aimed at reducing poverty in rural sectors have failed because local environmental knowledge and cultural values were not incorporated, but instead were supplanted with capital-intensive technologies, ostensibly intended to "modernize" these underdeveloped regions.[7]

Yet in many parts of the world the fragile social ecology of traditional communities is under siege as market and other development pressures encroach on the resource base that has sustained a way of life for hundreds of years or longer. In market economies, the values of water resources are well understood and can readily be expressed in quantified economic terms such as cost-to-benefit ratios.[8] Among competing values, economic values are the most often asserted, are most easily quantified, and have been the most subsidized. An example of such subsidization is the large public expenditure for hydropower infrastructure in the western United States to supply the huge amounts of energy required for industrial development, municipal expansion, and agribusiness welfare.

Next in the order of quantification are ecologic and environmental values. Most often, in the United States, these values are expressed in the promulgation of stringent controls against water pollution, protective measures to safeguard water habitats necessary for plant and wildlife species, and other similar environmental-protection initiatives. These programs are still growing in scope and enforcement resources, notably the Clean Water Act, the National Environmental Policy Act, the Wild and Scenic Rivers Act, and the Endangered Species Act. At the state level, most western states have enacted statutes requiring a minimum amount of instream flows designed to support ecologic values by keeping water conveyance channels, rivers and streams, wet and flowing year round. In turn, these policies expand receational and leisure uses for the more affluent consumers such as urban devotees of fishing, rafting, and other water sports.

In contrast, social, cultural, and historic values in American water policy and law are much more complex and the least quantifiable, if at all. In many settings, the perspectives, beliefs, preferences, and values of traditional people are not understood or appreciated by other water stakeholders. Often, the traditional uses of water are viewed as obstacles to development and economic progress. What may be a wholesome "rural culture lifestyle" to one group may be seen as a "pocket of persistent rural poverty" to another. At best, the agricultural practices of indigenous societies are measured as subsistence-level production with marginal or no potential for growth outside of the local community. These supposed "lower use yields" then become prime targets for conversion through one process or another.

During the coming century, increased growth in the surrounding economies, urban, national, and global, no doubt will heighten the conflict over water-resources use and approaches to management. Latent conflicts will surface more and more, not only in developing countries but in the western United States as well. While it is important for water stakeholders and the public at large to become familiar with alternative values and management systems, traditional peoples themselves need to assert their claims to water and to the land base that gave rise to their distinctive cultures. In particular, they need to express how local practices that maintain and repair the local irrigation system also bond the social life of the community. They know far better than anyone that continuance of the community and the culture requires them to serve as stewards and custodians of the watershed on which they as well as their heirs depend for their survival.

The reservoirs of local knowledge, as well as the potential for conflicts in values, can be found across many regions of the world.[9] Natural-resource exploitation exists everywhere, as does uneven development. This book presents the results of a regional field study and a series of documentary projects conducted from 1985 to 1997 in the uplands and desertic bioregion of the upper Río Grande and its northern tributaries. The bioregion originates in southern Colorado at the Río Grande headwaters near Creede, and plows through the middle of New Mexico all the way to El Paso, Texas. In the next century, this region and the adjacent border with Mexico will become even more dynamic and diverse. Population and economic growth will tax the resource base of the arid and semiarid environment. Debates over water-use priorities and other value-based questions most certainly will intensify and at times escalate into conflicts. From among the major stakeholders, the water-user group who will likely experience the brunt of rapid change is the acequia irrigation institution found in scores of river valleys in parts of southern Colorado and most of New Mexico.

This book would not have been possible without the support and assistance of many organizations and individuals. First and foremost, I should pay tribute to the acequia associations and their officials who gave of their time in providing information, sharing their documents, and contributing much of the knowledge presented in this volume. Their goals, I am sure, were the same as mine: to record the acequia experience for appreciation by contemporary readers while ensuring the transmission of this knowledge to succeeding generations as we enter the twenty-first century. I also need to thank the staff of the Southwest Hispanic Research Institute, University of New Mexico, where the book project began in 1985 under the title *"Acequias y Sangrías:* The Course of New Mexico Waters." Several years later, after additional fieldwork and archival research, the Center for Regional Studies at the university provided me with a half-time appointment during the crucial stages of data analysis and the beginning of the first manuscript draft.

Once the manuscript was completed, several colleagues and scholars read the draft, or key chapters, and provided invaluable comments and substantive recommendations: Anselmo Arellano, David Benavides, Malcolm Ebright, Frances Levine, Paul Lusk, Palemón Martínez, Michael Meyer, Devón Peña, Sylvia Rodríguez, and others. The outside reader engaged by the University of New Mexico Press likewise provided much guidance, as did David V. Holtby and the other editors at UNM Press. In the end, I am responsible for any inadvertent errors or omissions that may have resulted in the process. Last, but by no means least, I thank my *familia de Corrales*, who endured the fifteen months, with many long weekends, that I dedicated to the writing of the manuscript. They are María Elena, my wife, Anahí Daniela, Brisa Elena, Elvia Luz, and Mario José, our children.

Introduction

Throughout the upper Río Grande bioregion, from the uplands of the north to the more desertic and mesa lands to the south, watercourses and their tributaries stand apart as the most defining features critical to all forms of life, biotic and human. For centuries, this region has been a homeland to the aboriginal peoples, the Tewa, Tiwa and Keres (Pueblo) Indians, and the descendants of the first European settlers, the *hispano mexicanos*. These cultures revere water, treasuring it as the virtual lifeblood of the community. The upper Río Grande, the Río Chama, the upper Río Pecos, and other rivers and creeks stand out as the dominant natural systems of this southern Rocky Mountain province where it joins the great Chihuahuan Desert. Nestled within the canyons and valley floors, tiny villages and pueblos dot the spectacular, enchanting landscape. Their earthen ditches, native engineering works known locally as *acequias*, gently divert the precious waters to extend life into every tract and pocket of arable bottomland.[1]

On a comparative basis, these acequia communities aptly fit the classic subsistence mode of water control described by Donald Worster, in his study of irrigation societies throughout world history and civilizations:

> In the first and simplest type of irrigation society, based on the local subsistence mode, water control relies on temporary structures and small-scale permanent works that interfere only minimally with the natural flow of streams. The needs served by that simple technology are basic and limited: water is diverted to grow food for direct, personal consumption. . . . In such cases authority over water distribu-

tion and management remains completely within the local community, with those who are the users. They have within themselves,
which is to say, within their vernacular traditions, all the skill and ex-
pertise required to build and maintain their water system.[2]

For hundreds of years, the acequia irrigation systems of the upper Río
Grande have supported human subsistence in line with the typology of
functions described by Worster. But these systems have also performed
other important roles not often recognized or valued by other stakeholders: social, political, and ecological. As a social institution, the acequia systems have preserved the historic settlements and local cultures spanning
four major periods of political development in New Mexico: Spanish colonial (1598–1821), Mexican (1821–1848), territorial (1848–1912), and modern
(1912–present). The great majority of acequia villages are unincorporated.
In these instances the acequia institutions have functioned as the only form
of local government below the county level.

As biological systems, the acequias have served other important objectives: soil and water conservation, aquifer recharge, wildlife and plant
habitat preservation, and energy conservation.[3] This record of accom-
plishment runs counter to the notion put forward by critics that the
earthen acequia irrigation canals are wasteful, abusive to soils, inefficient,
and antiquated. Moreover, the fact that acequia communities continue to
support human and other habitats, without depleting the resource base, is
testimony to the existence and practice of a conservation ethic long ago
ingrained in the local value systems. As noted in later chapters of this
book, the acequia papers, consisting of organizational rules, minutes,
journals, and other documents, repeatedly express the values of resource
sustainability and the need to maintain the social fabric of the community.

Since the early 1960s, however, water markets and the demographic
forces behind them, such as population growth, inmigration, and land development pressures, have placed these fragile acequia communities at
great risk. No one disputes that emerging water markets, if left unchecked,
will sever water from the traditional agricultural uses in the region and
cause economic stress to rural villages. Water laws in New Mexico, as in
most western states, adhere to the doctrine of prior appropriation and the
principle of severability, where water can be transferred to alternative
beneficial uses. Like other property commodities, water rights can be
bought and sold in the open marketplace. Less well known, however, are
the broader impacts on the regional and state economies that can result if
these historic acequia villages literally dry up. Regional economies through-

out the upper Río Grande corridor are significantly dependent on the cultural-tourism businesses of the rural countryside and on the more recent high-tech industries that gravitate toward the urban centers. Interestingly, these industries often locate in the larger cities of the upper Río Grande bioregion because of the cultural, scenic, recreational, and other enchanting amenities that the rural landscapes provide.[4]

Purposes of the Book

The broad purpose of this book is to examine the proposition that acequia communities sustain the resource base that made initial occupation and settlement possible. The book begins by describing the acequia institution as the primary vehicle for community development formed by early *hispano mexicano* settlers in order to divert stream waters and regulate water-resources use. As part of the human-built environment, acequia canals were dug out of the natural landscape to create and then sustain human colonies. At the time of first occupation, each acequia system was the main force that established a distinct place, defined the community boundaries, and sought to maintain harmony with the natural environment. The early chapters of the book describe how these engineered systems historically provided a virtual lifeline from the watershed tributaries in the basin to the islands of human settlement dispersed alongside the hundreds of creeks and streams. The cultural imprints and the land-tenure patterns evident today in the river valleys and floodplains of the region resulted largely from this experience.

Throughout, the book also explores the acequia institution as a comparative case study of "common-property regimes" found in many parts of the world. According to criteria defined by Daniel Bromley, communal irrigation systems in particular represent the very essence of these types of regimes:

> There is a well-defined group whose membership is restricted; an asset to be managed (the physical distribution system); an annual stream of benefits (the water that constitutes a valuable agricultural input); and a need for group management of both the capital stock and the annual flow (necessary maintenance of the system and a process for allocating the water among members of the group of irrigators), to make sure that the system continues to yield benefits to the group.[5]

The acequia associations of southern Colorado and New Mexico aptly
fulfill the requirements of Bromley's definition. Long ago, the acequia appropriators crafted rules for the equitable allocation of water resources
while maintaining a place-centered conservation ethic. As physical systems, acequias literally created community places by demarcating the
boundaries of fruitful settlement, altering and channeling the streamflow
to set the land-use capacities of the community. In arid, uplands, and desertic settings, the acequia users designed micro environments for the support of human needs and habitats over many generations. Though acequias
are built systems, they mimic the physics of the natural watercourse systems as much as they alter them, relying on the benign technologies of
gravity flow.

Research Themes and Methodology

The main focus of this book is on the acequia settlers who migrated north
from the central valley of Mexico to establish water-based colonies in the
northern provinces, a development program requiring larger quantities of
irrigation water than had been harnessed by previous agriculturalists. The
research questions that prompted the writing of the book included a series
of intriguing themes. How did the *hispano mexicano* settlers who migrated
to the upper Río Grande basin plan their communities to accommodate
the resource requirements of an acequia-based culture:

- respect for and incorporation of the natural contours of the land?
- physical adaptations such as gravity-flow methods of irrigation?
- control of population densities through patterns of settlement
  dispersal?
- other strategies that set out to maintain sustainable communities
  by respecting the carrying capacity of the land and the watershed?

Of particular interest to the study were the governance tools adopted by
the acequia settlers for irrigation management. Did these early rules and
regulations of the acequia institution recognize the need to conserve the
resource base? Do the organizational papers express a water-conservation
and land ethic? Are water-rotation schedules, anti-pollution regulations,
and the acequia prohibition against wasteful uses evidence of environmental stewardship? Was there an ecological basis for the communal organiza-

tion of water management? Did the pattern of dispersed community settlements during times of expansion perhaps reflect the implied goals of sustainability? By design, the acequia insitition must provide for rules in support of sustainability of the community as a whole and to the individual *ranchos* on an equitable and long-term basis. How have these dual goals been achieved? What institutional arrangements did acequias develop in order to assign rights and responsibilities, build commitment, adopt rules and sanctions, and resolve disputes?

The methodological approach in the study favored the use of firsthand accounts and primary source documents: acequia journals, minutes of organizational meetings, records of the officers, *mayordomo* timebooks, oral history testimonies, public records of water hearings, transcripts of court proceedings, and other sources of retrospective data. The acequia papers, composed of organizational records originated and maintained by the local *parciantes* (the acequia irrigators) themselves, were examined to document important aspects of acequia self-governance. As presented in Chapter 4, the acequia rules provide for a system of direct democracy where all irrigators participate in the functioning and operations of their institution. The rules themselves, for example, are crafted by the entire membership. Any member can serve as an officer or as an election judge during the voting process; the officers, in turn, implement the general rules and enforce them with fines, penalties, or other sanctions established by the irrigators themselves.

When external sources were consulted, preference was given to accounts that recorded, documented, or codified existing practices and customs associated with acequia governance, as in the example of the acequia laws adopted by the territorial assembly in 1851 and 1852, some sixty years before New Mexico became a state. Occasionally, regional histories and ethnographic observations were used as sources of secondary data, but mostly in cases when these writers were eyewitnesses to the events or activities they described in their journals, diaries, or case studies.

The narrative text, thus, is interspersed with archival documents, acequia organizational papers written by the irrigators themselves, excerpts of *mayordomo* journals, public hearing testimonies, and other supplemental materials. Special attention is paid to the many practices and management devices utilized by the acequia irrigators to conserve water as the life-sustaining resource — "water is the lifeblood of the community," as they often say. Finally, no work on acequias can be accomplished without consultation of the background works that exist; for example, histories and special reports written by Wells Hutchins, Thomas Glick, Phil Lovato, Marc Simmons, Michael Meyer, Daniel Tyler, Malcolm Ebright, and John Baxter, as well as the more recent ethnographic documentaries and interdisciplinary studies by Sylvia Rodríguez and Devón Peña. Together, these secondary sources were consulted to provide historical and other information related to the origins, development, social organization, practices, and traditional governance of acequia institutions.

In addition to retrospective and secondary data sources, the book also utilized data obtained by regional field-study methods. As described by Walter Coward, the regional field study can mesh very well with the requirements of conducting irrigation studies of multiple systems over a wide area or territory.[6] Unlike the more limited socioeconomic surveys sometimes used in irrigation studies, the regional field-study method allows the researcher to broaden the scope of inquiry, paying attention to collective patterns, group actions, and institutional arrangements for irrigation that operate across systems in a larger region. "This information focuses on the social organization of irrigation and is gathered through discussions with key informants, observation of group activities (such as meetings and work parties), and the review of existing records and documents."[7]

As a setting for the acequia study presented in this book, the Río Grande bioregion contains a wide scope of irrigation activity while retaining many common elements needed to keep the study within a constant political and regional economy. Data for the study was collected during a twelve-year period, 1985 to 1997, in many localities and through diverse projects. From inception, the focus was on traditional water use within the region, its irrigation localities, and the scores of particular ditches. Organizational meetings of ditch associations were as common a source of information as were historic documents in museums and library archives.[8]

Some of the acequia papers and other related documents are included in Spanish to maintain the context in which they were produced. The texts in Spanish span the colonial, Mexican, territorial, and contemporary periods in order to preserve the linguistic dialects of the times and to convey meanings intended in the context of each historical period. The editing of these historic papers was minimal, intentionally. When intrusions were incorporated, it was mostly to correct obvious errors that would interfere with the original meaning; the more harmless "errors" were retained.[9] For the sake of consistency and comprehension, Spanish accents were added in instances where they had not been provided in the original sources. Some of the documents appear in the appendixes at the end of the chapters, either in their entirety or in excerpted form. In each instance, there were dozens of possible selections that could have been included; but due to limitations of space, preference was given to documents that are difficult for researchers and students to access or to those that remain unpublished. Some published materials were included simply because of their intrinsic worth for all audiences as well as their central contributions to the themes of the book.

Implications and Contributions

The explicit focus of the book is on the acequia institution and its role in community settlement, resource integration, and sustainability. As a physical system, the acequia has required communal upkeep and operations, but beyond this dimension, it has also bonded the community through self-help mutualism, governance, shared values, and traditions that formed a distinctive regional culture. As an irrigation institution, it has served the collective purposes for which it was established: distributing a valued resource in accordance with the accepted norms and customs of the members who contribute labor in exchange for the direct benefits of water use. By studying how acequias sustained themselves, both as organizations and as irrigation systems, we can learn more about collective-action enterprises that operate outside of government but serve public goals, suggesting public-sector policies that validate and empower self-government. There is no need for government itself to administer services when citizens' organizations possess the capacity and the interest to take care of critical needs in the community.[10]

Of special interest to the study, and featured as a major theme in this book, was the role of the acequia institution in promoting concepts of sustainability through a system of rules bonding the irrigators in a common enterprise devoted to the goals of survival and continuance. The results of this analysis are presented here and perhaps can shed light on other resource-management projects around the globe, particularly in support of trends toward decentralization, social participation, and the transfer of management responsibilies to users and user groups. In the arena of irrigation, for example, population growth in some countries has prompted enormous investments in new water-development projects, but disappointing results sometimes occur when planners focus their designs only on physical considerations while ignoring crucial elements of human organization.[11]

In the years ahead, according to research conducted by Elinor Ostrom and her colleagues at the International Center for Self-Governance, the development of irrigation systems will move beyond the design of blueprints for construction, the physical capital components. New processes identified by Ostrom will include the elements of institutional design, that is, principles that will help craft rules for self-government and the social capital needed to make projects work.[12] Evaluation studies lend support to Ostrom's thesis. In a comparative study of forty-seven irrigation systems around the world, Shui Yan Tang noted that total irrigated acreage tripled worldwide between 1950 and 1986. The cases he analyzed were quite diverse in terms of system type, both simple and complex, scale of irrigated hectares, from 3 to 628,000 hectares, and in organizational form, from community-based to bureaucratic systems.

Among other findings, Yan Tang reported that the community-based irrigation systems "tend to be more effective in maintenance and water allocation than the bureaucratic systems."[13] The ability to control and modify organizational rules to fit the specific social and physical environment, including the need to respond to contingencies during conditions of rapid change, was often an advantage, leading Yan Tang to conclude that in most situations "irrigators have the most intimate knowledge about their own physical and social environments . . . [enabling] them to utilize their knowledge effectively and to act quickly in solving problems."[14]

Numerous other studies support the need for irrigation systems composed of and crafted by irrigators themselves, where rules are established and enforced by the users rather than by a remote bureaucracy. When water-development projects have not involved existing local institutions or have not facilitated other forms of direct participation, many difficulties often arise shortly after the construction phase. The intended beneficiaries might not respond or participate as project irrigators, circumventing the system as planned and engineered; without a sufficient number of active irrigators, the project might not reach its operational targets; assumptions that the irrigators themselves will operate, maintain, and refurbish the physical infrastructure on their own often prove out differently than expected; the project may deteriorate and become financially insolvent.[15]

To counter the results of this dismal record, according to many critics, there is a need for social engineering to parallel and undergird the more technical, economic, and design aspects of water-systems planning. The focus of past projects solely on the physical infrastructure of dams, canals, and control systems, and on the economic feasibilities such as cost-benefit projections, should be expanded to include the human and social insitutions required to make projects work in the long term.

> The water flowing in irrigation systems is as much a social product of human organization as it is a natural commodity . . . [S]ociological issues are embedded in the operation of all irrigated systems, small or large: people must organize socially in order to secure water, transport it, divide it into usable shares, enforce rules for its distribution, pay for it, and dispose of unused portions.[16]

Major lending institutions such as the World Bank now require that local irrigators have to be involved not only in the operations and maintenance of projects after they are constructed, but these farmers must participate during the actual planning and construction phases as well.[17] In their own comparison of costs and benefits, Bagadion and Korten found that projects utilizing participatory approaches within the National Irrigation Administration [NIA] in the Philippines actually performed better on quantative and qualitative measures than NIA projects that did not include participatory methods. In brief, the participatory systems resulted in substantially greater increases in crop yields and in larger increases in dry season irrigated acreages. In addition, these systems were more likely to distribute water equitably when water became scarce, and very importantly, they demonstrated a better record of loan repayments when compared with nonparticipation systems.[18]

Scope of the Book's Chapters

The first four chapters of the book present background information critical to an appreciation of the acequia institution and of the acequia papers, in particular. Chapter 1 begins with a historical sketch of the acequia irrigation colonies in and around the Río Grande bioregion of "*el Reino de Nuevo México*" (Kingdom of New Mexico) prompted by the official taking or "*posesión*" of this borderlands Spanish province by Don Juan de Oñate in 1598. Chapters 2 and 3 describe the origins and traditions of acequia administration, from the Old World background in medieval Spain to the first written statutes during the Mexican and United States territorial periods. Chapter 4 then presents the acequia papers, from the 1911 ditch rules established by the Margarita Ditch in Lincoln County to the more modern set of rules adopted by the irrigators of the Acequia del Medio at El Prado near Taos in 1957.

The acequia papers presented in Chapter 4 and the documents excerpted or cited in other chapters should help contemporary readers and water stakeholders appreciate why the roots of custom and tradition permeate much of acequia political philosophy to the present time, and likely will continue to do so into the future. Chapter 5 analyzes the major issues that were salient during the latter quarter of the twentieth century, especially the clash between development and cultural values brought to light in water-transfer cases and water-rights adjudications. Chapter 6 concludes the book with a number of policy questions and possible new initiatives important to the continuation of the acequia institution into the next century. Some recommended action items will require government intervention and assistance, while many others lie within the ability and resources of the acequia irrigators themselves, putting self-governance in this part of the world to yet another test of endurance and sustainability.

For the moment, the earthen acequias of the upper Río Grande remain, and function as common property resource systems quite different from the modern, concrete-lined irrigation canals prevalent in the western United States and elsewhere. The *parciante* irrigators own the acequia watercourses, regulate them, police them, and maintain them from generation to generation, all the while perpetuating a sense of place and a system of direct, participatory democracy. As a model institution, the acequia is a modern-day treasure with roots in the medieval Old World, but with an opportunity to contribute to global cultural diversity well into the twenty-first century.

ACEQUIA CULTURE

Water, Land, and Community

in the Southwest

✜

CHAPTER ONE

Irrigation Communities
on the Río Grande

❖

The use of water-control systems to support agricultural societies in the upper Río Grande did not originate with the *hispano mexicanos*, a mixed *raza* (race) of people with Mexican, Indian, and Spanish heritage who migrated north from the central valley of Mexico beginning in the late sixteenth century. The first farmers in this region appear to have been the Anasazis, a Pueblo Indian culture of the Southwest associated with Mesa Verde and Chaco. Archaeological remains at Chaco, for example, document the fact that these prehistoric peoples built communities for long-term occupation. Their ingenious design technologies included thermally efficient pithouses and kivas, cisterns for domestic water storage, as well as outdoor hearths and roasting ovens.[1] For sustenance, they farmed on contoured terraces, grid-bordered gardens, and canyon floors. Their water supply depended on natural precipitation and runoff from the mesa tops, which they channeled to their fields and gardens via intricate systems of canals, diversion dams, and headgates.[2] For reasons not completely understood, these Anasazi settlements were abandoned after the peak population period of A.D. 1100. Archaeological evidence indicates that many Anasazis migrated south to the present sites occupied by the Pueblo Indians along the upper Río Grande, its tributaries, and other locations.

Prior to and with the entrance of the first Europeans, A.D. 1200–1600, the Tewa, Tiwa, and Keresan Pueblo Indians developed a variety of complex agricultural strategies over a wide range of settlements in the northern Río Grande region. Though the Spanish explorers, who entered the region in the middle and late 1500s, observed examples of Pueblo ditch-irrigation systems, most archaeological studies focus on the much wider use of dryland farming and water-harvesting techniques employed by Pueblo Indians throughout the region. These methods depended on the combination of snowmelt moisture, direct precipitation, intermittent runoff from mesa tops, and floodplain irrigation along the riverine bottomlands. Field studies point out that the Pueblo agriculturalists expended an enormous amount of time, energy, and resources to contruct an extensive network of water-harvesting and conservation systems. Their accomplishments were intricate and innovative for their times: (a) dense coverage of low mesas by installation of gravel-mulched fields, (b) complexes of rock-bordered rectangular grids and cobble-step terraces on the high mesas, (c) the use of stone-lined ditches to channel water from one feature or depression to another, and (d) the placement of cobble alignments as check dams across washes to impound and divert water from natural drainage channels to designated planting areas along the floodplain.[3]

Engineering of Community Ditches

The first Europeans to enter the northern Río Grande region were Spanish explorers and colonizers who migrated from central Mexico to establish frontier villages and towns on the northern outposts of Nueva España. Corresponding to points directly north of Ciudad Juárez, Mexico, and upstream on the Río del Norte (now the Río Grande), this territory came to be known as *La Provincia de San Felipe del Nuevo México*, later shortened to *La Provincia del Nuevo México*. Unlike the Anasazis or the Pueblo Indians, early Spanish-Mexican farmers did not limit settlement to areas dependent primarily on rainfall or the harvesting of natural runoff. The goals of Spanish colonization and the issuance of land grants to waves of petitioners demanded the harnessing of much larger quantities of water from permanent streams. To cultivate the valley bottomlands on the expansive land grants, the colonists had to engineer major diversions on the Río del Norte, the Río Chama, and the Río Pecos, as well as on the more minor tributaries and streams from present-day San Luis, Colorado, throughout New Mexico, and downstream to El Paso, Texas.

First and foremost, these colonizers were practical. While they were mindful of Spanish colonial settlement laws, most often they adapted town layouts and physical design to local conditions. If a ditch had already been dug by Tewa or other Pueblo Indians but later abandoned, they were as likely to reopen and expand it as to search for another location. This may have been the case, for example, when Santa Fe was built on the ruins of an abandoned Indian Pueblo in 1610.[4] But if an Indian ditch was still in use, Spanish laws prohibited any encroachment: "the lands in which [Indians] have made ditches for irrigation or any other benefit, with which by their personal industry they have fertilized, shall be reserved in the first place, and in no case can they be sold or alienated."[5]

Encroachment became a matter of interpretation, however, as when Capitán General Don Juan de Oñate established the first Spanish settlement and capital in 1598, at San Juan de los Caballeros on lands already occupied by Tewa Pueblo Indians. Within two years, Governor Oñate did move the colony to a new *villa* he called San Gabriel, on the west bank of the Río Grande opposite the Indian pueblo.[6] For the most part, however, the early *colonos* (colonists) actively sought locations where irrigation works could be constructed to make new settlements possible. Expanding from Indian practices, they diverted waters on the mightiest stretches of the Río Grande and other major rivers, building dams made of logs, brush, rocks, and other natural materials gathered nearby. Using wooden hand tools, the digging of earthen ditches and laterals would follow the construction of the main diversion dam, typically off both banks of the river to maximize the physics of gravity flow and continuing for several miles downstream.

Constructed of locally available materials such as forest timbers, brush, and rocks at the diversion point, these irrigation works included an earthen *presa* (dam) and inlet works, the *acequia madre* (mother ditch or main canal), *compuertas* (headgates), *canoas* (log flumes for arroyo crossings), *sangrías* (lateral ditches cut perpendicular from the main canal to irrigate individual parcels of land), and a *desagüe* channel, which drains surplus water back to the stream source. Repeated during each wave of expansion into new frontiers, these human carvings into the natural landscape shaped the identity and the spatial boundaries of each place of settlement, ultimately defining a unique cultural region distinct from the other *provincias* in the Spanish borderlands.

Working without the benefit of modern surveying instruments or machinery, the early settlers of the region relied instead on hand tools such as wooden spades, crowbars, hoes, plows, and rawhides pulled by oxen or mules.[7] The irrigation works were engineered by employing techniques of gravity flow that diverted water upstream from their fields, traversing the ditch around trees, large boulders, hills, and other physical obstacles. Frequently, gravity flow was determined by simply allowing water to run along its natural course at key intervals and channeling the ditch accordingly. Arroyos and other low elevations were either filled in or spanned by the use of hand-hewn flumes cut out of forest timber and supported by trestles of shorter logs arranged in a crib configuration to elevate and support the *canoas*, or flumes.

Higher points such as hilly areas were either dug through or avoided altogether by going around them. The *presa* at the diversion point upstream was built simply by placing layers of logs, juniper brush, rocks, and other local materials to contain the water flow sufficient enough to spill into the main headgate at the inlet section of the ditch. A more sophisticated technique was to raise the level of the streambed at the dam site by layering rocks and stones on the river bottom, lifting the water flow closer to the height of the headgate. Containment of the water by the *presa* would accomplish the rest of the task, with gravity flow pushing the water into and through the *acequia madre* system.

Construction of the community acequia was an absolute necessity and, along with the building of the local church, frequently was one of the very first tasks in the initial phases of occupation. The earliest Spanish ditch was built, with the labor of fifteen hundred Tewa Indians, in August of 1598, when Capitán General Juan de Oñate established the first colony at the Indian Pueblo of Ohke, naming it in Spanish as "San Juan de los Caballeros." This initial headquarters for Oñate and his party was located on the east bank of the Río Grande, near its confluence with the Río Chama. At this stage, Oñate's intention was to build a Spanish municipality, which he intended to name "San Francisco de los Españoles."[8] This capital city presumably would be sustained by crops to be grown on the fields irrigated by the ditch system then under construction near San Juan.

Later, however, Governor Oñate relocated the colony and capital when he laid out plans for the *villa* of San Gabriel, now Chamita, on the opposite bank of the Río Grande at the location of a smaller and partially abandoned Tewa Pueblo, Yunque.[9] Here, too, Oñate's party constructed an irrigation system, this time diverting water from the Río Chama. About ten years later, Oñate's successor, Governor Pedro de Peralta, relocated the capital to the Villa de Santa Fe, a more strategic center for the colonization of the expansive frontier to the west and east. Once again, the construction of a municipal irrigation system was a primary and early public-works project as two *acequia madres* were dug to irrigate fields on both sides of the river that passed through the center of the new capital city.[10]

The management of water resources in established towns such as Santa Fe was left to the *cabildos*, or municipal councils. In terms of political organization, however, most of New Mexico throughout the colonial period consisted of dispersed *ranchos* located within the larger agricultural *juris-dicciones* (jurisdictions), with no official government at the local level. As detailed below, the application of Spanish colonial laws, particularly as embodied and restated in the Laws of the Indies, combined with the practical necessity to modify plans according to local conditions, resulted in a unique and ingenious gravity-flow irrigation system that has sustained village life in the region for four hundred years.

Origins of Acequia Administration

Acequia technologies and irrigation methods employed by the *hispano mexicanos* in the new province were melded from diverse sources. Historians agree that these antecedents included the irrigation practices common to the arid regions in the south of Spain, particularly Andalusia and Valencia, based on traditions from the Roman period; the superimposition of Arabic customs and techniques during the seven centuries of occupation of Spain by the Moors; and the influence of Pueblo Indian agriculture as observed by early Spanish explorers and settlement pioneers.[11] Of direct significance were the Spanish medieval practices related to land and water use. These practices eventually became codified in the Laws of the Indies, promulgated in 1573 by Don Felipe, king of Castille, as a set of instructions governing the settlement and pacification of newly discovered lands and provinces in the New World. These historic, comprehensive laws were issued to colonial officials as the "*Ordenanzas de Descubrimiento, Nueva Población de las Indias dadas por Felipe II en 1573*" (Ordinances for the Discovery and New Populations in the Indies Issued by Felipe II in 1573).

Recompiled in 1681, the Laws of the Indies provided the framework for colonists and provincial governors to follow when selecting sites for development and occupation. A little-recognized element is the fact that Spanish settlement planning was ecologically based from the outset. Ordinance 35, for example, required that new settlements "should be in fertile areas with an abundance of fruits and fields, of good land to plant and harvest, of grasslands to grow livestock, of mountains and forests for wood and building materials for homes and edifices, and of good and plentiful water supply for drinking and irrigation." Ordinance 39 provided more detailed guidance on town site selection, requiring proximity to water for irrigation: "The site and position of the towns should be selected in places

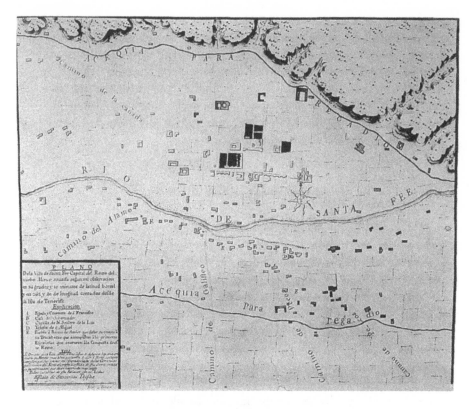

José de Urrutia's Map of Villa de Santa Fe, c. 1767,
Depicting Town Layout and Acequias.
Courtesy Museum of New Mexico,
Neg. No. 15048.

where water is nearby . . . [suitable] for farming, cultivation, and pastura-
tion, so as to avoid excessive work and cost, since any of the above would
be costly if they were far."[12]

Later, in 1789, the Plan de Pitic restated and clarified how Spanish colonial law was applicable to the new populations and towns projected for the
Provincias Internas de la Nueva España. The Plan de Pitic consisted of
twenty-four instructions governing the design of town master plans, the
allocation of lands for residential and agricultural uses, and the distribution of water rights. With respect to water and irrigation management, it
embodied many of the practices and principles evident in the acequia communities of New Mexico and southern Colorado. The Plan de Pitic stipulated that land should be divided into *suertes* (individual parcels) most

conducive to irrigation and agricultural productivity. Next, an *acequia madre* (principal canal) should channel sufficient quantities of water to each parcel; and a water *alcalde* or *mandador de aguas* (ditch superintendent) should be appointed to apportion the irrigation waters, based on principles of equity and justice. In addition, water lists and schedules should be established to ensure certain days and hours of irrigation for each irrigator. As to the responsibility for repairs and cleaning of the ditches, all users should share in the labor prorated to the number and size of their individual *suertes*, or irrigated plots.[13] These mandates are common features of acequia procedures for operations and management of irrigation waters that have been maintained into the contemporary period.

The *pobladores* who entered the Provincia del Nuevo México were also influenced by existing agricultural practices of the Pueblo Indians. Observations of their techniques were carefully noted by expedition parties and explorers who made the first contacts. In 1540 Francisco Vásquez de Coronado and his expedition came upon the Zuni Pueblo while searching for the fabled Seven Cities of Gold. At Hawikuh, he observed the abundant fields of maize and praised the ability of the Zuni Indians to produce it: "So far as I can find out, these Indians worship the water, because they say it makes the maize grow and sustains their life, and the only other reason they know is that their ancestors did so."[14]

In a later expedition some forty years later, Don Antonio de Espejo marveled at the large pueblo community he encountered at Acoma:

Acoma is built on top of a lofty rock, more than fifty *estados* high and out of the rock itself the natives have hewn stairs by which they ascend and descend to and from the pueblo. It is a veritable stronghold, with water cisterns at the top and quantities of provisions stored in the pueblo. . . . These people have their fields two leagues distant from the pueblo, near a medium-sized river, and irrigate their farms by little streams of water diverted from a marsh near the [San José] river.[15]

When the explorers with the Espejo expedition left Acoma and traveled four leagues upstream, Luxan's account compared Indian and Spanish irrigation practices, marveling at their direct similarities: "We found many irrigated cornfields with canals and dams, built as if by Spaniards."[16]

Observations of Pueblo Indian irrigation probably reinforced the necessity for the *hispano mexicanos* to build permanent settlements on the floodplains or in proximity to watercourses, as instructed by the Laws of the Indies. But these early colonists also knew that the much greater quantities and diversity of the crops they intended to cultivate would require more extensive and sophisticated irrigation works and distribution systems. This meant they would have to divert the larger river systems, as happened at numerous sites in the middle Río Grande valley. Like Santa Fe one hundred years earlier, the Villa de Alburquerque was also founded on the banks of a river, in this case the Río del Norte, the largest of all river systems in the region.[17] In the 1706 Certificate of Founding presented to the king of Spain, Governor and Capitán General Don Francisco Cuerbo y Valdez of the province of New Mexico declared his compliance with the royal instructions: "I founded a Villa on the margin and meadows of the Río del Norte in a goodly place of fields, waters, pasturage, and timber . . . keeping in mind what is prescribed by his Majesty in his Royal Laws of the *Recopilación*."[18] He also confirmed the construction of the most important institutions necessary for permanent settlement: "The Church [is already] completed, capacious and appropriate . . . the Royal Houses [are] begun, and the other houses of the settlers finished with their corrals, acequias ditched and running, [the] fields [already] sowed — all well arranged and without any expense to the Royal Treasury."[19]

If a suitable watercourse could not be immediately identified and diverted to support a new settlement, other solutions would be improvised to accomplish the same end. When Fray Francisco Atanacio Domínguez recorded his impressions of the Truchas community in 1776, he noted the presence of very good and fertile lands, but there was no river to divert for more continuous occupation and expansion:

> But since the Almighty gave man what he needs, those interested in these lands, with prodigious labor, dammed up in a small canyon the water of a little rivulet that came through it, which arises in the east in the sierra itself. By making it rise in the dam to a height of 60 or more *varas*, they succeeded in using it very freely for irrigation by means of a good ditch (which must be a league from the settlement). They have a copious harvest of good wheat and legumes.[20]

Land Policies and Water Petitions

Expansion of settlements to the upper reaches of the Río del Norte and beyond, to the west and east, frequently was accompanied with petitions by groups of restless *colonos* for more land and water to support the growing population in the region. These petitions also enabled the *pobladores* to respect the carrying capacity of the land and the watershed streams they believed were already fully developed and appropriated. Sustainability was part of the ethos of settlement, not only in legal Spanish codes but in actual practice. Repeatedly, settlers themselves took initiative to branch out in search of new territories just when the local natural resources, especially irrigation water from rivers and creeks, began to show signs of stress.

In the process of petitioning for lands, settlers had to specify the natural boundaries of the desired community land grant. The governor would then require an inspection to be conducted by the *alcalde mayor* of the jurisdiction. This official had to ascertain that the land in question was not already settled nor prejudicial to the welfare of an Indian pueblo. Part of his investigation also included an evaluation of the water supply needed for irrigation, for domestic use, and for the watering of livestock. To comply with Spanish land-distribution policies, the *alcalde* had to partition the land in a manner that would encourage "the tilling of the land and rearing of cattle."[21] If these and other conditions were met, the governor would then confirm the grant and authorize the possession ceremony.[22] This colonization policy resulted in a population-distribution pattern of community development alongside the watercourses and their tributaries farther and farther away from the main stem of the Río Grande in both westerly and easterly directions, eventually dispersing the population into semi-isolated *plazas, ranchos* and other water-based colonies. Access to irrigation water served as the guiding principle, a continuation of land policy implemented from the outset since the founding of the early *villas:* San Gabriel in 1600, Santa Fe in 1610, Santa Cruz de la Cañada in 1695, and Alburquerque in 1706.

Before petitioning for the more distant lands, however, residents in already established communities attempted to expand and conserve water resources from within the immediate vicinity. After eighteen months of occupation, for example, the settlers of Cañón de Fernández near Taos determined that the waters from the Río Fernando could no longer supply all of the water necessary for community irrigation.[23] To meet their growing needs, in 1797 they petitioned Governor Fernando Chacón and Taos Alcalde Mayor Antonio José Ortiz for *aguas sobrantes* (surplus waters) from two nearby sources, the Río Pueblo de Taos and the Río Lucero, to be channeled through a ditch constructed for this very purpose. If approved, the petition would allow the irrigators at Cañón de Fernández to take any surplus waters not used by the communities already holding water rights from the two streams, the Taos Indian Pueblo and Los Estiércoles (now El

Prado). Governor Chacón approved the request and Alcalde Ortiz subsequently issued the settlers "*Una Merced de Agua*" (a water-rights grant),
which allowed them the surplus water from the two rivers in question:

> By virtue of a petition made by the settlers of *Río de Don Fernando*
> to Lieutenant Colonel and Governor of this province, Fernando
> Chacón, praying might be pleased to do them (in the name of his
> Majesty – God preserve him) a favor and allow them the surplus wa-
> ter from the Taos River and from the Lucero River, and his excel-
> lency having given me the said Chief Alcalde the order to place them
> in possession, I do, in the name of his Majesty as aforesaid, giving this
> instrument for their greater security, to which I certify.[24]

At the close of the eighteenth century, there were some 164 community
ditches in the province of Nuevo México, a number that would continue
to grow at an even faster rate during the late colonial and Mexican periods of settlement expansion, 1800–1848.[25] By the early 1800s, the initial
colonial settlements near Taos on the western side of the Sangre de Cristo
Mountains had outgrown their initial sources of water, especially for agricultural uses. Thus began a long and eventful process of dispersal to other
river valleys, extending acequia settlements well beyond the Río Grande to
the more distant streams west and east.

In 1816 a group of *hispano mexicano* families occupying lands on the Picurís Pueblo determined that their future and that of their heirs would require them to seek new and permanent areas of settlement elsewhere. Led
by Antonio Olguín, several families trekked over the Jicarita Mountains
down to the fertile Mora River Valley on the eastern slopes of the Rock-
ies, a new frontier area that later would open the way for expansion into
the vast plains of northeastern New Mexico.[26] By around 1832, however,
even the Mora River and its tributary creeks were not sufficient to support
the additional and projected growth near this first Mora settlement, known
as San Antonio de Lo de Mora. Ingeniously, Antonio Olguín secured permission from the Picurís Pueblo to take water from the Jicarita Mountain
watershed, and with help from the other valley settlers, he devised a bold
engineering plan for a transmountain, interbasin water delivery system.
When completed, this unique system successfully diverted water normally
and naturally destined to flow westerly to the Río Grande, channeling it
instead by handmade ditches over and through the mountains and canyons
to the east, thereby causing waters to flow to an eastern basin connected
to the Arkansas River. The success and example of this transmountain di-

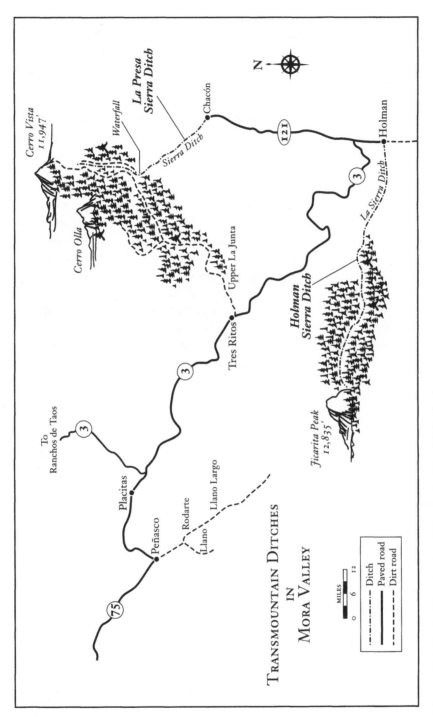

Cerro Vista
11,947'

Waterfall

**La Presa
Sierra Ditch**

Chacón

Sierra Ditch

N

121

Holman

Cerro Olla

Upper La Junta

3

La Sierra Ditch

To
Ranchos de Taos

3

3

Tres Ritos

Placitas

**Holman
Sierra Ditch**

Peñasco

Rodarte

Llano   Llano Largo

Jicarita Peak
12,835'

75

TRANSMOUNTAIN DITCHES
IN
MORA VALLEY

MILES

0   6   12

—··—·· Ditch
———— Paved road
—— —— Dirt road

Source: New Mexico Magazine (1979). Drawing by Richard C. Sandoval.

version project was replicated two more times farther upstream from Olguín's settlement at San Antonio (Cleveland) in order to accommodate
growth in population at El Rito de Agua Negra (Chacón) in 1865 and Agua
Negra (Holman) in 1879, when the Acequia de El Rito y La Sierra and the
Acequia de la Sierra were constructed in a similar fashion.[27]

Within the confines of available local resources, some physiographic
limitations, and many opportunities for creative engineering, the early
pobladores proved adept at implementing the goals of colonization expressed
in royal Spanish ordinances and continued through the period of Mexican
land grants. Initially borrowing from Pueblo Indian agricultural techniques, the *hispano mexicanos* expanded on the use of irrigation technologies on small and major river systems alike, creating a unique approach
to resource management which thus far has survived for four centuries.
With the active encouragement of government officials who liberally
implemented Spanish and Mexican land-distribution policies, the *colonos*
established permanent *ranchos, plazas,* and *villas* dispersed throughout the
narrow valley bottomlands of this northern frontier, La Provincia de San
Felipe del Nuevo México. The cultural imprints and the land-tenure patterns evident today resulted largely from these early community-develop-
ment strategies.

DOCUMENTS

Description of *Río del Norte* by Oñate's Party and the Taking of Possession of the Provincia de San Felipe del Nuevo México in 1598

The Río del Norte, now the Río Grande, was described by Capitán General Juan de Oñate's party on April 20, 1598, en route from the interior of Mexico to establish the first Spanish settlements at San Juan de los Caballeros and San Gabriel. The river had been named by earlier Spanish expeditions according to the direction of its headwaters, "corre del norte," meaning that its currents ran from the north. According to many sources, the possession ceremony took place on April 30, 1598, at a campsite some fifteen kilometers from the river south of present-day Cuidad Juárez and El Paso, just as Oñate was about to enter La Provincia de San Felipe del Nuevo México. After the ceremony, the expedition continued its incursions to the north along the banks of the Río del Norte. The full text of Oñate's possession declaration can be found in Capitán Gaspar de Villagra's epic poem *Historia de la Nueva México*; for an English translation, see Hammond and Rey, eds., *Don Juan de Oñate*, 1:329–36. The source here for the two excerpts is Ma. Luisa Rodríguez-Sala, Ignacio Gómezgil R. S., y María Eugenia Cué, *Exploradores en el Septentrión Novohispano* (Miguel Angel Porrúa, México, 1995).

... es Río mayor que el de Conchas y aún de más agua que el de las Nazas, aunque no es de tanta madre, va cocinado en estos parajes y turbio por pasar por tierra muerta, es de gran frescura y alameda, muchísimo pescado bagre, mohote, robalo, armado, apujas y un pescado blanco de casi media vara, parece jurel, y matalotes, hay algunos sauces, mezquite grande y pequeño, jarales espesos y algunas salinas de muy buena sal como la de Guadalquivir y es muy semejante a él. Corre del norte y de esto toma nombre y da vuelta hacia el Levante hasta que cobra nombre de Río Bravo con el de Conchas y otros que se le juntan. (20 abril, 1598) [Ma. Luisa Rodríguez-Sala et. al., *Exploradores*, pp. 222–23, citing Itinerario de las minas de Caxco ... AGI, Patronato 22, R. 13, fol. 15.]

[Yo, don Juan de Oñate, gobernador y capitán general y adelantado de la
Nueva México y de sus reinos y provincias,] tomo y aprehendo, una y dos,
y tres veces . . . y todas las que de derecho puedo y debo, la Tenencia y posesión real y actual, civil y natural en este dicho Río del Norte, sin excep-
tuar cosa alguna y sin alguna limitación, con los montes, riberas, vegas,
cañadas y sus pastos y abrevaderos . . . tomo y aprehendo, en voz y en nombre de las demás tierras, pueblos, Ciudades, Villas, Castillos y casas fuertes
y llanas que ahora están fundadas en los dichos Reynos y provincias de la
Nueva México, y las a ellas circunvecinas y comarcanas, y adelante, por
tiempo se fundaren en ellos, [con sus montes, ríos y riberas, aguas, pastos,
vegas, cañadas, abrevaderos, y] con todos los indios naturales que en ellas
y en cada una de ellas se incluyeren, y con la jurisdicción civil y criminal,
alta y baja, horca y cuchillo . . . desde la hoja del arbol y monte, hasta la
piedra y arenas del río, y desde la piedra y arenas del río hasta la hoja del
monte. [Rodríguez-Sala et. al., *Exploradores*, p. 224, citing CODOIN, tomo
XVI, pp. 98–99.]

De Vargas Letter, 1691

In the early summer of 1691 Governor Diego de Vargas was headquartered
at El Paso. From this location he complained to the Spanish viceroy that
the kingdom of New Mexico was severely wanting for provisions and infrastructure necessary to harness the waters of the mighty Río del Norte.
This letter excerpt is part of the hundreds of documents in the De Vargas
Papers archived in the University of New Mexico collection. The letter
was provided and translated courtesy of History Professor John L. Kessell,
ed., The Vargas Project, Zimmerman Library. The source of the letter was
credited to the Archivo General de la Nación (México), Historia, vol. 37,
exp. 2.

Gov. Diego de Vargas to the Viceroy Condo de Galve,
El Paso del Río del Norte, June 20, 1691

Most excellent sir,

   I have informed Your Excellency of my arrival at this *plaza de armas* of
El Paso del Río del Norte and at the same time reported the supplies of
weapons and horses I found and that this kingdom is without provisions.
Because the season was so advanced, I had to direct attention and aid to
repair of the irrigation ditches for the fields. I spent two months on these

repairs, and the main dam is still not to the point that it will control the river and not let it misdirect its current. Since the run-off is very heavy during the springtime because of the snows that melt in the ranges and mountains of New Mexico, it does great damage when the current strays from its course, refusing to enter the irrigation ditches. For this reason it is necessay to build next year's dam in time, so that it will channel part of the river current into the ditch, and when there is no such occurrence, it can take it all. Because of these repairs, the fields were planted late with the modest amount of wheat that is sown in May and the maize during this month of June. This is because of the fear that irrigation would be lacking at the height of the growing season.

> *Don Diego de Vargas Zapata Luján Ponce*
> *de León, Governador y Capitán General*

Alburquerque: 1706 Certificate of Founding

In compliance with the Laws of the Indies, the Villa de Alburquerque was founded at a site providing the necessities to build and sustain a permanent colony. The Certificate of Founding in 1706 confirms the presence of meadows, pastures, timbers, and river waters to irrigate the fields. By the time the certificate was issued by Governor Cuerbo y Valdez, the acequias were already dug and running. This translation of the certificate was excerpted from Lansing B. Bloom, "Alburquerque and Galisteo Certificate of Their Founding, 1706," 10 *New Mexico Historical Review* 1 (January 1935), pp. 48–49. Bloom states: "The document was found in the Archivo General de la Nación (México), sección de las Provincias Internas, tomo 36, ramo 5." The document also appears in Charles Wilson Hackett, ed., *Historical Documents Relating to New Mexico, Nueva Vizcaya, and Approaches Thereto, to 1773* (Washington, D.C., 1937), 3:379.

[I,] Don Francisco Cuerbo y Valdez, Caballero of the Order of Santiago, Governor and Captain General of this Kingdom and [the] provinces of New Mexico, and Castellán of his forces and Presidios for H[is] M[ajesty] &c. CERTIFY to His Majesty (whom may God guard for many years), to his Viceroys, Presidents, Governors, and other Officials:

That I founded a Villa on the margin and meadows of the Río del Norte in a goodly place of fields, waters, pasturage, and timber, distant from this Villa of Santa Fe about twenty-two leagues, giving to it as titular Patron

the most glorious Apostle of the Indies San Francisco Xavier, calling it and
naming it the Villa of Alburquerque. [I located it] in a good site, keeping
in mind what is prescribed by his Majesty in his Royal Laws of the Recopilación, Book IV, Title VII, and there are now thirty-five families settled there, comprising 252 persons, large and small. The Church [is already]
completed, capacious and appropriate, with part of the dwelling for the
Religious Minister, the Royal Houses [are] begun, and the other houses of
the settlers finished with their corrals, acequias ditched and running, fields
[already] sowed — all well arranged and without any expense to the Royal
Treasury.

> [signed]
> FRANCISCO CUERBO Y VALDÉS
> [rubric]
> By order of the Sr. Governor and
> Captain General:
> [signed] Alfonso Rael de Aguilar
> Secretary of government and war

Colonial Land Use and Irrigation Practices at Nambe, San Ildefonso Pueblo, and Truchas — Observations and Descriptions by Fray Francisco Atanasio Domínguez, 1776

Eleanor B. Adams and Fray Angélico Chávez translated and annotated the
observations of Fray Francisco Atanacio Domínguez when he was sent to
New Mexico in 1776 on a special visitation. According to Adams and Chávez, Fray Domínguez had been charged by the Mexican Province of the
Holy Gospel to document the spiritual and economic status of the missions. This broad mandate entailed the gathering of much geographical
and ethnological data, providing a rich source of information regarding the
social ecology of the dozens of *ranchos*, *plazas*, and Indian pueblos extant at
the time. As such, the Domínguez descriptions are probably the earliest
records of land-use and irrigation practices evident in colonial Nuevo
México. By the time of the visit, both the Spanish and the Pueblo Indian
communities had developed relatively sophisticated irrigation systems, diverting water from large and small streams alike, by constructing dams upstream from their villages or, as in the case of Truchas, literally creating a
stream source by damming up a small canyon at some distance from any
river. For the description of all the missions visited by Fray Domínguez, see

The Missions of New Mexico, 1776: A Description by Fray Francisco Atanasio Domínguez, translated and annotated By Eleanor B. Adams and Fray Angélico Chávez (University of New Mexico Press, 1956).

NAMBE: Nambe is about 7 leagues from Santa Fe and lies north quarter north-northeast from it. . . . They have almost as much land above the pueblo as below it. . . . They irrigate the upper lands with a mother ditch from well upriver, and they take water for the lower lands from the same ditch a little before the said arroyo empties into the river. The lands are fairly fertile and everything sown in them yields a crop, with a sufficient harvest of everything. . . . The natives of this pueblo are Teguas. . . . Some ranchos of citizens are attached to this mission for spiritual administration. They comprise two very small branches called Cundiyó and Pojoaque. In relation to the pueblo, the first [*rancho*] is up east-northeast at the foot of the aforementioned sierra in a small cañada which runs from south to north there with a rapid little river through the center. The water is crystalline and good and there is trout fishing. It has sufficient farmlands for the number of inhabitants. They are fairly good, are irrigated by the said river, and . . . there is a fairly good harvest of all that is sown in them. . . .

SAN ILDEFONSO: Said pueblo is in the form of a very large plaza, clean and without any impediments. It consists of four tenements with three large passageways to the east, south, and north at their respective corners, and a small one to the west to lead to the church. . . . Around the plaza at proportionate distances are the corrals, ovens, and henhouses. . . . The Indians of this pueblo have lands in all four directions, but not divided equally, for the east, north, and south there are a little less than three-quarters of a league. To the west, indeed, they have even more than a league, occupying both banks of the Río del Norte, since it runs through them. Those on the west side of the river are irrigated from this very river through adequate ditches taken from it where necessary. Some of those on the east side, where the pueblo is, are irrigated from the river, and others from the spring in the little swamp I mentioned when I was speaking of the convent lands. Still others are irrigated from the Nambe River, which is very scanty by the time it reaches these parts, because everyone located beyond Nambe bleeds it, as is understood, and when it dries up, there are hardships for those of these lands. . . .

TRUCHAS: Truchas, much higher up the cañada than Chimayó, is to the east-northeast in relation to the above villa and about 4 leagues from it. This settlement is on a high level site provided by a ridge of the afore-

said sierra, with very good lands, although there is no river. But since the
Almighty gave man what he needs, those interested in these lands, with
prodigious labor, dammed up in a small canyon the water of a little rivulet
that came through it, which arises in the east in the sierra itself. By making it rise in the dam to a height of 60 or more *varas*, they succeeded in
using it very freely for irrigation by means of a good ditch (which must be
a league from the settlement). They have a copious harvest of good wheat
and legumes. . . . This settlement is not of *ranchos*, but around two plazas
because Governor Vélez Cachupín issued orders to this effect since they
are almost on the borders of the Comanche tribe, whose people make incursions from that vicinity.

Excerpts from *El Plan de Pitic de 1789* y las nuevas poblaciones proyectadas en las Provincias Internas de la Nueva España

The Plan de Pitic was drawn by the office of the General Comandante in
1789 for the founding of a new town at Pitic (now Hermosillo), Sonora.
The plan contained twenty-four provisions to guide the future development of military jurisdictions and contiguous local settlements in the internal provinces of Sonora, California, Nueva Vizcaya (now Chihuahua),
and Nuevo México. The instructions pertaining to land and water resources coincided with the ordinances previously stipulated in the Laws of
the Indies. In the area of water management, however, the Plan de Pitic
provided more details as to the construction of the acequia irrigation systems, the regulation of water distribution to ensure access by all landowners, the communal process for ditch operations and maintenance, and
other matters important to acequia governance.

To administer the system of self-government, each community would
have to select annually a water *alcalde* or *mandador* (boss), responsible for
the implementation of a water-rotation schedule and the supervision of
ditch-conservation practices such as the *reparos* and *limpiezas* (repairs and
cleaning). Irrigators would have to adhere to their assigned turns for
the use of ditch waters, taking no more into their headgates than necessary.
They must also provide their share of community labor in proportion to
the amount of land irrigated and benefits received. These elements of ditch
administration continued as the customary practices and rules through the
rest of the colonial and Mexican periods and became codified in the terri-

torial laws of New Mexico in 1851 and 1852. To a large extent, the Plan de Pitic simply restated a number of Spanish laws already in effect, and there is some question as to the extent to which the Plan de Pitic might apply to New Mexico, but most scholars agree that it was an historic document at the time, codifying water-irrigation practices up until its promulgation in 1789. (See Richard E. Greenleaf, "Land and Water in Mexico and New Mexico, 1700–1821," 47 *New Mexico Historical Review* 2 [April 1972], pp. 97–104; and Michael Meyer, *Water in the Hispanic Southwest: A Social and Legal History, 1550–1850* [University of Arizona Press, 1984], pp. 30–37.)

The Spanish language excerpts below appeared in 2 *Colonial Latin American Historical Review* 4 (Fall 1993). These excerpts pertain to acequia irrigation management and are presented courtesy of Joseph P. Sánchez, the editor of the journal, who also transcribed and edited the *Plan de Pitic*. Sánchez cites the Archivo General de la Nación (AGN), México, D.F., Sección Californias, tomo 9. In addition to the English summary provided above and in the text, the reader may wish to consult Greenleaf, "Land and Water in Mexico and New Mexico," and Meyer, *Water in the Hispanic Southwest*, who both provide translations of and commentary on key articles in the Plan de Pitic.

> Ynstrucción 19: . . . Siendo el beneficio del Riego el principal medio de fertilizar las Tierras y el mas conducente al fomento de la Población pondrá particular cuidado el Comis[ionad]o en distribuir las Aguas de modo q[u]e todo el Terreno que sea regable pueda participar de ellas especialmente en los tiempos y estaciones de Primavera y Verano en que son mas necesarias á las sementeras para asegurar las Cosechas, á cuyo fin valiéndose de Peritos ó inteligentes dividirá el Territorio en Partidos ó heredamientos señalando á cada uno un Arbollón i Azequia que saldrá de la Madre ó principal con la cantidad de Agua que se regule suficiente para su regadía en los enunciados tiempos y en los demás del año, q[u]e los nesesitaren; por cuyo medio sabía cada Poblador la Yla y Azequia con que deve regarse su heredamiento y que no puede ni tiene facultad para tomar el Agua de otro distinto ni en mayor cantidad que la que cupiere a la suya; a cuyo fin y el de q[u]e no se aumente en perjuicio de los herederos situados en el Terreno posterior ó mas bajo será conveniente que los Arbollones ó repartidores se construyan en la Azequia Madre de Cal y canto á costa de los mismos Pobladores.
>
> Ynstrucción 20: . . . Para que estos disfruten con equidad y justicia el beneficio de las Aguas a proporción de la necesidad que tuvieren sus respectivas Siembras se nombrará anualmente por el Ayuntamiento un Al-

calde ó Mandador de cada Yla á cuyo cargo estará el cuidado de repartir-
las en las heredades comprendidas en el Partido ó heredamiento que se
regare con ellas á proporción de la necesidad q[u]e tuvieren de este beneficio, señalando por lista que formará las [h]oras del día ó de la noche en
que cada heredero deverá regar sus sembrados; y p[ar]a que por descuido ó
desidia de los dueños no queden sin riego los q[u]e los necesitaren ni se
pierden las Cosechas, en lo que además del perjuicio particular resulta también el Público y común, que produce la falta de provisiones y Vastimien-
tos será también del cargo del Alc[ald]e ó mandador de cada Yla, tener un
Peón ó jornalero instruido en la hora del día ó de la noche señalada para el
riego á cada Tierra ó sembrado el qual á falta de su Dueño cuidará de re-
garlo regulandose después por el Comisionado ó por la Justicia el Justo
precio de su Trabajo q[u]e se le hará pagar inmediatamente por el Dueño
de la Tierra ó heredad regadas.

Ynstrucción 21: . . . Los repartos y Limpiezas que necesitase la Azequia
Madre p[ar]a su conservación se harán á costa de todo el Vecindario en los
tiempos q[u]e señalaren el Comisionado y Ayuntamiento concurriendo á
ellas cada Vecino con sus asistencia y trabajo personal ó en su defecto con
la cantidad q[u]e por repartimiento y prorrateo equitativo se le señalare
para pagar y satisfacer á los Peones y por lo respectivo á los reparos y
limpias de los Arbollones repartidores y Azequias destinadas al riego de
los Partidos ó heredamientos en que deve dividirse el Terreno, serán del
Cargo de los Hacenderos ó herederos cuyas suertes y posesiones se regarén
con ellas entre los quales se repartirá el gasto que ocasionaren a prorrata
del número de Suertes que cada uno poseyese en aquel Partido ó
heredamiento correspondiendo al Cavildo ó Ayuntam[ien]to de acuerdo
con el Comisionado determinarlos en q[u]e sin perjuicio de las Sementeras,
deven hacerse las enunciadas limpias y reparos.

Ditch Engineering at Valdez, c. 1815

The mountain village of Valdez, New Mexico, was established in the early
1800s. A compiler from the Works Progress Administration (WPA), Simeón Tejada, took down the oral history of several villages of Taos County
during the late 1930s. In the excerpt below, he recorded how the first
pobladores of San Antonio, now Valdez, engineered a ditch to irrigate the
plains of Desmontes by using a crude transit along with wooden shovels
and crowbars. The ditch is now known as La Acequia de la Cuchilla. The

Cuchilla is a main canal diverting water from the Río Hondo above Valdez. At the top of Hondo Canyon, it divides to form the Rebalse and Desmontes acequias. Baxter notes that the construction of the Cuchilla was a remarkable feat for its time and is still viewed with awe by professional engineers. Per his description, the ditch "climbs up the south wall of Hondo Canyon more than two miles before reaching the plain at the top, where it divides into several laterals that water fields at Desmontes." According to Tejada, Baxter, and local residents, this topographical alignment creates the impression that the ditch seems to run uphill. See John O. Baxter, *Dividing New Mexico's Waters, 1700–1912* (University of New Mexico Press, 1997), p. 16, and Baxter, *Spanish Irrigation in Taos Valley* (New Mexico State Engineer Office, 1990), pp. 26–27.

Simeón Tejada, 8-25-39. Palabras. HISTORIA DE VALDÉS. La población de Valdés se encuentra 12 millas al norte de Taos, estado de Nuevo México, 5 millas al este de la carretera no. 3. La población de Valdés se llamaba San Antonio hasta el año 1894 en honor del primer poblador que se llamaba Don Juan Antonio Valdés. . . . Tan pronto como se pobló la población de San Antonio, hoy Valdés, los vecinos pensaron en hacer una acequia para regar el llano que llaman Desmontes, y buscaron para agrimensar esta acequia un instrumento en forma de triángulo con un hilo puesto en una de las esquinas, y en la punta de este hilo un pedacito de plomo para que marcara el nivel. Y los instrumentos que usaron para hacer esta acequia heran de madera. Sin embargo de usar esta clase de instrumentos, hoy hasta los ingenieros quedan admirados al ver la acequia tan derecha, y a la simple vista parece que el agua sube hacia arriba. Esta acequia tiene una milla de larga, y al principio que la usaron ponían un buje de un carro para medir el agua. Hoy riega un terreno extenso y con mucha agua.

[Simeón Tejada, 8-25-39. Palabras. HISTORY OF VALDÉS. The settlement of Valdés is located 12 miles north of Taos, state of New Mexico, 5 miles east of highway no. 3. Until 1894, the settlement of Valdés used to be known as San Antonio, in honor of its first settler, Don Juan Antonio Valdés. . . . As soon as the community of San Antonio, now Valdés, was settled, the villager citizens planned on constructing a ditch to irrigate the plains they called Desmontes. To grade the ditch, they used an instrument configured as a triangle with a thread tied to one of the corners. At the other end of this thread was a piece of lead to site the level. And the tools they used to construct this ditch were made of wood. Notwithstanding the use of these types of tools, nowadays even engineers stand in awe to see the ditch so straight, and at a simple glance it appears that the water runs uphill. This ditch is one mile long. When they first put it to use, they used to place a cartwheel from a wagon to measure the water flow. Nowadays the ditch irrigates extensive properties with abundant water. (Works Progress Administration Records — Taos County History, Folder 233b, State Records Center and Archives, Santa Fe, N.M.)]

Petition to Take Possession of
Valle de Guadalupita,
Río del Coyote, 1837

Population growth and policies in support of colonization prompted *hispano mexicanos* to seek new lands for development well into the Mexican period. Availability of water was always of paramount concern. On February 20, 1837, a group of *vecinos* from the Valle de Santa Gertrudes (Mora) petitioned the *alcalde* at Las Trampas for additional lands a few miles to the east, permitting them to take possession of the Guadalupita Valley on the Río del Coyote, a tributary of the Mora River. In honor of God and his divine laws, the petitioners proclaimed that new cultivable lands were necessary to sustain themselves and their families due to the scarcity of water at their current location in Mora. The *alcalde* of the jurisdiction, Juan Nepumuseno Trujillo, acknowledged their petition a few weeks later and requested that the *colonos* (colonists) appear before him on April 1 of that same year, clearing the way for eventual approval of the new settlement at Guadalupita.

San Fernando 20 de Febrero de[e]ste año de 1837

Señor Alc[al]de Co[n]stitucionado de Las Trampas de nuestro padre San José y lustre Corporación de alluntamiento:

   Nosotros los C.C, entre los [A]crisolados Respectos de sus Señorias, que la necesidad de vernos tan recortados las aguas en esta recidencia hasemos una proclama a su Caridad de que pidemos en obsequio de Dios y las divinas leyes. El que se dignen de conseguirnos el tomar la poseción del Valle de Guadalupita Río del Coyote para cultivar y sostener nuestra posección. Si merecemos el honor de consequir lo que pretendemos para deramar nuestra Sangre en obsequio de la nación y ciendo de su atrivación de V. [usted] el dar aviso de lo que resuelva bien conosemos que los ricos podrán — enbarasar o quedrán mas vien que perescan. [N]uestras familias y con toda severación de la Nación se dignen de admitir esta nuestra nesecidad la lista que devidamente a Conpaña dará a conocer el número de indevidos [individuos] que declaramos al abrigo de su Caridad y por eso a semos [hacemos] esta introgación a ves Señorias y se sirban en obsequio de la Justicia de decretar su voluntad.

José María Silva + Pedro Antonio
Gallegos + José Rafael Saenez

Valle de Santa Gertrudes de lo de mora

Marzo 9 de 1837. Vista con reflección la anterior presentación que el tereno que solicitan de mi Jurisdición es publicada a los principales de este punto adataron a dicha solecitud.

Por no ser en perjuicio de terreno de viende [deben de] presentarse los Colones [colonos/*colonists*] para el día 1 del entrante abril.

Juan Nepumuseno Trujillo

[San Fernando, February 20, 1837

Sir Constitutional Alcalde of Las Trampas of our father Saint Joseph and illustrious Town Council:

We the citizen colonists, among your Lordship's proven subjects, upon finding ourselves very cut back in water supply at this current place of residence, appeal to your kindness in the name of God and his divine laws, if you could be magnanimous and grant us the right to take possession of the Valley of Guadalupita, at the Coyote River, to cultivate and sustain a settlement there. If we are worthy of the honor of being granted that which we seek so that we may shed our blood in tribute to the nation, and it being in your power to give notice of what you justly [will] resolve, we know that those with money can impede or will remain better off than they seem [admit]. [To sustain] our families and in all reverence to the nation, with dignity please accept our stated need with the list attached so that you may know the number of individuals that we submit for your kindness, and that is why we place this request to see if you can serve in the name of Justice to decree your wishes.

José María Silva,
Pedro Antonio Gallegos,
José Rafael Saenez

Valley of Saint Gertrudes of Mora

March 9, 1937. In reference to the above request, the land that they solicit from my jurisdiction has been communicated to the principals in this case as adopted [stipulated] in this request.

Without prejudice to the lands, the colonists should present themselves before me the first of this coming April.

Juan Nepumuseno Trujillo]

TWO

Evolution of the Acequia Institution

❖

Spanish legal instructions for the settlement of the *provincias internas* focused mainly on physical-design ordinances and related guidelines to be followed in the selection of locations suitable for habitation. Criteria included proximity of the proposed colony to vital natural resources in the vicinity; the development of master plans to locate town facilities, buildings, and streets; and the adoption of land-use regulations to support agricultural production. On the other hand, prescriptions for social and political organization, outside the official town governments (*cabildos* such as Santa Fe and a handful of other municipal jurisdictions), were not dictated by ordinance or by other precise laws. Instead, early settlers in the outlying and agricultural *jurisdicciones* relied on the customs, practices, and social institutions most familiar to them, transplanted as they were themselves, from Mexico and Spain.

The land-grant petitioners and other colonists who arrived in La Provincia del Nuevo México prior to 1680 established the basic framework for adaptation to be followed by the subsequent waves of immigrants. As agropastoralists, they brought their farming, irrigation, and ranching institutions, introducing them to the Pueblo Indians in the process. The main commodities they brought to the region included horses, cattle, sheep, goats, vegetables, grains, fruits, and other diverse agricultural products, which the Indians quickly incorporated into their own staples of maize, beans, chile, cotton, and squash.[1]

Old World Traditions

The agropastoral practices that the *colonos* imported to the region, via Mexico, were principally those that had been developed in similar climatic areas of Spain, particularly in Andalusia and Valencia. As Thomas Glick and other historians have noted, the allocation, distribution, and administration of irrigation waters during the colonial period, and continuing into the present, have been strikingly similar to those of medieval Valencia, practices which have survived there as well.[2] A *Tribunal de Aguas*, for example, still manages the irrigation affairs of the Valencia *huertas* (fields and gardens), closely resembling the functions of the governing body of *comisionados* (ditch commission) in New Mexico. The *cequier* (water chief) or *partidor de aguas* (water distributor) during Spanish medieval times compares with the popular *mayordomo* (ditch boss or water superintendent) of New Mexico. As described by Glick, the duties for this medieval officer are virtually identical to the role of the New Mexico *mayordomo* even in modern times:

> The chief irrigation officers of the kingdom were the *sobrecequiers* and *cequiers*. . . . The canals of the Valencian *huerta* were administered by a *cequier* delegated by each community of irrigators at the general meeting. . . . The duties of *cequiers* [included]: see that no one dare steal water, nor disturb the canals, . . . clean the main canals from head to tail, . . . [maintain] bridges and . . . repair the diversion dam whenever it was breached. . . . Besides his enforcement activities, the *cequier* oversaw the normal distribution of water. . . . The daily activities of the irrigation community were necessarily directed by someone who knew the topography, regulations, and local traditions intimately.[3]

Another comparable official is the overseer, or *veedor*. In medieval Spain, the *veedor* was employed an an inspector who assisted the *cequier* with his responsibilities to oversee the operations of the irrigation system and to settle disputes. Glick points out that these *veedores* were not subordinate to the *cequier*, and conversely, their function was to represent the rights of the *comuna*, the community of irrigators. "Frequently the *cequier* counseled with the inspectors before rendering a decision, and thus the inspectors provided an added guarantee for the observance of customary practice and for the probity of the *cequier*."[4] In Spain, as in colonial New Mexico, the job of these local water inspectors, called *veedores* or *hombres peritos* (expert men) in New Mexico, was to ensure that customary practices were being followed, especially under conditions of water scarcity or in the settlement of disputes.

In 1722, for example, Alcalde Don Francisco Bueno de Bohórquez y Corcuera appointed two *veedores juezes* (overseer judges) to examine the fields in the Santa Fe vicinity and to distribute the water when the river was running extremely low, in accordance with the established principles of equity and fairness to those in greatest need.[5] A century later, the practice of appointing water judges or other inspectors to observe compliance with accepted norms and standards was still evident. In 1829 the *ayuntamiento* (town council) of Santa Fe appointed a *repartidor de agua* (water distributor) to ensure that water was not wasted, that the acequias were cleaned and maintained, and that adequate bridges (as livestock crossings) were constructed.[6]

In addition to role similarities with the major irrigation officials, other parallels with Old World traditions can be noted at the organizational level. In medieval Valencia, the basic irrigation unit in the society was the *comuna*, defined by Glick as a group or community of irrigators all irrigating from a single main canal.[7] The idea of a common ditch for all irrigators in any new settlement was replicated in the province of New Mexico from the outset of colonization and, in fact, was the key to both the development and upkeep of local acequias. As late as the territorial laws of 1851–52, each local ditch in New Mexico was still described as the *acequia de común*. Glick's description of the Spanish medieval *comuna* also could be used to describe the functions of the acequia institutions of Nuevo México. According to Glick,

> The primary business of the commons as a whole was to enact regulations for the distribution of water and maintenance of the canal system and then to elect the executive and administrative officers to whom authority for the day-to-day running of the canal's normal affairs was delegated. Ordinances [of 1435] established the duties of the *cequier* and his assistants, set fines for various misdemeanors, and stipulated obligations of the *hereters* regarding observance of turns, maintenance of the canal, and contribution of dues.[8]

Acequias and Environmental Ethics

Spanish medieval patterns of water use and the institutional framework for arid-lands irrigation have survived essentially intact into the modern era of agropastoral farming on the upper Río Grande. Unlike the fate of the community ditches in San Antonio, Texas, where the once indispensable network of mission acequias has been destroyed or reduced to tourism sites as remnants, the active acequias of New Mexico and southern Colorado still number well over one thousand. With pressures of population growth and large parts of the world still undergoing development, these ancient systems of the arid American Southwest can perhaps illuminate practices and value perspectives for application elsewhere. There are many aspects of acequia irrigation systems that lend themselves to replication.

A good starting point is to consider the conservation ethics and environmental values that acequia irrigators inherited and transplanted from Old World irrigation systems. Guided initially by Spanish and Mexican water laws, and in some places by the provisions stipulated in Spanish and Mexican land grants, the early settlers were mindful of conserving the resource base for themselves and for future generations, especially when the existing water supply could no longer support additional community growth. As described in Chapter 1, petitions for new lands and water-resource locations were submitted to the proper authorities with admirable regularity as population densities and increased agricultural production outstripped the carrying capacity of the resource base.

Petitioners had to satisfy the governor and *alcalde mayor* that the areas proposed for new land grants were not already occupied or prejudicial to the welfare of an Indian pueblo. The governor would not otherwise confirm the land grant. Further, *vecinos* who already occupied land-grant communities in the vicinity could file a protest if they determined that the boundaries for a new petition encroached on their resources. Such a protest was filed in 1795 in the lower Taos valley, when the neighbors of the proposed Río Grande del Rancho Grant appealed to Taos *alcalde* Antonio José Ortiz that approval of the petition would curtail flow from the already scanty stream they depended on for their own sustenance at downstream Trampas. Baxter's account of this controversy relates the adverse claims brought forth, in poignant terms, to the *alcalde* by the Trampas citizens: "the *vecinos* pointed out that additional irrigation would bring diminished harvests, leading to decreased tithes and first fruits for the Church, and great risk for their own livelihoods."[9]

In his ongoing study of Spanish colonial agriculture in the upper Río Grande, Estevan Arellano[10] attributes the strong land and water ethic to the enduring impact of environmental laws established from the outset of settlement in the Spanish *Leyes de las Indias* (Laws of the Indies). Pointing out that these laws defined the relationship of land and water to the culture that developed in the region, Arellano cites Book Four as the primary source of environmentalist ethics adopted by the settlers. The first law within Title Five of Book Four ordered that lands selected for settlement should be healthy, good for planting and foraging, the sky of good and joyful constellation, clean and benign, with pure and sweet air, without impediments or alterations, and with good grazing for livestock, forests and trees for firewood and building materials, and a plentiful supply of good waters for drinking and irrigation:

> Ordenamos, que . . . tengan los pobladores consideración y advertencia a que el terreno sea saludable . . . y de tierras a propósito para sembrar, y coger . . . el Cielo es de buena y feliz constelación, claro y benigno, el aire puro y suave, sin impedimentos, ni alteraciones . . . si hay pastos para criar ganados: montes y arboledas para leña: materiales de casas y edificios: muchas y buenas aguas para beber, y regar.[11]

Title Seven of Book Four reinforces the requirement that settlers should look for land and a surrounding environment that is not only fertile and healthy in soils, but contains abundant pasture, firewood, lumber, materials, sweet waters, and is free from the corruption of winds and waters:

> Ordenamos, que el terreno y cercanía, que se ha de poblar, se elija en todo lo posible el mas fértil, abúdante de pastos, leña, madera, materiales, aguas dulces, gente natural, acarreos, entrada y salida, y que no tengan cerca lagunas, ni pantanos en que se crien animales venenosos, ni haya corrupción de ayeres, ni aguas.[12]

Spanish environmental laws were respected and upheld by water officials when necessary at the local community level, even prior to the Laws of the Indies. In medieval Spain, for example, water-use laws prohibited the pollution of ditch waters, authorizing local *cequiers* to impose fines in cases where water was being polluted or wasted. In his study of the most common water misdemeanors documented in two account books of Castellón for the years 1443 and 1486, Glick found that along with the taking of forbidden water, the two other most frequently imposed fines were for wasting water and the unauthorized washing of clothing, sheets, or wool in the ditch.[13]

Water-quality protection and conservation were also taken seriously in the *acequias de común* that flourished centuries later in the upper Río Grande, carrying forward the water ethic evident in the irrigation societies of medieval Spain. In his review of customary practices transplanted from Spain to New Mexico, Ebright found evidence that the environmentalist ethic was woven directly into the very fabric of custom and public law in the Spanish-Mexican land-grant communities. The 1705 decrees in Santa Fe, Ebright points out, mandated that villagers should not drive their livestock onto a marshy wetland and public commons known as the *cienega*. Later, in 1717, the village pigs and other loose animals were rounded up so as not to damage planted fields or the highly valued grass meadows found at the *cienega* commons.[14]

At the founding of Pitic (now Hermosillo, Mexico) in 1789, Spanish colonial law for all new towns required settlers to conserve water by establishing rotation schedules where irrigators would equitably share available water by taking turns. The ordinance simultaneously prevented waste and mitigated conflicts. Later, during the Mexican period, the Provincial Statutes of 1824–26 authorized local *alcaldes* to impose a one-*peso* fine, plus the cost of repairs, on any irrigator who caused the flooding of roads and fields by not closing off his ditches when they overflowed.[15] A much more comprehensive set of acequia statutes was adopted in 1851 and 1852, at the start of the territorial period in New Mexico. Here again, water conservation was mandated. Section thirteen of these written laws stipulated that the *mayordomo* should apportion the available waters to a particular irrigator, but not only according to the amount of cultivated land he owned; the *mayordomo* should also take into consideration "*la naturaleza de las semillas, cosechas y de las legumbres que se cultivan . . .* " ("the nature of the seeds, crops and plants to be cultivated . . ."). Furthermore, each irrigator was entitled to retain all native plants of any description growing naturally on the ditch banks bordering and running through his property.[16]

Other territorial laws specifically addressed the need to maintain water purity and quality in local ditches. The laws of 1868 and 1872, enacted for communities in Valencia and Socorro counties, authorized local *mayordomos* to levy fines against persons who befouled acequia waters by washing dirty clothes, bathing, or allowing swine to wallow inside the ditch.[17] By the turn of the century, a series of general laws had been enacted, in 1880, 1897, and 1899, that applied to all acequias of the territory. These laws prohibited the pollution of streams, lakes, and ditches by any number of means or the discarding of objects that would endanger the public health of the community. The penalties, upon conviction, were gradually made more severe, up to one hundred dollars and/or a sixty-day jail sentence in the 1897 laws.[18]

Water conservation became a frequent concern as the number of ditches and irrigators increased in some of the more populated valleys. The solutions and arrangements for the sharing of available water were primarily of local design. For example, an 1895 legal agreement between two community precincts in Taos County provided for the conservation of water during periods of shortage by establishing, at the time of cultivation, a schedule of water delivery for mutual benefit. One precinct could take the water for the exclusive use of irrigation of crops weekly, "on Friday evening at sunset and keeping the same in the ditch all day and night Saturday and until Sunday at 12 O'clock noon," when the overseer of the the ditch would turn the water over to the people of the second precinct for their use the rest of the week. Per terms of the agreement, this rotation would be repeated through the remainder of the irrigation season, lasting until the fifteenth day of September every year.[19]

Water-rotation schedules have continued as a practice into the contemporary period, and are evidence of the persistent conservation ethos among acequia *parciantes* as well as a reflection of the need to maintain the common good. Passed on through oral traditions are instructions for individual irrigators to always tend to their waters in the *sangrías* that flood their fields during their water turns. "You have to watch your *sangrías* and move with the water until your parcel is irrigated; then, at that time, you turn the water over to your *vecino*."[20] Moreover, conservation values repeatedly have been inscribed into formal ditch rules since the time they began to appear in writing. Among others, the Corrales Ditch Rules of 1928 prohibited the destruction of berms on the mother ditch so as not to lose water in the ditch and cause damage to the irrigator's planted fields or those of a neighbor: *"Nadien tendrá derecho de destruir los bordos de la acequia madre a modo que [h]aiga peligro de que se rompa la acequia [h]acerse perjuición a si mismo o al vecino."*[21]

Rules have also been crafted by the irrigators to protect and enforce water quality standards in the ditch. Just before statehood in 1911, the *parcionistas* (landowner irrigators) of the Margarita Ditch in Lincoln County charged the *mayordomo* with enforcing the *"Reglas de Limpiesa"* (Rules for Cleanliness). These rules prohibited anyone from discarding junk in the community ditch, namely *"garras, cajetes, puercos cueros, barriles o otras porquerillas que sean en prejuicio de la saludbridad de los ha[b]itantes"* (rags, tubs, pig hides, barrels, or other filthy objects which might endanger citizen

health).[22] Public health was likewise a concern in the Jacona Ditch Rules
during the 1950s and well into the modern period, before clean water and
concern for other environmental resources became more widespread in
the general society: "No garbage, trash, rubbish or other objectionable
matter may enter the ditch, and each [irrigator] is responsible to keep the
ditch on his property free from the same."[23]

More recently, the environmental contributions of acequia irrigation
methods of the agropastoral farmers in the upper Río Grande have caught
the attention of conservation biologists, environmental scientists, historians, and other social science scholars. According to work in progress conducted by Devón Peña, Rubén Martínez and a team of interdisciplinary
researchers, the benefits of acequia-based farming extend well beyond the
consumptive needs of the irrigators themselves. Preliminary results from
this unique research indicate that acequia-based agropastoral farming increases the local biodiversity, extends the riparian zone, and protects the
hydraulic integrity of the watershed.[24]

Though little recognized in the public discourse, acequia irrigation
technologies actually serve more than one public purpose. The impacts on
the landscape, local hydrology, biodiversity values, and wildlife are multiple. The earthen acequia watercourse itself helps to recharge the local
aquifer through the natural process of seepage. Aided by gravity flow, water that continues to flow in the ditch, in turn, serves to extend the stream
to a new, wider landscape, resulting in a benign irrigation technology
which helps to control soil erosion. Water that percolates down to the
aquifer aids in the cleansing of groundwater. Seepage throughout the ditch
system nourishes the cottonwood bosques as well as native shrubs such as
plum, *capulín*, and willows, which, in turn, provide shelter for wildlife.[25]
Any unused waters are returned to the stream as *sobrantes*, or surplus waters, destined to support other values or users downstream.

Putting stream waters to beneficial use through acequia-based farming
also helps to maintain instream flows for the protection of fish habitats.
Other water-use alternatives, especially water-rights transfers from surface use to groundwater pumping deplete hydrologically connected stream
flows. This application can result in the lowering of the flows to levels potentially adverse to fish and other wildlife depending on river systems that
are wet year round.[26] Acequia systems, on the other hand, contribute to
the health of the river by flushing silt, creating a hydraulic head, and taking surface water in the season when it is available, as opposed to groundwater pumping, which often creates deficits of water quantity by depleting
the aquifers well into future years.

Disputes and Public Regulations

The institutional framework for acequia administration was transplanted from the Old World, but most scholars agree that local arrangements evolved from a process of customary usage rather than through a set of prescribed laws or ordinances. Spanish and Mexican water laws pertinent to water management were implemented as guidelines and, more often than not, were elaborated to fit prevailing norms, customs, traditions, and local circumstances. In the frontier environment of the Spanish border-lands, the legal and judicial systems were informal or decidedly more casual than those elsewhere. As Ebright points out, the customary process of *conciliación* (conciliation) compensated for the lack of trained legal professionals. *Conciliación* was a localized procedure where each of the disputants in a case was free to appoint an *hombre bueno* (a good and honest man), who would represent his interests before the *alcalde* hearing the dispute.[27] As their charge, these two men would be asked to recommend a fair settlement so that the *alcalde* could render a decision acceptable to the original parties in the dispute and avoid a formal trial. Presumably, the *hombres buenos* would design workable solutions not according to a formal set of codified laws they knew little about, but according to the standards and informal precepts acceptable to the majority of *vecinos* in the locality. Following Ebright's analysis, local officials and other lay persons took the place of a more formal legal system of justice and acted, as they were often requested, as the arbiters of custom in their particular localities.[28]

Thus, to a significant degree, acequia customary laws were probably improvised and then more broadly applied on a case-by-case basis. They became formalized gradually, after a period of time and as local conditions required official interpretation of specific rules and standards of conduct. Before water judges were appointed and sent out to investigate a dispute or oversee the distribution of irrigation waters, government officials would likely articulate the principles and requirements acceptable in the affected locality or jurisdiction, as was done by Santa Fe Alcalde Don Francisco Bueno de Bohórquez y Corcuera in 1722 (see case details below). The results of these deliberations and subsequent field inspections were often made public in proclamation orders issued by the *alcaldes* where the disputes arose, making compilation possible at a later date. With the exception of the provincial statutes enacted during the early period of Mexican jurisdiction, comprehensive rules pertaining to acequia governance and operations remained unwritten until the territorial period. (Acequia laws, as we now know them, were not codified until the territorial laws of 1851 and 1852; see details in Chapter 3.)

Were it not for a few dozen known cases that document irrigation disputes as they were brought forward for judicial resolution, the accepted practices of each time period prior to 1851 would have remained even more obscure. In most cases, the disputes were brought forward as complaints and to the attention of the *alcalde mayor* of the jurisdiction and, on occasion, were presented directly to the governor. Typical disputes during the colonial era included friction over inequitable apportionment of water, claimed damages to the acequia, locations of acequia rights-of-way, noncompliance with ditch-labor participation, alleged theft of water, and damage to crops resulting from overflows or flooding.[29]

An early recorded set of public regulations were issued in Santa Fe in July of 1722, when Alcalde Francisco Bueno de Bohórquez y Corcuera determined to allocate irrigation waters diverted from the Río de Santa Fe during the summer months, when shortages frequently occurred.[30] In his order, the Santa Fe *alcalde* sought to avoid discord among *vecinos* of the fledgling *villa* concerning their need to irrigate fields and gardens. Accordingly, he appointed two *veedores juezes* (water judges or overseers) to inspect the *milpas* and *huertas* (fields and gardens) and to distribute the water under the established principles of equity and fairness, rules which presumably reduced to writing the norms and customs that prevailed at the time. To guide them in their task, the *alcalde* instructed the judges to keep in mind that:

1. distribution should first go to those in greatest need such as widows;
2. the quantity allocated should be in proportion to the size of the irrigated fields;
3. a rotation schedule should be followed on a use it or lose basis, until the next turn;
4. irrigators who failed to control for weeds would not receive water until the problem was deemed corrected by the water judge;
5. the judges must not allow the improper taking of water from others, nor should they favor relatives or in-laws.[31]

To enforce these provisions, the *alcalde* empowered the water judges to imprison anyone who disobeyed or was rude to them. Any *vecino* who did not show respect or did not obey determinations made by the *veedores* could be fined twenty-five *pesos* and be ordered to serve eight days in jail on the first offense.[32]

In another jurisdiction, a widow from Abiquiu, Margarita de Luna, appeared before the governor and capitán general of New Mexico in 1769, pleading successfully that he order the Zalasares (a family) to not block her use of ditch water needed to irrigate her cultivated fields. She also succeeded in obtaining a stipulation that the Zalasares should help her clean and maintain the ditch. Both parties consented, but a year later, 1770, the widow wrote a letter to the governor recounting her complaint and alleging that the Zalasares had not allowed the passage of waters to her fields after all, causing her to lose her yearly crop that season. In addition, she noted that the dams built by them had flooded lands of other residents of Abiquiu. Her new petition was that the Zalasares be ordered to not use her ditch at all and that they be required to dig their own or use another.[33]

Here too, the ruling by the governor expressed the prevailing norms and acceptable practices for the entire community to follow, which he applied to the case at hand:

1. the watercourse should not be blocked or dammed in detriment to downstream users who have water rights;
2. all water users should share in the maintenance of the ditch;
3. violations of these rules could be appealed to higher authorities.[34]

The settlement of water disputes, cases recorded as they were within the particular orders of judgment by the hearing official, probably helped to develop and document the customary laws that later would be made more explicit in statutes. In some rural jurisdictions, water officials actually found it useful and even necessary to issue general instructions for everyone to follow, based on past and cumulative experience with individual cases. In 1813, for example, Don Ygnacio María Sánchez Vergara, *alcalde mayor* of the Jemez jurisdiction, issued a broad proclamation covering a variety of local situations that heretofore had proven troublesome to his authority and damaged the welfare of the community. Complaining of vagrants and other shiftless persons "who aspire to wrong-doing," he ordered that persons who did not toil in the fields would be obliged to leave the district; and masters should supply all worthy servants with a plot of tillable ground to permit them the means with which to maintain their families.[35]

Alcalde Sánchez Vergara went on to note that roaming livestock had been causing destruction along the edges of fields and ditches:

> In vain have the superior authorities demanded compliance with orders which prohibit grazing-stock from being pastured alongside cultivated fields or along the banks of irrigation ditches, even under the pretext that they are milk animals. . . . And in spite of what has been ordered, [irresponsible owners] continue to pay no attention to these very reasonable restrictions.[36]

Accordingly, the *alcalde mayor* stipulated, under the threat of punishment for the careless:

1. during the spring planting season, the ditch cleaning and throughout the growing season, livestock raisers must pasture their animals away from the cropland and the banks of irrigation ditches;
2. animals should be kept out of farmlands belonging to the Indians under all circumstances with severe penalties to be imposed on any transgressors; and
3. flumes and bridges should be constructed where needed to prevent the theft of waters from one ditch to another and to provide for livestock crossings.[37]

Stiff penalties were noted in the proclamation; for example, masters who did not allocate plots of cultivated lands to their servants would be fined eight *pesos fuertes*; owners of livestock who did not keep their animals under care and away from the cultivated fields would be fined one-half of a *real* of silver for each head; worse yet, irrigators who did not build the necessary flumes to cross over other ditches would pay the consequences, "suffering four days of imprisonment in the public jail."[38]

By the start of the early Mexican period, the body of rules and the system of how officials should handle ditch and irrigation infractions were sufficiently developed that the Provincial Deputation, the legislative council of the period, adopted formal statutes that would apply to all jurisdictions. In these 1824 statutes (revised in 1826), all *alcaldes* of the province were instructed to administer a uniform schedule of penalties and method for the collection of fines under specified types of violations:

1. Owners of loose cattle and other animals which cause damage to the cultivated fields and property of others would be assessed two *reales* for each head plus actual damages;

2. Those who flooded the roads and fields by not closing off ditches when they overflowed would be fined one *peso* plus the costs or repairs;

3. A greedy irrigator who took water out of turn by shutting water off from the designated user would be fined twelve *reales*, one *peso* for the collection fund, and four *reales* for the owner of the water;

4. The supervisor of the *acequia madre* who did not comply with his duties would be discharged and fined three *pesos*; and

5. Those who failed to contribute to the work of the village, such as maintenance of the *acequia madre* and the church, were to be fined four *reales*, "two for his disobedience and two for the work which he should have lent."[39]

The provincial authorities were formalizing the precepts and standards that were based on customary practices, but which may not have been clear in actual law or uniformly applied across all of the *alcalde* jurisdictions.[40] These precursor acequia laws thus sought to identify the more common violations and specify the appropriate penalties, while at the same time creating a public fund to facilitate further compliance and to provide for local needs such as ditch repairs. The preface to the revised statutes of 1826 stated these objectives quite precisely:

These [means] are those derived from mature experience, whereby the disorders and problems with which the authorities are occupied are found to result from the failure of light penalties or those minor transgressions which are committed indifferently, by not having a clear law which states the penalties deserved by those who commit them; thus there is formed a list of these failings, with a monetary punishment designated for each, obtaining the avoidance of harm and the establishment of funds which are to the benefit of the same public, in behalf of whom, and in behalf of compliance with the exactitude which this important matter requires, now the following are submitted.[41]

As official orders, proclamations, and regulations became more formally established and widely circulated throughout the New Mexico province, the administration of the irrigation system itself also developed in maturity and sophistication. Though government officials and legislative bodies were beginning the process of codifying irrigation laws in this distant outpost, it would be up to local *mayordomos* and their acequia or-

ganizations to implement them. The operations and management of acequia systems would also increase in complexity with the passage of each
period and the adoption of explicit laws, a process described further in
Chapter 3.

Vernacular Traditions and Local Customs

In public testimony provided at a court hearing in the early 1990s, historian Daniel Tyler noted that the isolation of irrigators during earlier periods of settlement resulted in usages and practices that may have varied
somewhat site by site.[42] Knowledge of local rules was essential to successful implementation and, if necessary, enforcement. To survive, these informal rules had to be clear, locally understood and accepted by the users,
continuously applied, reasonable, and remain largely undisputed in order
for *alcaldes* to make rulings that would carry the force of law. Factors of
need, noninjury, equity, and a concern for the common good were usually
considered when it came time to apportion community water. To Tyler,
this explains, in part, why the rules and regulations during the earlier periods of acequia history did not have to be reduced to writing on a more formal basis.[43]

More often than not, the weight of time, "time immemorial," would
create acceptance of customary standards. The official rulings by water inspectors, *jueces*, and *alcaldes* would follow traditional procedures for water
management. In his extensive analysis of land grants and actual litigation
cases involving land and water issues, Ebright concurs with Tyler:

> During both the Spanish and the Mexican Periods, disputes over
> land and water were settled primarily according to the customs fol-
> lowed in the remote frontier that was New Mexico. Records of liti-
> gation reveal once again that local custom was more often the basis
> for decision than were the formal rules of Spanish law.[44]

In the area of water-law petitions, Ebright describes in great detail the
classic ditch dispute in 1832 involving Don Manuel Martínez and his Abiquiu neighbor, Ramón Martínez.[45] Interestingly, disputes such as this left
a paper trail of fragmentary documents revealing the intricacies of how
custom and tradition prevailed in the judicial administrative process, even
when high-level officials were brought into the case. Ebright's painstaking
review of the documents surrounding the Martínez ditch dispute led him
to conclude that water-use conflicts were worked out and resolved more

through customary legal forms based on tradition than on legal codes.[46] Though the series of petitions in this case, by Don Manuel Martínez of Abiquiu, were addressed to the highest official in the land, New Mexico Governor Abreu, the governor disposed of the case by refering it to the *ayuntamiento*, with the stipulated order that this local administrative body "decide [the case] according to what you believe is just and . . . according to the uses and customs which have been observed in that jurisdiction in such cases."[47]

Some of the very first narrative accounts of acequia customs and practices came from the diaries and journals of Anglo-Americans who entered the region from the East more than two centuries after Oñate supervised the construction of the first Spanish ditch at San Juan de los Caballeros in 1598. In 1807, Lieutenant Zebulon M. Pike of the U.S. Army led an expedition into the plains territories in search of the headwaters of the Arkansas and Red rivers. On March 7 he arrived in Albuquerque, a village on the east side of the Río del Norte. In his diary entry for that day, he marveled at the communal labor and festivities associated with the spring opening of the irrigation ditches:

> Both above and below Albuquerque the citizens were beginning to open the canals to let in the water of the river to fertilize the plains and fields which border its banks on both sides, where we saw men, women, and children of all ages and sexes at the joyful labor which was to crown with rich abundance their future harvest and insure them plenty for the ensuing year. Those scenes brought to my recollection the bright descriptions given by Savary of the opening of the canals of Egypt. The cultivation of the fields was now commencing and everything appeared to give life and gaiety to the surrounding scenery.[48]

A more complete description of the irrigation systems and the supervision required to maintain the *acequia madre* appeared in the journal narratives of Josiah Gregg, when he wrote his firsthand accounts of New Mexican agriculture. Traveling with merchant caravans on the Santa Fe Trail from 1831 to 1840, he noted the relatively primitive state of agriculture: cultivation was accomplished by hoes alone or with ploughs rudely constructed from sections of tree trunks with protruding branches.[49] Nonetheless, Gregg credited acequia farmers with mastering the "art" of irrigation:

All the acequias for the valley of the *Río del Norte* are conveyed from
the main stream, except where a tributary of more convenient water
happens to join it. As the banks of the river are very low, and the de-
scent considerable, the water is soon brought upon the surface by a
horizontal ditch along an inclined bank, commencing at a convenient
point of constant-flowing water — generally without [a] dam except
sometimes a wing of stones to turn the current into the canal.[50]

The *acequia madre*, Gregg noted, suffices to convey water for the irrigation of an entire valley or settlement, and is "made and kept in repair by
the public, under the supervision of the alcaldes."[51] Though written in narrative form, Josiah Gregg's journal captured some of the basic rules and
procedures of acequia irrigation already in effect, anticipating the more
formal territorial water laws written a decade or so later: labor to maintain
and repair the ditch is shared by the public users; each proprietor runs a
minor ditch over the most elevated part of his field; when there is a shortage of water, each farmer is allotted his day or portion of a day; completing the process, the cultivator lets water into his minor ditch and floods
his fields a section at a time by causing the water to spread regularly over
the surface.[52]

Josiah Gregg's observations reflected a period when the *acequia de
común* was still the central institution in the agropastoral economies of the
New Mexico province. The community ditch, and the water flowing
through the main canal and into the lateral *sangrías*, defined the interdependence between the natural landscape and the society of irrigators.
Since each system was different, the crafting of rules to work out effective
arrangements for the community as a whole became very much a local
process that obviated the need for a uniform set of written laws issued by
a higher level of authority. Rather than a codified set of laws, the irrigators
needed a small number of rules that were clear, fair, and understood by all
the users. During the pre-territorial periods, water was viewed as essential
to the sustenance of community, not as a commodity property subject to
the forces of economic markets and government regulation. The allocation or irrigation was communal, not private. Lastly, the dispersed pattern
of settlement insulated the more outlying *ranchos* from outside governance
and the more formal legislative process, a condition that would start to
change with United States territorial status and statehood.

DOCUMENTS

Acequia de Chamita at San Gabriel, c. 1612–13

The Laws of the Indies instructed colonists to establish settlements in sites with access to plentiful supplies of clean and pure waters for irrigation and domestic purposes. In addition, the lands and the surrounding environment should be replete with the natural resources necessary to sustain permanent colonies: forests to supply fuel wood and building materials, abundant pasturelands for the grazing of livestock, lands with healthy and fertile soils for the planting and harvesting of crops, and a sky with clean and pure air.

After Capitán General and Governor Juan de Oñate decided to abandon his first colony at San Juan, he did not have to go very far to locate a site that complied with the royal ordinances. Across the Río Grande, at its confluence with the Río Chama entering from the west, Oñate found an ideal site at *el Yunque*, a partially abandoned Tewa Pueblo, which he renamed the villa of San Gabriel in c. 1600. Here, too, one of the first tasks of the Oñate party was to construct an irrigation ditch sufficient to irrigate the fields to be cultivated in the fertile valley between the two rivers.

Most scholars agree that San Gabriel was located in the community now known as Chamita and that the Oñate ditch at this location is the present-day Acequia de Chamita. When Franciscan historian Fray Juan de Torquemanda visited San Gabriel a decade or so after its founding, he observed a thriving agricultural community during the period of his visitation, as he reported in an historical volume written c. 1612–13 and published in 1615. See *Monarquía Indiana por Fray Juan de Torquemada*, 3 vols., Tercera Edición (México, D.F.: Editorial Salvador Chávez Hayhoe, 1943), 1:678.

Libro Quinto, CAP. XXXX. Donde se da fin a las Relaciones de el Nuevo México, y se dicen en particular las cosas tocantes a sus Moradores.

Ya hemos dicho, que el Lugar principal donde el Governador Don Juan de Oñate hizo su Población, y sentó su Real, le puso por Nombre San Gabriel, y que está situado en treinta y siete Grados de altura, y que tiene por vanda dos Ríos, uno de los cuáles es de menos Agua, que el otro. Este chico riega todas las Sementeras de Trigo, y Cebada, y Maíz, que ay de Riego, y todas las demás cosas, que se siembran en Huertas, porque se dan en

aquella Tierra Coles, Cebollas, Lechugas, y Rábanos, y la demás verdura
menuda, que en esta: danse muchos, y buenos Melones, y Sandías. El otro
Río es mui grande, y llámanle de el Norte, dase en el mucho Pescado. . . .

[Book Five, Chap. 40. Wherein concludes the accounts of New Mexico
and where things related to her settlers are mentioned in detail.

We have already mentioned that the principal location where Governor Don Juan de Oñate established his settlement and capital, he called by
name San Gabriel. And this is situated at thirty-seven degrees latitude,
and its sides consist of two rivers, one of which has less water than the
other. This small one [the Río Chama] irrigates all the varieties of wheat,
barley, and corn, in cultivated fields, and other things that are planted in
gardens, because those lands produce cabbage, onions, lettuce and beets,
and other small vegetables than in this one: producing many and good
melons and watermelons. The other river is very large, they call it [Río] de
el Norte, which provides a lot of fish. . . .]

De Vargas Proceedings in the Settlement of
Santa Cruz de la Cañada, 1695–96

The next villa to be founded after Santa Fe was "La Villa Nueva de Santa
Cruz de la Cañada de Españoles-Mexicanos del Rey Nuestro Señor Carlos Segundo." On April 19, 1695, Governor Don Diego de Vargas issued a
proclamation founding this new settlement some twenty miles to the
north of the capital city, allowing settlers to occupy the land and establish
homesites and farms. According to Baxter, De Vargas carefully chose the
site at La Cañada valley because of its known fertile soils and plentiful
water supply for irrigation. See Baxter, *Dividing New Mexico Waters*, pp.
5–6. These resources were needed to sustain the growing populations,
newly arrived families from Zacatecas and Mexico City, that could no
longer be supported by the acequias and cultivated fields established earlier in the century at Santa Fe. In his proclamation of the Santa Cruz land
grant to the Spanish-Mexican families, De Vargas designated to them not
only the town site for the new Villa but also the use of the "cleared agricultural lands, drains, irrigation ditches and dam or dams" as well as access
to the "woods, pastures and valleys" within the La Cañada environs. A
few days later, he placed the families in possession of the Nueva Villa de
Santa Cruz, escorting them to the site himself and conducting the appropriate land grant ceremonies.

Around a year later, on May 8th, 1696, De Vargas issued a decree allowing a second group of Spanish-Mexican families to move from Santa Fe to Santa Cruz because the irrigation water supplies continued to be inadequate to handle more growth at the capital city. Translated excerpts from this decree appear below, and together with the proclamation, illustrate the Spanish colonial policies of town site planning, common lands use and the reciprocal interdependence involving land grants, irrigation and community in the emerging acequia culture of the upper Río Grande province. The decree can be found in its entirety at the Spanish Archives of New Mexico, SANM I Translations, archive no. 817, State Records Center and Archives, Santa Fe, NM. The April 19, 1695, proclamation and the subsequent possession ceremony are at archive no. 882.

Having recognized that in this villa of Santa Fe there is not the supply of water which is requisite to insure the irrigation of the cultivated fields, in order to maintain the families domiciled thereon; and having recognized that this said villa has better accommodations for the reception of the families which the King, our Lord, whom God preserve, has seen fit to send for the settlement of this said kingdom and its frontiers; and finding the Villa Nueva de Santa Cruz already inhabited by the Mexican-Spanish subjects of the King, our Lord, Carlos Segundo [Charles Second], I assign them to said villa for the aforesaid reasons.

I, the said Governor and Capitán General, have decided to go personally to the said Villa Nueva de Santa Cruz, not only to prepare and order them, but also to inform them that they need four houses; and likewise to examine the lands, whose sections are uncultivated, being naturally fertile, and being under irrigation as they are, and able to use the water which the rest have had generally in great abundance, assured by their ditches, clean and running, which have been established at my own expense, as I have also repaired and made their dam secure.

I order and command the nineteen families of the forty-four which arrived on the 9th day of May of last year, one thousand six hundred and ninety-five, who are the following, whom I appoint, choose, name, order and command to go and settle in said Villa Nueva, enjoying the same freedom, privileges and respect that the King, our Lord, whom God guard, is able to grant them.

... After their arrival at the said Villa, I, the said Governor and Capitán General, will go in person and place them in the said four houses, and I will also order the Alcalde Mayor to divide the aforesaid lands that he showed me and assigned to them. I will likewise give each one three almudes of corn for planting. . . .

. . . likewise this will serve them as a patent to be residents belonging and assigned to the said Villa Nueva of Santa Cruz, and as such will further their use of the said lands, and their right to the pastures, woods, waters and minerals, as it appears in the grant made to the said Mexican residents of said Villa Nueva, and that the said order made in their favor will be sufficient title for the privileges derived from the grant that I, the said Governor and Capitán General have assigned to them in the name of his Majesty.

> *Don Diego de Vargas Zavala Luján*
> *Ponze de León*
> *(Rubric)*
>
> *By order of his Excellency, the Governor*
> *and Capitán General.*
> *Domingo de la Barreda*
> *(Rubric)*
> *Secretary of Government [and] War*

Margarita de Luna vs. Zalasares, Abiquiu, 1770 Ditch Dispute

Much of what is known about irrigation customs, especially during the Spanish colonial period, is attributable to the fact that disputes over any number of practices arose from time to time, causing the aggrieved parties to take their complaints to higher officials. This process of judicial administrative review helped to preserve fragments of written evidence, such as petitions, rulings, decrees, or other official documents, which provide insightful information on the customary laws acceptable to the society of the times. In the document below, a widow from Abiquiu, Margarita de Luna, petitions by letter to the governor, reporting that his ruling in her favor a year earlier had fallen on deaf ears. The defendants and her neighbors in the case, the Zalasares, continued to block her use of irrigation waters, causing her to lose her yearly crops.

The English translation by Anselmo Arellano is based on Spanish language document, SANM II, Reel 10, Frames 619–623, New Mexico State Records and Archives Center.

Sir Governor and Capitán General:
Margarita de Luna, widow of the military commander, Pedro Martín, appeared before your excellency in the best agreeable manner, and I state

that last year your excellency was pleased to pass sentence on the dispute I had with the Zalasares with regard to my irrigation ditch, whereby you ordered them not to block or prevent me from using the necessary water I need for my cultivation, to which ditch I hold exclusive rights, and that as long as they helped me with the ditch cleaning they could use the water without prejudice on my part, and that if they did not allow me to pass the water I needed, they would be excluded from the ditch. And we were notified of this decision, and we consented to it. But it was not enough to contain the Zalasares with the order, as they prevented passage of my water, and for lack of irrigation I lost my crops. And being that neither through my pleading nor any other means did they allow passage of the water, I went to see the *alcalde* who was Don Antonio Joseph Ortiz. The testimony contained in the sentence was manifested, and since he was busy, he sent Don Salvador García who was the commander. He recognized my farmland and obligated the Zalasares to follow the order in the sentence, that which was executed by our commander, and seeing the field and finding it dry and lost, he told me that even if I were to irrigate it with holy water, it had no remedy. And therefore, they let me irrigate for eight days, or to water that part which could be salvaged and that afterwards I would let them irrigate for that year, to which I protested that the following year, which is the present, I would not consent to them irrigating from my ditch and that they would lose the condition of the sentence by having violated the order completely, and since last year the Zalasares had two or three dams. I could not irrigate my land as is presently the case in which many residents from Abiquiu find their lands flooded by the Zalasares, for which I ask and beg your excellency that the Zalasares be ordered not to use my ditch and that they dig their own or use another without prejudice to me with respect to the reasons which are already provided in said sentence which should be executed with mercy and justice. And I ask and swear not to possess malice in that which is necessary.

Margarita de Luna
February, 1770

Algodones Ditch Dispute, 1829, Testimony

In this dispute, representatives from the Santa Ana Indian Pueblo and Don Pablo Montoya appeared before Alcalde Pedro José Perea to determine the obligations of Don Pablo with respect to water access on a shared acequia. Following the established process of *conciliación*, the *alcalde* employed the services of *"dos hombres buenos nombrados por ambas partes"* (two good men named and approved by both parties). After hearing from these advisors, the *alcalde* agreed with their interpretation of the law: Don Pablo should no longer be provided water unless he helped the Santa Ana Pueblo to clean the ditch. Accordingly, the *alcalde* instructed the *alcalde de agua* (water judge) that Don Pablo should be obligated to work the ditch along with the Santa Ana Pueblo.

The translation by Anselmo Arellano is based on Spanish-language document, Julius Seligman Collection, 1791–1872, University of New Mexico Zimmerman Library, Center for Southwest Research.

Bernalillo, July 18, 1829

On this date, the sons of Santa Ana Pueblo and Don Pablo Montoya presented themselves before this court of justice, and enforcing the law before us, I had two good men [*dos hombres buenos*] brought forth approved by both parties. And after having heard the complaint both parties gave in my presence, it was decided through justice, and presented to the *Alcalde de Agua* [water judge] who runs it that Don Pablo Montoya must work the ditch with all the Pueblo [Santa Ana]; and he was obligated, if it becomes necessary, to give them all the assistance they request, and which he can provide, without dispute or repugnance, something which before now was prohibited to the sons from the Pueblo. And that they work the acequia, with Don Pablo making haste beginning with the first cleaning. And the two associates, realizing that the management which had previously been made to give him water without providing any labor was something contrary to law, and they ordered that from this day forward Don Pablo Montoya shall work in the acequia, being that this was found and decided; = this is a copy of the original which is found in these Archives to which I refer, = Pedro José Perea, Alcalde

In testifying to the same, I certify the present copy, with the power vested in me by the law, being duly recorded for constancy and I sign and seal it in this Villa of Algodones, County of Santa Ana, being the Alcalde of said county, on this 13th day of October, present day of Our Lord, 1848.

Jesús Miera
Alcalde
[Seal]

W. W. H. Davis, Description of
New Mexico Acequias, 1857

During the middle 1850s, W. W. H. Davis traveled through New Mexico, then a young territory under U.S. jurisdiction, and marveled at the engineering accomplishments of the acequia farmers who maximized every tract of land that could possibly be irrigated in the narrow and hilly terrain. This description of the New Mexico acequias, as well as Davis's description of the Mexican plow and use of oxen which follows, appeared in his book published in 1857, based on the diary he had kept during his two and a half years stay in New Mexico. In his preface, Davis noted that "the matters contained in it are either drawn from careful personal observation, or other reliable sources."

Davis's descriptions are from his *El Gringo: New Mexico and Her People* (University of Nebraska Press, Lincoln, 1982; 1st ed.: Harper and Brothers, 1857).

The system of acequias, or irrigation ditches, is a subject so new to the American farmer, that an explanation at some length of the manner in which the land is cultivated by means of them may not be uninteresting. It must be borne in mind, as we have already remarked, that all the land capable of being farmed lies in the valleys through which runs a river or other stream large enough to supply the necessary quantity of water. . . . The valleys are generally narrow, approached on either side by hills, and it is customary to cut the ditch along their base, when only one is required for a given tract of country, so that after the water shall have been distributed, the surplus can find its way back to the river. The main ditch is sometimes several miles in length, and resembles a miniature Erie Canal; and it is dug by the joint labor of all the proprietors along the line, each one being required to furnish a number of hands in proportion to his land to be irrigated. . . .

The whole management of irrigating ditches is now governed by a law of the Territory in pretty much the same manner as roads in the States. The several justices of the peace are authorized to call together annually the owners of ditches, and the proprietors of the land watered by them, to elect one or more overseers . . . to superintend the erection and repairs of ditches. . . . In all that devolves upon the overseer of ditches, he has about the same duties to discharge as a supervisor of roads in the several states. Hence it will be seen how much importance is attached to the system of irrigation; and, inasmuch as the entire cultivation of the country depends upon the ditches and the supply of water they furnish, they are deserving of great attention. (pp. 196–99)

W. W. H. Davis, Description of Mexican Plow and Use of Oxen, 1857

The manner of cultivation is exceedingly rude and primitive. Until within a very few years all their agricultural implements were wooden, and the use of iron for this purpose was hardly known. At the present day many of the peasantry cultivate with the hoe only, and plows are alone seen among the larger proprietors. The native plow is a unique affair, and appears to be identical with the homely implement used in the time of Moses to turn up the soil of Palestine. The following description of one of them is a true picture to the very life. "The Mexican plow is an implement of a very primitive pattern, such as perhaps used by Cincinnatus or Cato; in fact, it is probably a ruder instrument than the plow used by these great ancients. It is not seldom the swell *crotch* or knee timber of a tree, one branch of which serves as the *body* or *sale* of the plow, and the other as the handle; or, still more frequently, it is made out of two sticks of timber. The body is beveled at the point, which is shod with a piece of sharp iron, which answers for a share. It has also, mortised into its upper surface about midway of its length, an upright shaft, called a *tranca*, which plays vertically through the plow-beam. This beam, which is a ponderous piece of timber not unlike a wagon-tongue, is fastened to the plow at the junction of the handle with the body, and, being raised or lowered at pleasure upon the *tranca*, serves to regulate the dip of the share-point. To this beam is attached a yoke of oxen, no other plowbeasts being known here." The above implement is in general use where the hoe has been laid aside, except with the wealthy proprietors, who have purchased more modern plows from the United States, but not of the latest pattern. In some instances as many as twelve or fifteen of these homely affairs, drawn by as many yoke of oxen, will be in use at the same time in a single field. Two men are required to each plow, one to hold up the handle and guide the machine, while the other is employed in goading up the oxen with a long pole shod with a piece of sharp iron. Such is plowing in New Mexico. (pp. 201–2)

THREE

Acequia Governance and Administration

By the time Brigadier General Stephen W. Kearny claimed New Mexico as a territory of the United States in 1846, following the American military invasion of the republic of Mexico, acequia irrigation practices in the Spanish-Mexican province had evolved for more than two centuries. Seeking the allegiance of all *nuevo mexicanos*, Kearny promised that their property rights covered under former and existing laws would be protected. With respect to water rights, the Kearny Code, as the laws of his provisional government came to be known, decreed that the "laws heretofore in force concerning water courses . . . shall continue in force."[1]

When the territorial legislative assembly convened for the first time in 1851, the right of the people to construct "*acequias de común*" (communal ditches) was engraved into article one, chapter one of the *Leyes Generales del Territorio de Nuevo México* (New Mexico Territorial Laws). The legislature also crystallized in New Mexico water law other water-use customs and precepts already in place, following more than two centuries of acequia evolution: the irrigation of cultivated fields "*debe preferirse a todas los demás*" (should be given preference above all others); all owners of tillable lands, "*propietarios*," shall labor on the public ditches in proportion to their land; animals should be kept under the care of a shepherd so as not to cause injury to the field, otherwise damages will be paid; finally, as an underscore to the Kearny Code, "the course of ditches already established shall not be disturbed."[2]

Less than six months later, the legislative assembly continued with the task of codifying and enumerating the extant acequia customs and making them law. The act of January 7, 1852, provided more detailed guidance relating to acequia management, governance, elections, and procedures for appeals. The duties and responsibilities of the ditch *mayordomo* were outlined, as were the requirements for communal labor on the ditch, with penalties authorized in cases of negligence. Also included in these comprehensive laws were other causes for the imposition of fines and penalties and how fines were to be appropriated and spent for beneficial improvements, as well as procedures of compensation for the taking of land.[3] Together, the laws of 1851 and 1852 confirmed twenty-six provisions for all acequias of New Mexico to follow. These enactments were exceptionally significant because they reduced to writing and in perpetuity the acequia practices that had evolved in the former Spanish-Mexican province for two and a half centuries, from 1598 to 1851.

In case of any doubt as to the force of customary rules promulgated by the *acequias de común*, and presumably to legitimize any ditch regulations not yet covered in these very first territorial laws, section twenty-one of the 1852 laws stipulated:

> *El arreglo de las acequias que ya están trabajadas quedará establecido tal como se hizo y permanece hasta hoy, y las prevenciones de este acto, serán vigentes y en observancia desde el día de su publicación.*

> [The regulations of ditches (acequias) which have been worked, shall remain as they were made and remain up to this day, and the provisions of this act shall be in force and observed from the day of its publication.][4]

With such explicit recognition of the powers of acequia institutions, historians, lawyers, water engineers, and scholars alike credit these communal associations with having crafted the first set of water laws in New Mexico. In a 1928 report published by the Office of the State Engineer, for example, economist Wells Hutchins conceded that the early American legislatures "did little more than crystalize and adopt an amalgamation of long-established Moorish, Spanish, and Indian customs."[5] Earlier, in 1909, the Territorial Engineer of New Mexico, Vernon L. Sullivan, had reached a similar conclusion: "In a great many cases the people [Pueblo Indians and descendants of the Spaniards] still pursue their ancient methods of irrigation. . . . [W]hen the legislature took up the matter and enacted its first irrigation laws, these were based entirely upon the old customs in vogue on the small community ditches."[6]

Still earlier, a water-rights report, issued in 1898 by a special commission which studied irrigation and water rights in New Mexico, affirmed that the territorial laws of 1851–52 "were largely the crystalization into statutes of the principles theretofore governing such questions, and the customs arising thereunder. . . . The continuance of this system, admirably adapted to the necessities of the people living in the most thickly inhabited parts of the territory, has been productive of good results."[7] Historians, contemporary scholars, and legal experts continue to maintain the importance of custom and tradition in the evolution of acequia water laws.[8]

Expansion of Acequia Powers

Subsequent territorial laws expanded the powers of acequias beyond their preexisting scope of customs and traditions. In 1880 the legislative assembly provided for the optional election of three ditch commissioners in the case of the more extensive acequias, ultimately requiring these officers for all systems, large and small, in 1895. Prior to these dates, the *mayordomo* had functioned as the sole authority in the policy and management affairs of the acequia institution. Now these matters and issues would be shared with a new ditch commission. The *mayordomo* was still designated as the principal executive officer and water superintendent; henceforth, he would report to a policy body of three commissioners.

The 1895 laws were also significant because they elevated the status of the acequia associations to that of quasi-public "corporate bodies" with the broad powers, by authority of the ditch commission, to sue and be sued, to enter into contracts, to assess fees and to promulgate bylaws, rules, and regulations for the governance of the acequia. Relative to the past, this expansion of acequia administrative powers was important since it empowered the institution to act on behalf of the common interest as a public corporation and to legally represent its collective interests.[9] The powers of property condemnation, to acquire easements with just compensation for ditch construction, had been granted earlier in 1884. To coincide with the increased base of legal authority, the acequia institution would now be required, through a stipulation in the 1895 laws, to secure bonds for the *mayordomo* and the treasurer.

Two years later, the 1897 laws conveyed nearly all the remaining and necessary authorities for the governance of acequia corporate affairs: "The officers of such community ditches or acequias shall consist of three commissioners and one mayordomo, or superintendent. . . . said commissioners shall organize, by election of one of their number as chairman, another as secretary and another as treasurer."[10] Among many other duties, these ditch officers were instructed, explicitly in 1903, to provide for written ditch rules, to keep records and other organizational papers, and to issue reports to the members. Entering the twentieth century, and approaching the year of statehood for New Mexico in 1912, the development of the acequia as a modern water-management institution was formed and complete, leading Wells Hutchins to report in 1928:

> The community ditch as it exists today in contemplation of laws, and for the most part in actual practice, has changed considerably from its original form, being no longer an element or even an adjunct of the municipality but coming to have an independent organization of its own.[11]

Acequias de Común

The structure and form of the community acequia as a corporate body developed in tandem with the evolution of the customs, traditions, and practices, and, eventually, the more formalized rules and regulations of self-government. During the colonial period, the political status of the ditches was simply that of *"acequias de común,"* as noted by historian Michael Meyer,[12] a name and informal description befitting the times and the role of the ditches. First and foremost, they were communal. Given the harsh, arid surroundings, they were an element of sheer necessity for the establishment and subsequent survival of the entire human settlement. Their construction, maintenance, and magnitude of operations were beyond the capabilities of individual cultivators and irrigators. Ownership in common and the shared responsibilites for the cyclical labor was essential for the economic welfare of the entire community.

The necessity of communal responsibility for village irrigation did not escape the attention of the first legislative assembly. Section five of the 1851 laws, for example, restated the customary requirement for the provision of ditch labor in proportion to benefits: *"Que todos los asociados en una acequia de común, ya sean propietarios o arrendatarios de tierras, contribuyan a trabajar según la proporción de sus labores,"* meaning that "all those associated with a common ditch, be they proprietors or lessees of lands, shall contribute to work according to the proportion of their cultivated fields."[13] *"De común"* was derived from *"de comun(idad),"* or "of community," as was made clear in section one of these first written laws. This section stated that all inhabitants possessed the right to construct either acequias *"par-*

ticulares" (private ditches) or *"comunes"* (community ditches). Six months later, the laws of 1852 reiterated the necessity of shared communal labor:

> *Que desde y después del pasaje de este acto toda persona o personas, siendo labradores de tierras regadas, habiendo comenzado a trabajar en una acequia pública con el común de trabajadores, son y lo sean por el presente acto obligados en unión de aquel trabajo hasta la conclusión de la limpia de dicha acequia.*

[That, from and after the passage of this act, every person or persons, being tillers of irrigated lands, who shall have commenced the work on any public acequia in common labor, are and shall be by the present acts obligated to continue on that work until the completion of the clearing of said acequia.][14]

Prior to the territorial period, the management of the *acequias de común* had been more informal, based on local customs, and was centered on the ditch superintendent, eventually called the *mayordomo* in New Mexico. In the handful of townships that existed during the colonial period, according to Meyer, the operation of the community ditches was undertaken by the *cabildo de regidores* (town councils) directly or through water judges they appointed as *jueces de agua* (water judges) or *alcaldes de aguas* (literally, water mayors): the ditch cleaning, repairs of public acequias, and distribution of irrigation water to the surrounding meadows, pastures, and cropland.[15] On the other hand, Meyer notes that the more typical arrangement in the rural *jurisdicciones* (subordinate districts or jurisdictions), under the supervision of an *alcalde mayor* appointed by the governor, was the formation of voluntary associations, or *mancomunidades*.

The purposes of these voluntary associations, per Meyer's account, were to contruct the *acequias de común* during the early stages of settlement and to continue working the ditches during the annual cleaning and when repairs were necessary.[16] Loose and informal as they undoubtedly were, the *mancomunidades* laid the foundation for the evolution of the ditch associations recognized and empowered later in the territorial laws as corporate bodies. They were, in effect, the first acequia associations, as they came to be known later. Reference to the ditches as *"acequias de común"* after the early territorial period appears to have declined, but the concept of "the community ditch" survives.[17]

Other scholars generally agree with Meyer. In his study of land use and settlement patterns during the colonial period, Marc Simmons found that

New Mexico was essentially a dispersed rural province. Only four towns were recognized as *villas:* Santa Fe, Alburquerque, Santa Cruz de la Cañada, and El Paso del Norte. No municipality in the region ever attained the rank of *ciudad*.[18] The great majority of settlements were loosely grouped *ranchos*, generally called *poblaciones* or *lugares*, consisting of homesteads with adjacent irrigated bottomlands for gardens, orchards, and crop production in the fields, a reflection of the fact that site development was constrained by the geography of the narrow river and stream valleys.[19] Despite contrary instructions to build more compact defensive *plazas*, the early *pobladores* preferred to live near their fields, owing to the importance of economic needs above others, as Governor Pedro Fermín de Mendinueta (1767–1778) discovered when he tried but failed to compel *nuevo mexicanos* to abandon their scattered farms and move to *plazas* that could be better fortified and defended.[20]

In his study of water administration in Hispanic New Mexico, Daniel Tyler clarifies that the goal of settlement was to inhabit the vast reaches of the province based primarily on agropastoral economies, a land use-practice resulting not in the establishment of towns but in the dispersal of the population throughout hundreds of loosely defined "*estancias, parajes, poblaciones, ranchos* and *pueblos*" that eventually dotted the landscape.[21] In case of disputes or other issues related to the administration of water resources, these outlying settlements could seek the intervention of the *teniente alcalde*, a subordinate official responsible for local-government affairs of a *partido* or portion of a larger *alcaldía* district. Typically, according to Tyler, these officials would defer to local conditions, politics, social pressures, and the particular customs in force at the time.[22]

The dispersed pattern of land tenure in the outlying *ranchos* was offset, in part, by the construction and maintainance of community institutions that united the irrigators and the other *vecinos:* the local church and the acequia. Whereas the church provided spiritual nourishment, the acequia was the economic backbone of agropastoral subsistence for the extended families bent on surviving the arid and otherwise harsh natural conditions. The proper functioning of the irrigation system, from the outlet works at the *presa* and through the hand-dug *acequia madre* and *sangrías*, was absolutely essential. Maintaining and operating the system collectively would bind the *ranchos* in their common quest for survival. Small wonder that this goal demanded that the *vecinos* work out arrangements for the equitable use and rotation of acequia waters. The collective welfare depended on the establishment of democratic rules for all irrigators to follow and the installation of respected overseers of ditch operations to enforce them on their behalf.

Role of the *Mayordomo*

The exact steps in the evolution of water officials to superintend the ditches are not totally clear. Most historians point to any number of early role types that existed from time to time in Nuevo México and in other provinces of northern New Spain: *zanjero, acequiero, aguador, mayordomo, mandador, alcalde de agua, juez de agua, repartidor de agua, veedores jueces, comisionados, la junta del agua,* and other designations.[23] The process for their selection is not completely clear, nor is it uniform in all instances. Some of the ditch overseers were appointed by the *alcalde mayor* of the particular rural *jurisdicción,* the official who was accountable to the governor for the management of land and water resources. The authority of the *alcalde mayor* included the administration of water rights and the settlement of disputes over water, especially in the rural districts, where the *alcaldes mayores* themselves, directly or through their assistants, exercised broad jurisdiction over irrigation affairs.[24]

In other jurisdictions, water officials were appointed when the *alcalde mayor* or the *ayuntamiento* (town council) determined that particular circumstances warranted an on-site solution as allowed under Spanish laws. The Plan of Pitic in 1789, for example, instructed local officials of new towns to appoint a water *alcalde* or a *mandador* (water boss) charged with distributing water to all irrigators according to a list and water schedule rotating days and hours for each turn. In most of the province of New Mexico, however, the outlying communities were too small in scale to require a formal water bureaucracy, much less a town government with comprehensive powers and specialized leadership. As noted earlier, the *teniente alcalde* occupied the lowest level of government authority in the outlying *jurisdicciones,* but even he was not likely to contravene the established water practices in any given locality.

At some stage in the development process of each New Mexican village, the irrigators probably began to appoint or elect a ditch superintendent of their own choice, as was the case already in the *villas* such as Santa Fe, where a *repartidor de agua* (water master) was elected by each of the *barrios* to distribute water, organize ditch cleanings, police the flow of waters, and order the construction of flumes.[25] Ultimately, the most frequent title given to this type of water official in New Mexico became *"mayordomo"* (ditch boss). Though Simmons does not provide a precise date, he concludes that the first *mayordomos* were elected by the village acequia members originally under the call and direction of the district *alcalde.*[26] A process of annual elections presumably followed from that point forward, and these elections were subsequently codified in the territorial laws of 1852, where the justice of the peace was instructed to convene all local ditch irrigators yearly for the purpose of electing their *mayordomo* overseers.

Michael Meyer reports that by the close of the eighteenth century the *acequias de común*, though small in size, had proliferated in the rural jurisdictions of New Mexico and were all supervised by local *mayordomos*. He cites documents from 1813 and 1819 that use the term *mayordomo* to refer to the ditch supervisor in rural communities.[27] These may be the earliest records known to have adopted *mayordomo* as the term of choice. The fact that the 1852 laws incorporated the term and institutionalized the process of annual elections on a formal basis suggests strongly that the usage of "*mayordomo*" versus other variants was consolidated earlier on, perhaps during the early 1800s.

As is still the case today in most villages of the upper Río Grande region, these ditch associations were the only form of local government in the dispersed agricultural *jurisdicciones*. Thus, the powers delegated by custom and circumstance to the early *mayordomos* likely were very broad, particularly in the absence of a detailed role discription or a formal set of ditch rules and procedures for *mayordomos* to administer. As noted earlier, written ditch rules emerged gradually through a series of local proclamations by the *alcaldes mayores* in colonial times and then were consolidated somewhat in the provincial statutes of 1824 and 1826 issued to all *alcaldes* by the Provincial Deputation at the start of the Mexican period. The fact that *mayordomos*, from at least 1800 to the territorial laws of 1880 (when other officers were instituted), were able to execute their duties without major changes in the system attests to the strength of the oral traditions and the local knowledge of customs for ditch operations and administration. Absent the presence of other government authorities in the locality, the circumstances produced a strong *mayordomo* type with almost abolute power over water affairs.

Without a written charter to prescribe his every duty, the early *mayordomo* nonetheless had ample guidance from other sources. By 1800 the duties of the *mayordomo* were an amalgamation of responsibilities inherited from earlier roles and residual Spanish water laws woven into local practices for some two centuries. At minimum, by this date, *mayordomos* would have been responsible for:

1. distribution of water on an equitable basis utilizing a water schedule or some other form of rotation to assure everyone would have a turn;

2. convening of the irrigators for the annual spring cleaning and for occasional repairs to the *presa* or the *acequia madre;*
3. policing of the irrigation system guarding against waste and violations of traditional rules, including the authority to levy fines against those who committed infractions; and the
4. settling of conflicts and other disputes among *vecinos.*

The absence of written rules likely required a strong *mayordomo* who was familiar with local practices, norms, and informal rules, and was willing to enforce them equitably. His authority to interpret and enforce these standards would have to be absolute, absent any other officials in the immediate area. On almost all matters, he was accountable only to the irrigators who selected and, in some cases, paid him. To be selected, he would have to enjoy widespread support and a reputation for fairness and impartiality, characteristics still a part of the *mayordomo* tradition in modern-day New Mexico. With little definition as to exact duties, scope of authority, or other statutory guidance, the *vecinos* no doubt would select someone already familiar with local customs and the precedents unique to each system. Curiously, the earliest written policies by a superior government, the Mexican Provincial Deputation of 1824–26, actually stated that a *mayordomo* could be fined by the higher authorities if he did *not* perform his required duties: "The supervisor of the mother ditch . . . who does not comply exactly with the duties of his employment will be removed from it and charged . . . three pesos."[28]

As noted in Chapter 2, the provincial statutes of 1824 and 1826 (revised) were the very first set of uniform ditch rules written by a legislative body. Though issued as instructions to all of the *alcaldes* of the province on how to determine penalties when adjudicating some of the more common transgressions, preventive enforcement on a day-to-day basis probably was left to the local ditch *mayordomos.* In other words, part of the *mayordomo's* duties, presumably, included educating his water users as to the types of infractions prohibited by the statutes, enforcing them whenever violations occurred, and collecting the fines in order to also establish a ditch maintenance and repair fund as authorized in the provincial statutes.

More precise duties for the *mayordomo* were not defined in written statutes until the territorial assembly of 1852 under United States jurisdiction. The 1852 laws stipulated that acequia *mayordomos* should be elected by the local *propietarios* (landowners with irrigated properties) at a convocation called by the justice of the peace of each precinct. The proprietors should also establish the pay and other benefits at this time. Section thir-

teen of these laws then enumerated the duties of the *mayordomo*, formalizing the practices already well established at the local level: superintend repairs and excavations; apportion the quantity of laborers needed; regulate
the laborers according to the amount of irrigated land of each proprietor;
apportion the waters in proportion to the amount of cultivated lands and
the types of crops cultivated; and conduct the distribution of waters with
"*justicia e imparcialidad*" (justice and impartiality).[29]

As in earlier times, the powers and authority of the *mayordomo* during
the early territorial period were broad and required strong but prudent
leadership beyond reproach. Heretofore, the role had not been subject to
restrictive laws or much outside supervision by higher authorities; local
autonomy was more the norm, necessitated in large part by the dispersed
nature of settlement in the outlying jurisdictions of provincial New Mexico. Even at the start of the territorial period under United States rule, the
regulation of *mayordomos* was limited to sanctions that could be imposed if
they did not fulfill their duties in a fair and proper manner. Expanding on
the provincial statutes from the Mexican period, section fifteen of the
1852 laws made clear how important it was to have a dedicated and impartial *mayordomo*:

> If any overseer of any public ditch (acequia), after having undertaken
> to serve as such, shall wilfully neglect or refuse to fulfill the duties
> required of him by this act, or conduct himself with impropriety or
> injustice in his office as overseer, or take any bribe, in money, prop-
> erty, or otherwise, as an inducement to act improperly, or neglect
> the duties of his office, he shall be fined, for each of said offences, in
> a sum not exceeding ninety dollars . . . and on being convicted a sec-
> ond time, he may be removed from his office by the justice of the
> peace of the precinct, on the petition of two-thirds of the proprie-
> tors of the land irrigated by said ditch (acequia).[30]

Other *mayordomo* duties were clarified by the territorial assemblies of
subsequent years either as simple amendments, resulting from new ditch
rules that would need local application or enforcement, or in response to
unique problems in certain sites. The 1864 laws, for example, responded
to the need in Santa Ana County for year-round vigilance by *mayordomos*,
due to continuing and constant water flows that were required there.[31]
The laws of 1867 required that the *mayordomos* of the new Hormigoso
ditch in San Miguel County combine their powers with the *mayordomos* of
the San José de Antonchico acequias to arrange for the joint community

labor necessary to construct a new *atarque* (diversion dam) and provide for its repairs whenever necessary.[32]

Commissioners and Officers

The authority of the *mayordomo* was supreme well into the territorial period, subject only to his election, reelection, or recall due to nonperformance of required duties. In 1880, however, the legislative assembly made possible the election of a three-member *comisión* (commission) in the larger ditch systems, while retaining the *mayordomo* as the principal officer.[33] Commissioners had been authorized previously, but their role had been ad hoc and limited, such as in the 1863 and 1865 laws when three-member commissions, "*hombres peritos*," could be appointed by probate judges or justices of the peace to inspect water flows ("*vigilar corrientes*") and damages on ditches and to evaluate disputes.[34]

In 1895 the territorial laws mandated the election of a three-member commission for all acequias regardless of size, coinciding with the transition of acequias to the status of "corporate bodies."[35] This expansion of powers presumably necessitated a more careful system of checks and balances. Following 1895, the *mayordomo* would serve as the executive officer or superintendent of irrigation waters, but at the policy direction of the three commissioners, an arrangement that continues to the present. The division of labor, policy responsibilities, and reporting relationships were made very clear:

> The commissioners shall assess fatigue work or tasks of all parties owning water rights in said community ditches or acequias, and shall have general charge and control of all affairs pertaining to the same, together with the power to receive money in lieu of said fatigue or task work at a price to be fixed by them, and shall . . . provide by-laws, rules and regulations for the governing of said ditch or acequia. The mayordomo or superintendent shall, under the direction of said commissioners, be the executive officer of said ditch and have the superintendence of all work thereon and the distribution of the waters thereof, with the collection of fines, if any, and of amount to be paid in lieu of fatigue or task work, and shall perform such other duties in connection with said ditch as may be prescribed by the rules and regulations of the same or as may be directed by the commissioners.[36]

The 1895 laws also organized the ditch commission into three officers: a chairman, a secretary, and a treasurer. The treasurer and the *mayordomo* were both to be bonded under this corporate legal form of organization.[37] With the expansion of powers and a mandated system of governance, the acequias of New Mexico entered the new century and modern period with a much more defined administrative structure and a corporate responsibility to promulgate a set of formal rules, keep records, issue reports, and document their transactions, all mandated in the 1895 laws.

Just after the turn of the century, the 1903 statutes further strengthened the powers of ditch commissioners by granting them the authority to contract and be contracted with, to levy assessments for the payment of the salary of the *mayordomo* and other legitimate expenses incident to the operations and maintenance of the acequia, and to contract for obtaining irrigation waters for their ditches. In his meticulous examination of these and other territorial laws, historian Ira Clark concludes that the laws of 1903 established the administrative structure for community ditches on a permanent basis with only relatively minor changes thereafter.[38]

Competing Water Institutions

Through most of the territorial period, the acequia institution enjoyed the sustained protections enacted by the New Mexico legislative assembly. For decades, numerous laws and special irrigation reports validated the special status of New Mexican acequias. In the closing years of the nineteenth century and into the period just before statehood, however, changes were already underway that were destined to complicate water-policy affairs for all stakeholders, especially the centuries-old acequias. A series of new water institutions began to emerge which together constructed a new and more turbulent policy environment for the *comisionados* and *parciantes*.

Authorized by New Mexico statutes, these new players in the water-administration arena came to the fore in response to a number of interrelated forces: technological, economic, and political. With the advent of sophisticated technologies for groundwater mining, such as the installation of pumps and sprinkler irrigation systems, commercial-scale agriculture became more feasible in the arid West and Southwest. In addition, other industries expanded their operations, induced in part by the availability of rail transportation and access to markets east and west, permanently linking New Mexico to the national economy. Sawmills, commercial agriculture, coal mines, the oil and gas industries, coupled with the blossoming of towns and municipalities in many parts of the upper Río Grande region, all required substantial amounts of water and huge public expenditures for modern diversion dams and concrete-lined canal systems. This increased demand created the need for an institutional process for the acquisition of legal rights to use and distribute the water resources of the growing territory.

In relatively short order, when compared with the stablity of the pre-1848 regimes, the territorial and state legislatures of New Mexico greatly expanded the institutional framework for water-resources administration and politics. In 1887 the territorial assembly authorized the incorporation of irrigation companies, permitting private individuals, with their own capital, to construct, operate, and maintain reservoirs, canals, ditches, or pipelines for the purposes of large-scale irrigation. Subsequent legislation at the turn of the century and into the 1920s supported growth and development policies by approving the formation of irrigation districts, water-users associations or mutual ditch companies, and conservancy districts.[39] In future years these new institutions would compete more and more for the acquisition and control of water resources in the different basins of the region. Financed in large part with federal funds, reclamation projects would bring new lands under canal-system irrigation, threatening the centuries-old system of independent ditches, self-government, and local control.[40]

To balance the entrance of new water institutions, the territorial legislatures did provide the acequia associations with additional measures of protection, or at least they tried to do so. The Water Code of 1907, for example, declared all surface water as belonging to the public and required all individuals or entities to apply for permits in order to obtain rights to use the water and put it to beneficial use. Water rights in use prior to 1907, however, were confirmed as historical uses and were granted status as "vested water rights," meaning that these rights would be automatic rights with a pre-1907 priority date. Protected uses included areas where "local or community customs, rules and regulations have been adopted" for the governance of ditches and laterals. In addition, these local or community customs "shall not be molested or changed" unless so desired by the ditch users practicing the customs.[41] The effect of these provisions meant that the preexisting rights of the acequia *parciantes* would remain in force and undisturbed into the twentieth century, a potential advantage considering the turbulent institutional environment that was emerging.

According to Robert Clark, the legislative assembly very much contem-

plated the possibility of impairment to historic water rights by the onslaught of increased demands following the Reclamation Law of 1902 and
other federal activism in western land and water projects. To safeguard
preexisting rights, Clark concludes, the legislature strengthened the provisions of the Water Code of 1907 by a subsequent law in 1909, which sought
to prepare the rural-community acequias for the changing economic and
political order. While recognizing the need of the state to undertake water-conservation, reclamation, and flood-control projects, the legislation
stipulated that these initiatives should not interfere with vested rights nor
the "natural right of the people living in the upper valleys of the several
stream systems to impound and utilize a reasonable share of the waters
which are precipitated upon and have their source in such valleys and superadjacent mountains."[42] Though never tested in case law, these provisions were historically significant because they foretold many of the
conflicts over proposals later in the twentieth century to transfer rural
water rights to other uses or to more distant locations. In addition, with
statehood on the horizon, the local acequia associations henceforth would
have to compete with other water institutions for legislative attention and
support.

DOCUMENTS

TERRITORIAL ACEQUIA LAWS, 1851 AND 1852

The first laws enacted under U.S. jurisdiction in 1851 and 1852 codified into written statutes the extant acequia customary practices as they had gradually evolved since the first Spanish settlement was established in 1598. Due to the importance of such a compilation, the acequia laws of those first two sessions of the territorial assembly are presented below in the language of the times. With a majority population of *nuevo mexicanos*, the proceedings of the assembly during this early period were recorded in Spanish first, and then were translated into English, as was the case with these acequia laws. Presentation in Spanish is also necessary in order to preserve the original meaning of terms, phrases, and other content of contextual significance that may be lost or altered somehow in translation. For example, note the terms and revealing descriptions in Spanish: *acequias de común, acequias públicas, los asociados, regadío de las labores, propietarios o arrendatarios de tierras, porciantes de acequias, trabajos comunes de acequias, en beneficio común, mayordomos, repartir y proporcionar el agua, repartición con justicia, tres hombres peritos, labradores, plantillos, multas y confiscaciones recobradas,* and many others. The English translations are not provided here since a summation of them appears in the text, pp. 49–50. For complete translation, readers may wish to consult the official translations published simultaneously alongside the Spanish versions in the Laws of 1851 and 1852. See *Revised Statutes and Laws of the Territory of New Mexico* (Studley 1865).

Artículo I. Capítulo I.

Acto de Julio 20 de 1851. Foll. p. 190

Acequias

SECCION I. Que todos los habitantes del Territorio de Nuevo México, que tengan tierras de labor en su propia residencia, o en otros puntos, tengan derecho a construir acequias particulares y comunes, y tomar el agua para dichas acequias de donde se pueda, con la precisa obligación de pagar al dueño por donde puedan pasar las dichas acequias, una compensación justa y tasada al equivalente del terreno invertido.

Sᴇᴄ. 2. Que ningún habitante de dicho Territorio tendrá derecho a construir finca alguna con perjuicio del regadío de las labores, o siembras, como son molinos, u otras que impidan el curso de las aguas, pues el regadío de las siembras debe preferir a todos los demás.

Sᴇᴄ. 3. Se prohibirá toda senda or vereda por las labores sopena, de multa o castigo.

Sᴇᴄ. 4. Que todo habitante que sea dueño de tierras de labor, sea exijido a los trabajos comunes de acequias, en perjuicio de que haga o no haga siembra.

Sᴇᴄ. 5. Que todos los asociados en una acequia de común, ya sean propietarios o arrendatarios de tierras, contribuyan a trabajar segun la porporción de sus labores.

Sᴇᴄ. 6. Que siendo impracticable o de absoluta imposibilidad que las labores del Territorio se cerquen, los animales se tengan con pastores para no dañar las siembras, y lo que fuere dañado se pagará por los causantes.

Sᴇᴄ. 7. Que en caso de que un común de gente necesite construir una acequia en cualesquiera parte del Territorio, y resultare en que los contruyentes son ellos mismos los dueños de todo el terreno en donde se ha de sacar la acequia, entonces no se debe obligar a nadie a recompensar ninguna, por razón de que todos los porciantes de dichas acequias, que se contruyan como arriba dicho, es en beneficio común de todos los que las componen.

Sᴇᴄ. 8. Que de las acequias ya establecidas no se embaraze su curso.

Acto de Enero 7 de 1852. Foll. p. 279

Sᴇᴄ. 9. Que todos los ríos y corrientes de agua en este Territorio, anteriormente conocidos como acequias públicas, son por este decreto establecidos y declarados a ser acequias públicas.

Sᴇᴄ. 10. Que desde y después de la publicación de este acto, será la obligación de los varios jueces de paz de este Territorio de convocar cada uno en su precinto o demarcación, cuando sea conveniente a los propietarios de las acequias a los mismos propietarios de tierras regadas con cualquiera acequia pública, para el fin de elejir uno o mas mayordomos de tal acequia para el mismo año.

Sᴇᴄ. 11. El modo de conducir las elecciones y el número de mayordomos, será arreglado por el alcalde o juez del precinto, y en tales elecciones podrán votar solamente los dueños propietarios o arrendadores de tierras regadas con dichas acequias.

Sec. 12. La paga y otro extrasueldo de los mayordomos será arreglado por una mayoría de los propietarios de las tierras regadas con tal acequia.

Sec. 13. Será la obligación de los mayordomos de superintender los reparos y las escavaciones de tales acequias; de proporcionar la gente o el número de labradores para este fin suplidos de los propietarios; de regular los mismos conforme a la cantidad de tierras de cada uno que debe regarse con tal acequia; de repartir y proporcionar el agua de la misma en la proporción a que cada propietario tiene derecho según la cantidad de tierra cultivada por él, teniendo también consideración a la naturaleza de las semillas cosechas y de las legumbres que se cultivan; y de conducir y llevar tal repartición con justicia e imparcialidad.

Sec. 14. Será obligación de tales propietarios de poner cada uno por su parte el número de labradores requeridos por el mayordomo para el fin mencionado en la sección anterior, en el tiempo y lugar señalado por tal mayordomo, y por el tiempo que lo juzgue necesario.

Sec. 15. Si cualquier mayordomo de cualquier acequia pública, después de haber comenzado a obrar como tal, voluntariamente descuida o rehuza desempeñar cualesquiera de sus deberes confiados a él por este acto, o se maneja de mala fé y con injusticia en su oficio de mayordomo, o toma o se ofrece a tomar cualquier cohecho, ya sea de dinero o de propiedad o de cualquiera otra clase, como un inducimiento para de este modo descuidarse o manejarse de mala fé en su empleo, él será multado por cada una de tales ofensas en una suma que no esceda de noventa pesos, los cuales serán recobrados delante de cualquier juez de paz del condado, la mitad de la suma cobrada será entregada al condado, y la otra mitad a la persona que haya puesto la demanda por la misma; y sobre una segunda convicción, podrá ser removido de su empleo por el juez de paz de su precinto o demarcación sobre petición de dos tercios de los propietarios de las tierras regadas con tal acequia.

Sec. 16. En todos los casos de deposición como proveído en la sección precedente, el juez de paz mandará inmediatamente una nueva elección para llenar la vacante ocasionada por tal deposición, que será conducida del mismo modo que está prescrito en el sección tercera de este acto.

Sec. 17. Si algún propietario de tierras regadas con cualesquiera de tales acequias, descuida o rehuza de suplir el número de labradores requeridos por el mayordomo, como preveído en la sección sesta de este acto, después haber sido legalmente notificado por el mayordomo, pagará por cada una de tales ofensas para el beneficio de tal acequia, una multa que no esceda de diez pesos, los cuales serán recobrados por el mayordomo delante de cualquier juez de paz del condado; y en tales casos el mayordomo será un testigo competente para probar la ofensa o cualquier hecho que sirva a constituir la misma.

SEC. 18. Si alguna persona durante el tiempo de cultivación obstruye o de cualquiera manera interfiere o disturbe cualesquiera de tales acequias, o usa el agua de la misma sin el consentimiento del mayordomo, pagará por cada una de tales ofensas una suma que no esceda de diez pesos, los cuales serán recobrados como proveído el la última sección, para el beneficio de tal acequia; y a más de esto, pagará a las partes injuriadas todos los daños que hayan recibido; y la persona o personas que no tengan con que satisfacer la multa o perjuicios causados, serán sentenciadas a quince días de trabajos públicos.

SEC. 19. Todas las multas y confiscaciones recobradas para el uso y beneficio de cualesquiera acequia pública, serán aplicadas por el mayordomo para los fines de mejoras escavaciones y puentes de la misma en dondo esté cruzada por un camino público por donde sean necesarios tales puentes.

SEC. 20. En todos los casos de convicción bajo este acto, una apelación será permitida a la corte de pruebas, que debe ser tomada y conducida como en todos los casos de apelación de las decisiones de jueces de paz.

SEC. 21. El arreglo de las acequias que ya están trabajadas quedará establecido tal como se hizo y permanece hasta hoy, y las prevenciones de este acto, serán vigentes y en observancia desde el día de su publicación.

SEC. 22. Si alguna acequia se trabaja de nuevo o se saca la primera vez con necesidad de romper tierras de alguno y algunos particulares, se contará primero con su consentimiento, y se les dará si ellos lo solicitan por la comunidad de la dicha acequia, una justa compensación por el sanjeó de sus tierras, cuya estimación se hará por los dueños en términos racionales que no escedan a una cantidad conveniente.

SEC. 23. Si los dueños o dueño de tierras en donde se hace un nuevo sanjeó para acequias, solicitan un precio excesivo por compensación que no acomode a la comunidad, será deber del juez de pruebas en el condado donde sucede, nombrar tres hombres peritos de conocida honradez para que hagan el avalúo de la indemnización, la cual hecha, la hará ejecutoria, y sin apelación el juez de pruebas que conozca en el asunto.

SEC. 24. Todos los plantillos de cualquiera clase que sean que fuesen emanados en las márgenes de las acequias, pertenecerán a los dueños de las tierras por donde las acequias están ubicadas.

SEC. 25. Todos los actos y partes de actos repugnantes ó inconsistentes con este acto son por este abrogados.

SEC. 26. Este acto tomará efecto y será en fuerza, desde y después de su publicación.

Report of Commission of Irrigation and Water Rights, December 15th, 1898, Santa Fe, New Mexico, New Mexican Printing Company

On March 18, 1897, the Legislative Assembly of the Territory of New Mexico created a Commission on Irrigation and Water Rights, directing it to "inquire into the conditions existing in different portions of the territory, with reference to irrigation and water-rights, [and] to examine the laws upon this subject in force in this territory." The end purpose of this investigation was to deliver an informational report to Territorial Governor Miguel A. Otero and to recommend possible legislation for the assembly to consider. Among other significant findings, the commission confirmed that the early territorial acequia laws were merely a crystallization of customs, principles, and vested rights that previously existed and should not be disturbed. At one point, the report refers to these practices as "community ditch laws" that have been easily understood by the people themselves, have been put into effect, and have been uniformily interpreted by the courts. The fact that these laws were so widely accepted and justly implemented no doubt resulted from the process of self-government that had crafted and implemented them well before the territorial Commission on Irrigation and Water Rights undertook to study their value and effectiveness.

To the Honorable Miguel A. Otero, Governor of New Mexico.

Sir: The undersigned, constituting a Commission of Irrigation and Water Rights in the Territory of New Mexico, appointed pursuant to the act of the legislative assembly, approved March 18, 1897, respectfully submit the following report:

. . . There is a widespread and largely justifiable impression prevailing that the result of changing the present irrigation laws of the territory in any essential respect would be to disturb vested rights, and to unsettle public confidence in legal rights which have long been owned and beneficially used in the great portion of the waters of our streams. For this reason it

was determined by the commission, after thoroughly canvassing the subject at its first meeting, that any and all recommendations from the commission along this line should be of the most conservative character, and
that, before any change in the laws was recommended, there should be a
close study of the laws and methods of enforcing them as now existing, and
unless it was apparent that changes could be recommended which would
be of considerable advantage to the public at large, it would be better to
recommend that no changes whatever be made. . . .

The first statutory law we have on the subject is the provision of the
Kearny Code of 1846, to the effect that all laws in force at the time of the
promulgation thereof, concerning water courses, should continue in force.
[Code is cited here.] This reference was, undoubtedly, to the Spanish-
Mexican laws then in force with reference to the control of waters; and
. . . it is believed that such reference thereto was intended to apply to the
system of community ditch laws, which at that time regulated the rights of
the owners thereunder in this territory . . . and that, at such time, almost
all rights claimed by the citizens of New Mexico in the waters of any of its
streams were by virtue of such community laws, and that the individual
rights of private owners of ditches had not at that time assumed such value
as to attract the necessity of legislation to protect the same.

The assumption that the language referred to in the Kearny Code was
directed particularly to rights owned under the community system, received additional strength from the fact that the legislative assembly of 1851
and 1852, following close upon the promulgation of the Kearny code,
adopted a set of laws with reference to the community ditch system, which
laws were largely the crystalization into statutes of the principles theretofore governing such questions, and the customs arising thereunder. [1851
and 1852 laws are cited here.]

It is to the Spanish-Mexican laws, therefore, and to legislative enactments beginning in 1851, continuing more or less to the present time, that
we owe the present acequia laws of the territory. The continuance of this
system, admirably adapted to the necessities of the people living in the
most thickly inhabited parts of the territory, has been productive of good
results, where the spirit of the law has been enforced. . . . [Amendments to
and other acequia laws, 1861–1893, are cited and highlighted here.]

Few laws have been deemed necessary other than the community system of laws above mentioned, and these have, as above stated, been enacted. The principles of these laws are easily construed by the courts, and
very little difficulty is found in following and putting them into effect.
There is no subject with reference to which the laws of the territory (both

the community and private water appropriations) are better understood by the people, or with reference to which principles are more definitely established. . . .

After the fullest consideration which the commission has been able to make of the laws of our territory, and those of the various western states and territories, it is our deliberate and unanimous conclusion, that the principles governing the law of water and the rights connected therewith in force in this territory are sufficiently just, progressive and simple, and that the courts have sufficient jurisdiction and authority at present to fully determine and enforce the same with justice to all, and that no change of any of the principles so enforced, would be advisable; and it therefore recommends that no legislation with reference to any of such principles is at present advisable. . . .

> Dated December 15, 1898
> *Respectfully submitted,*
> > *Antonio Joseph, President*
> > *Joseph E. Saint, Secretary*
> > *Frank Springer*
> > *W. A. Hawkins*
> > *George Curry,*
> > *Commission*

Reglas y Regulaciones de la Asequia Madre de Arroyo Seco, 1956

More than half a century after the 1898 report by the Territorial Commission on Irrigation Water Rights, acequia rules at the local level continued to be adopted by democratic processes, again resulting in direct, clear, and enforceable language. The 1956 rules and regulations of the Arroyo Seco Ditch in Taos County are presented in the original Spanish to illustrate the continuance of style, substance, and traditions. Note that the early spelling of "*asequia*" was still in use in Arroyo Seco even at this late date. Much of the terminology is likewise familiar to expressions and customs from earlier periods, for example, "*vesino,*" "*los regadores,*" "*dueños de propiedad de regadío,*" "*reparto de la agua,*" "*limpia de la asequia,*" and many others. Although they cover many complex social processes, the ten sections of rules are remarkably clear. The emphases on democratic participation, self-government, and the local administration of water affairs,

from the distribution of waters to the settling of disputes, are particularly
noteworthy. Section one, for example, leads off with the stipulation that
all landowners with water rights who belong to the ditch should meet the
first Monday of December every year to elect the officers. Later, section
seven clarifies that the elections are to be conducted by secret ballot so as
to maintain complete harmony among the members. Interestingly, the
voting process does allow for some informality: the secret ballots at the
time of voting can be placed in either "*una caja o en un sombrero*" (a box or
a hat). The incumbent ditch commissioners serve as the designated election judges. In section eight, the commissioners are also empowered to
settle disputes and other types of complaints brought forth by any of the
irrigators. Earlier, section four delegated the settling of disputes over water use and the taking of turns in rotation to the *mayordomo*, though his
rulings would be subject to appeal directly to the ditch commission. Appropriately, section ten closes the rules by affirming that said rules were
developed at the call of the landowner irrigators from the acequia district
and presented at an open meeting where the irrigators had the opportunity to either approve or reject the rules by majority vote.

Sec[c]ion 1. Todos los dueños de propiedad de regadío debajo de la
Asequia Madre de Arroyo Seco tendrán que juntarse para elijir sus oficiales
de la Asequia Madre de Arroyo Seco el primer lunes de diciembre de cada
año. En ese tiempo elijirán tres Comisionados de la asequia por el término
de un año entrando en sus deveres oficiales el primero del año o sea el primero del mes de enero de cada año, y elijirán un Mayordomo para dicha
asequia por el término de un año comensando en el desempeño de sus deveres el primero del año.

Sec[c]ion 2. Los Oficiales arriba mencionados serán electos por la
mayoría de votos dados a cada uno el ellos. Los cuatro que saquen la mayoría mas grande de votos serán declarados los nuevos oficiales, por hese
año, y desempeñarán los deveres de su cargo a lo mejor de su capacidad y
entendimiento y sin miras de Partido Político y con imparcialidad para todos los dueños de propiedad debajo de la arriba mencionada asequia.

Sec[c]ion 3. Será de dever del Mayordomo de suvir al reparto de la
agua a las sies de la tarde todos los días durante el tiempo del regadío. Y los
que sean asi[g]nados por el Mayodomo para regar hese día serán los que
ocupen la agua por el tiempo designado a ellos por el Mayordomo, y ellos
tomar o harán uso de la agua el día siguiente a las seis de la mañana.

Sec[c]ion 4. Cuando bengan asuntos de desputa entre los regadores
de la Asequia Madre de Arroyo Seco, New Mexico, el Mayordomo será el

que tendrá que arreglar estos asuntos por medio de requerir a persona o personas de no entervenir con su vesino en cuanto al uso de el agua. El Mayordomo es el autorizado para arreglar tales asuntos. Y si alguno de los litigantes no comviniere con la desición del Mayordomo, entonces apelará a la Comisión de la asequia para de este modo quedar satisfecho con el fallo de la Comisión.

Sec[c]ion 5. Será el dever del Mayordomo de cuidar que otras personas no corten la agua cuando la estén usando los que han sido asignados para usarla hese día. Y si alguna persona o personas violaren esta regla tan sustancial para todos los dueños de propiedad debajo de la Asequia Madre de Arroyo Seco, le impondrá una multa por la arriba mencionada ofenza, en la suma de $5.00 for la primer ofenza. Y si la persona o personas que tomar la agua sin el consentimiento del Mayordomo después que hallan sido multados por el Mayordomo en la suma arriba indicada, entonces y en tales casos el Mayordomo los multará en una suma que no exceda la suma de $10.00. Esto lo hará el Mayordomo en la segunda ofenza.

Sec[c]ion 6. Todos los dueños de propiedad debajo de la Asequia Madre de Arroyo Seco pagarán la suma de $3.00 como derechos de la asequia cuando falten en mandar un peón a la asequia para la limpia de la asequia cuando sean avisados por el Mayordomo para la limpia de la asequia. Y pagarán la suma de 40 centavos por cada un acre de terreno que tengan bajo la antedicha asequia; este dinero será colectado por el Tesorero de la asequia. Teniendo que ser asignado uno de los Comisionados de la Asequia Madre de Arroyo Seco como Tesorero de la asequia arriba dicha. Este dinero será para los fines siguientes. Para el pago del Mayordomo a quien se le pagar[á] la suma de $300.00 por el término del regadío. El Mayordomo también puede ser autorizado para colectar las cuotas de los dueños de propiedad, y en cambio se las entregará al Tesorero quien las guardará en un lugar segura para usarse cuando el tiempo se presente, para haser uso de los fondos de la Asequia Madre de Arroyo Seco, New Mexico.

REGLAS DE LAS ELECCIONES DE OFFICIALES DE LA
ASEQUIA MADRE DE ARROYO SECO, NEW MEXICO

Sec[c]ion 7. Las elecciones de oficiales de la Asequia Madre de Arroyo Seco se condusirán en la manera siguiente como sigue a saber: Será condusida por medio de boleto secreto para que nadie quede desatisfecho con la votación. Se echarán los boletos de la elección en una caja o en un sombrero, y el Presidente de la Comisión designará a una persona para que saque los boletos de la caja o sombrero y el votante escrevirá el nombre del candidato por quien él está votando. Serrada la elección, los Comisionados serán los Jueces y ellos contarán las voletas y después de hecho esto, anunciarán qu[i]enes fueron los elejidos para Comisionados y para Mayordomo. Y tomarán cargo de sus deveres oficiales el primero del año entrante.

Sec[c]ion 8. En cuestiones de disgustos entre los usadores de agua de la asequia antedicha, entonces los disgustados presentarán sus quejas a la Comisión de la asequia, y los Comisiondos serán los Jueses de la causa presentada a ellos. Si las personas quejantes no quedaren satisfechos con la desición de la Comisión, apelarán a la corte un Juez de Paz, el Juez de Paz mas cercano a su domicilio de el Districto de Regadío de Arroyo Seco, New Mexico. La Ley dise que si no hay un Juez de Paz en al Precinto en que la ofenza fue cometida, entonces tendrán que ir a presentar su queja al presinto mas cercano en donde heiga un Juez de Paz.

Sec[c]ion 9. En las reuniones de los dueños de propiedad de la Asequia Madre de Arroyo Seco al llamado del Mayordomo o al llamado de la Comisión de la Asequia Madre de Arroyo Seco, se desedirán las questiones presentes ante una audencia de 10 personas dueños de propiedad dentro de los limites del regadío de la Asequia Madre de Arroyo Seco; esto constituirá un quorum; estas 10 personas interesadas en el bienestar de su comunidad podrán transar todos los asuntos concernientes a todos los asuntos que fuerén presentados ante dicho quorum. Proveído además que tendrán que estar presentes la mayoría de los miembros de la Comisión de la Asequia Madre de Arroyo Seco en tales juntas y el Mayordomo para que todos se interen de lo que esté pasando en dicha junta.

Sec[c]ion 10. Estas Reglas son hechas a pedido de dueños de propiedad en el Districto de Regadío de dicha asequia, y son para ser presentadas en junta abierta de todos los dueños de propiedad bajo la Asequia Madre de Arroyo Seco para su aprovación o su recasamiento por la mayoría de los dueños de propiedad de regadío en el Districto de Regadío de dicha asequia.

APRODABAS POR LA MAYORÍA DE LOS DUEÑOS DE PROPIEDAD DE REGADÍO DENTRO DEL DISTRICTO DE REGADÍO DE DICHA ASEQUIA: FIRMADAS POR LOS COMISIONADOS DE LA ASEQUIA MADRE DE ARROYO SECO.

Joe T. Fernández   Presidente
José E. Romero   Miembro

ATESTADA POR EL SECRETARIO DE LA JUNTA HOY ESTE DÍA ___ DE 1956.
DE ESTA FECHA EN ADELANTE ESTAS REGLAS QUEDARÁN EN PLENA

FUERZA Y VIGOR HAVIENDO SIDO APROBADAS SIN OPOSICIÓN O POR LA
MAYORÍA DE LOS PAGADORES DE IMPUESTOS EN DICHA ASEQUIA. SI SON
RECHASADAS POR LA MAYORÍA DE LOS PAGADORES DE IMPUESTOS EN
DICHA ASEQUIA, ENTONCES QUEDARÁN NULAS Y SIN NINGÚN VALOR. Y
NO SERÁN FIRMADAS POR NINGUNA PERSONA O PERSONAS.

Rules and Regulations of the Asequia
Larga de Jacona, c. 1950s

The Asequia Larga de Jacona takes its waters from the Río Pojoaque. This version of their rules was in effect during the 1950s and were written in English as they appear here. Democratic principles apply in the Jacona rules as they did in Arroyo Seco. Members, or shareholders as they are called in the Jacona Ditch Rules, not only elect the commissioners and the *mayordomo;* they also have sole authority, by majority vote, over major expenditures such as ditch repairs. With such broad authorities, however, the irrigators also have to act responsibly. Rules eight and nineteen, for example, require that all irrigators practice water conservation, maintain water quality, and keep watch over the water when it is their turn so that it does not get wasted or damage other properties should there be an excess. Rules fourteen and fifteen require the keeping of record books for the ditch cleaning and ledgers or registers for all financial transactions. The last rule, number twenty two, is particularly significant since it underscores the adaptive and local nature of all ditch rules: the Jacona Ditch Rules are based on custom; they serve as guides; if ambiguities exist, the commissions can step in with full authority and act with complete impartiality for the good of the whole.

1. The new Commissioners (hereafter indicated by C) and Mayordomo (hereafter indicated by M), who are elected on the first Monday in December, shall be sworn in and bonded before a Notary Public before the end of the same year. In the event that no new officers are elected or the new officers fail to be sworn and bonded, the former officers still hold office under the law. . . .

3. At the beginning of each year, the C shall estimate, to the best of their ability, the probable cost of cleaning, upkeep and normal repairs on the ditch; and they shall assess each shareholder for his share according to

the water rights. The C shall inform the M of the assessments. The C will decide how the monies, services or other payments are to be made and collected. Anyone who fails to comply will be considered delinquent.

4. In any year, a shareholder may take none or only part of his water. *Provided* he so informs the C at the time the M calls the men in the spring and before the water is on rights, the C may allow him to pay only 25% of the assessment on that part of his water right that he will not use that year. This 25% payment is an assessment which must be paid *in advance* by everyone on the unused part of his water right, in order to retain such right on the ditch.

5. In the event that any large expenditure, big repairs or improvements on the ditch become necessary or desirable, the shareholders must have an opportunity to consider and vote upon the matter, either at the annual meeting or at a special meeting called during the year. The C, M, and shareholders shall abide by the majority vote.

6. The M or his assistant is directed to inform all the right owners of said ditch of the number of workers, or other assessment, that each must send, using his own judgment as to the day, hour and place, according to the list given him by the C. He who fails to do the said work shall pay his assessment, as set by the C, before using the water of the ditch; and if the M does to the contrary, he is responsible for the said payment.

7. The M, upon completing the work of cleaning the ditch, and making necessary repairs, will begin to divide the water between its shareholders, according to the rights which each one owns (with the greatest fairness that he can and without favoritism), and in this manner he will start it from the bottom toward the top.

8. Each irrigator is responsible that the ditch, regulators and watergates on the property shall be kept in good condition, so that the water may pass along the ditch without loss, and without causing damage to the property. No garbage, trash, rubbish or other objectionable matter may enter the ditch, and each one is responsible to keep the ditch on his property free from the same; or, if someone else has allowed same, to inform the C immediately. When it is not the turn of the right owner, he must keep his water gates closed and in good repair. When a right owner shall not do in the manner of this rule, then he shall be responsible for whatever damage is caused, unless there come an excess of water which the ditch cannot support; but if the irrigator shall put in such a quantity, then the irrigator is responsible. . . .

14. The M shall keep a permanent record of all the work of each share-holder from the beginning of the cleaning until the end of the irrigation period; this includes cleaning, labor, improvements and repairs of said ditch; likewise a register of all monies that pass through his hands. These records and monies must be handed immediately to the Treasurer for safe keeping.

15. Legal receipts must be given and obtained for all money transactions carried out by the C or M. The Treasurer shall keep a proper record of credits and debits of the ditch, entering every item daily as incurred so as to keep the record up to date. The Treasurer's accounts shall be available to any shareholder upon request, and shall be presented to share-holders at the annual meeting in December.

16. The rates of pay for labor, teams of horses, hire of vehicles, value of rock, brush, posts and other services and materials, will be determined by the C at the beginning of the year. Teams that do not or cannot do the work equal to the other teams will be withdrawn, likewise young boys or men who cannot do the work will not be permitted, upon notification by the M. . . .

19. No shareholder shall wantonly allow his water to run to waste. If a shareholder cannot use his water, he must pass it to the next in turn. . . .

22. Many of the rules on the ditch are by custom and it is not possible to set down a rule for every contingency. These rules are for a guide. In cases of doubt or dispute, the C have full authority to act at their discretion, to the best of their ability and with complete impartiality to all concerned. . . .

Hay Harvest at Cañón de Fernández, 1904, Depicting Communal
Labor in Acequia Agriculture.
Courtesy of Ben Tafoya family.

Acequia and Farm at Tesuque, ca. 1925.
Courtesy of New Mexico State Records Center and Archives,
Virginia Johnson Collection No. 33351.

Canoa Logs with Trestle, 1938. Acequia de los Espinosas near Chimayó.
Courtesy Museum of New Mexico, Neg. No. 9051.

Acequia Aqueduct at Las Trampas, 1979. Old wooden flume still in use.
Photo by Alex Harris, reprinted by permission.

Blessing of the Fields Procession at Rancho de las Golondrinas, 1978. San Isidro, woodcarving at center, is known as the patron saint of acequia farmers.
Photo by Nancy Hunter Warren, reprinted by permission.

Ditch Cleaning at El Cerrito, 1977. The annual *limpia* of the acequia bonds the community.
Photo by Nancy Hunter Warren, reprinted by permission.

Irrigated Fields at Sena, 1986. The ditch shapes the landscape and boundaries of
the community and extends the riparian zone of the Río Pecos at Sena.

*Photo by Paul Logsdon, reprinted by permission. All aerial photos by Paul Logsdon were
made possible by a grant from Sunwest Bank (now NationsBank) of Santa Fe.*

Chimayó Landscape below Santa Cruz Lake and Dam, 1986.
Photo by Paul Logsdon, reprinted by permission.

Velarde Fruit Orchards on the Río Grande, 1986.
Photo by Paul Logsdon, reprinted by permission.

Irrigated Long Lots at Hernández on the Río Chama, 1986.
Photo by Paul Logsdon, reprinted by permission.

Holman Sierra Ditch in Mora Valley, 1986. Built by cutting through dense
forest to take water from La Jicarita Peak watershed for the expansion
of acequia settlements on the eastern frontiers.
Photo by Paul Logsdon, reprinted by permission.

La Presa Sierra Ditch above Chacón, 1986. This transmountain ditch
and waterfall at center divert water from the Río Grande basin to the
Mora River on the eastern slopes of the Sangre de Cristo range.
Photo by Paul Logsdon, reprinted by permission.

Burros at Acequia Madre, Santa Fe. c. 1915.
Photo by T. Harmon Parkhurst, Courtesy of Museum of New Mexico, Neg No. 11047.

FOUR

Water Democracies:

The Acequia Papers

The granting of corporate powers to acequia associations in the 1895 laws established the modern framework of legal-political governance. Acequia commissioners would have to be elected by and held accountable to the irrigators on a formal basis; but they would also enjoy broad legal powers usually reserved for political subdivisions of the territorial (and later, state) government. Subsequent laws, state Supreme Court cases, and attorney-general legal opinions in time would clarify and define these unique powers even more.[1] Concomitantly, the associations would be required to formalize their activities and document their actions. In 1903, for example, the legislative assembly explicitly required acequia officials to keep financial records, issue transaction reports to the membership, and document all proceedings in writing:

> [The] mayordomo shall make full written reports of all moneys received, expended and how expended, and of all his doings as such officer, to the commissioners of said ditch. . . . The treasurer of said ditch commissioners shall make such reports to the ditch commissioners of the moneys received, expended and how expended, and kept in his custody as such treasurer and of all his doings as such officer. . . . The commissioners shall receive and pass upon the reports of the mayordomo and the treasurer herein provided for before their term of office expires, and if the same are found to be true and correct they shall approve them, otherwise they shall reject them, respectively. All proceedings of the commissioners relating to all subjects whatever shall be reduced to writing in a book or books kept for that purpose.[2]

By this time, however, the acequia tradition in New Mexico was three centuries old. Precedence, customs, norms, and other standards were so permanently embedded in the administration of water resources that the ditch officials and the membership had not felt compelled to keep written records. Moreover, literacy abilities had been limited, as was access to paper and journal ledger books, especially during the Spanish colonial period.[3] Even as late as the decade of the 1920s, some associations were still not maintaining a written set of records, and in cases where no commissioners had ever been elected (another technical violation of the 1895 laws), the *mayordomo* continued to interpret the acequia rules based on custom and tradition, rather than on a prescribed set of written rules and regulations. In the 1926–28 biennial report of the State Engineer, Wells Hutchins reported that 21 percent of the ditches still had no commissioners, a situation even more prevalent in the heavily Hispanic counties of Río Arriba, San Miguel, Taos, Valencia, and Mora, where the largest concentration of ditches were located.[4]

Hutchins also attested to inadequate systems of record keeping in some of the smaller acequias:

> Officers of small acequias usually keep loose records or none at all. The lack of system found in connection with so many community ditches is a natural result of the illiteracy of many ditch officers in the early days, at a time when the only records anyone was especially concerned over related to the performance of a landowner's annual labor on the ditch. One method of crediting labor in those times was to keep a stick for each landowner and to cut a notch in it for each day's work performed. The more important acequias, however, keep records of minutes of landowners' and commissioners' meetings, labor debits and credits, transfers of rights where permitted, and other matters of permanent value.[5]

Gradually, however, the acequia officers began to document the affairs of the ditch association. From the viewpoint and priorities of the commissioners, the official ditch rules, the *mayordomo*'s timebook, and the treasurer's ledger would receive the greatest attention. Minutes of meetings were and continue to be taken, but often these entries simply register the most important actions, such as the results of the annual election, the adoption of a formal resolution, or the acceptance of a grant or loan. Discussions of issues or needs are not particularly recorded in the minutes of commission or general membership meetings, though this varies from ditch to ditch.

In many ditches *mayordomos* are charged with keeping and updating a strict accounting of labor credits and debits, not only at the time of the annual *limpia* (ditch cleaning) but throughout the irrigation season. Marc Simmons speculates that these formal lists were rare, especially during the Spanish colonial period, but he did locate one such record from the mid-nineteenth century that tabulated acequia frontages and debits of labor owed by each proprietor,[6] much like the timebooks kept with greater regularity after the turn of the twentieth century. Usually, the task of keeping track of communal labor has required the *mayordomo* to keep a separate journal or timebook. The treasurer, too, has been responsible for maintaining a ledger of his own devise. Ditch rules and regulations, minutes of meetings, copies of resolutions, and other transactions have been more loosely maintained, though many of these often have been recorded in a central journal from season to season.

Acequia papers and organizational documents prior to around 1950 are sparse, when they can be found at all. As officers completed their terms — sometimes a decade of service or more — the journals they kept would not necessarily pass on to the next generation of officers, except for the treasurer's ledger. Mostly, these books would remain in the home, packed away in a trunk or in some other location where they could later be easily lost or discarded inadvertently. Without a central office to collect, store, and preserve the diverse set of materials, the great majority of historic acequia papers have been lost permanently. Below is a description of some papers that have survived and are now archived.[7]

Ditch Rules and Regulations

Sometime after the Laws of 1903, acequia associations began to demonstrate cognizance of their legal obligations to maintain a set of written rules, and some of them began the process of reducing to writing their customary local rules and regulations. Commonly, these rules documented the process for the election of officers and their compensation schedules, clarified member voting rights, the provisioning of work and labor, the system of dues and penalties, and other matters of local need and importance.

One of the earliest acequia associations to promulgate a set of written rules, that we know of, was the Margarita Ditch in the village of San Patricio, Lincoln County. In 1911, just a year before statehood for New Mexico, the commissioners of the Margarita Ditch convened a meeting on January 28 for the explicit purpose of arranging their *reglamentos* (rules, or regulations) in conformance, they said, with the Laws of 1903 and the Water Code of 1905. Presumably, a set of informal rules already existed, loosely written or by way of oral tradition, but the commissioners felt it was time to assure full compliance by documenting their most important procedures, fourteen carefully enumerated rules in all. Among the rules were stipulations that complied with other legal obligations they knew of, such as the bonding of the *mayordomo* and the treasurer as well as the maintenance of a revenue ledger complete with receipts for all collections.

Handwritten in Spanish by the irrigators (*parcionistas*, as self-described in the Margarita rules) themselves, the fourteen rules also included procedures long associated with acequia governance in the former Provincia de Nuevo México:

1. the *mayordomo* should require all *parcionistas* to construct and maintain adequate headgates on the main ditch;
2. he should ensure that livestock do not trample on or obstruct the acequia;
3. all families benefiting from domestic uses of ditch waters should contribute one day's labor during the annual cleaning;
4. the *mayordomo* should be watchful that the ditch is kept free of trash and other debris that could threaten the health of the inhabitants who have to use ditch waters for domestic purposes;
5. the *mayordomo* is authorized to impose a penalty of $1.50 per day when laborers do not participate in the work of maintaining the ditch;
6. on February 6 the *mayordomo* should begin to distribute the waters on a schedule of one and a half days per each *derecho de agua* (water right), starting downstream on a rotation turn basis;
7. Sundays, however, should be reserved exclusively for the irrigation of gardens under one acre in size.

The Margarita rules also established the method and rate of payment for the many services to be performed by the *mayordomo* throughout the irrigation season. The rules of 1911 authorized the commissioners to impose an annual tax or assessment of four dollars per water right, stipulating that each owner would have to pay this pro-rated amount to the treasurer, making sure to obtain a receipt. Failure to pay the stated amount would result in the termination of the water right and inability to use water until the amount was paid. This special tax would then be used to pay the *mayordomo*'s annual compensation.

Reglas y Reglamentos   Por el año 1913

Nosotros los Abajo firmados

Comisionados nombrados por los Asociados de la Asequia Conosida Con el nombre Margarita del Precinto No 2° San Patricio Condado de Lincoln y Estado de N. Mex

Teniendo su Voca Asequia. En Terreno de Oscar Anderson y su desague. en Terreno de T.A. Briscoe

Nos Emos Reunido hoy 6 de Enero A.D. 1913

Con el fin de Poner Nuestros Reglamentos Segun la Ley de 1905

1° El Mayordomo es Requerido de dar fianza y El Tesorero de dicha Asequia Margarita Al Estado de Nuvo Mexico En Una suma Segun Acordados por la Comision

2° El Mayordomo es Requerido por la Comision Comision de dicha Asequia de Exijir a todos los Dueños de Terrenos en dicha asequia que tengan su Regadillo en la misma de poner sus Compuertas en la asequia principal de 5 Pies de Ancho y de Largo. y sus Tarjetas en sus Sangrillas de 2½ de Ancho y 5 Pies de Largo. Para que de este. de Esta Manera se priben las Escalaciones del Vordo de la asequia. Y El que No lo haga Segun Requerido por El Mayordomo Quedara Entedido que desde Luego quebra la Ley que Autorisa En dichos Casos.

3° Que todas las Personas Que Viven en Las Margenes de dicha Asequia Sellan Exijidas a un dia de trabajo en la Limpia General de dicha asequia Por El uso de la agua para sus familias Oh Usos Domesticos en la Misma

4° El Mayordomo es Requerido por la Comision de Vijilar que No Vajen Partida de Ganados a Vrevar en dicha asequi Para que No sea Obstruida de Ninguna Manera

5° Sera dever del Mayordomo de Vijilar que No se echen porquerillas en dicha asequia Como Son garra Cajetes puercos ho otros Porquerillas que Sean en prejuicio de la Solobridad de los Havitantes que tengan uso para usar la Misma y la Persona Oh Personas que No cumplan con esta Orden del Mayordomo Quedaran Sujetas A la Ley que Abla Sobre estas Reglas de Limpiesa

6° Se hace el Dever del Mayordomo de Imponer Multas y de Colectarlas el mismo. Segun la Ley de 1903. y Entregarlas dichas Multas al Tesorero. de dicha

Reglas y Reglamentos, 1913, Margarita Ditch Journal.

Para cuando Venga Inscsor, y Descargarce el de Responsabi-
lidad. y descargarce de tal Cargo

7° El mayordomo es ordenado por la Comiscion de Tasar
un Peso y Veinte y sinco Centabs $1.25. Por Cada dia que falte
al Trabajo en dicha Asequia de los Trabajadores que
esten Obligado a trabajo en dicha Asequia.
Si Cualesquera Persona Alligrada al trabajo en dicha
asequia faltare Quedara Sugeta alos Requisitos de la Ley
que Abla sobre Multas. Por Enflijer la Ley en tal Caso......

8° Es ordenado por la Comiscion de dicha Asequia Al Mayordomo de Comenzar el Trabajo General de dicha asequia por el
dia de   1915 ah a desposicion de la Comiscion
Firmado Hoy   de   a D 1913

                                Presidente
                                Tesorero
                                Secretario
                                Mayordomo

9° Ahora es Acordado por dicha Comiscion de la Asequia
de la Margarita que para el dia   de   1913
Comenzara el mayordomo de la asequia Margarita
a Repartir el agua Por Derechos dandoles a cada Dueño
Oh Autorisado a dicha Agua un dia y medio por cada
Derecho Entero

10 Se hace el dever del mayordomo de Vijilar la
asequia y la agua que este en Buena Orden para
que Comence Con dicho Regadillo. Comenzando
del Primer Regadillo harriba que es el Terreno de
Oscar Anderson. Y de alli para Abajo por su orden
asta el Terreno de F. A. Briscoe que es el Desague.

11 Si Alguna Persona de los parsionistas no
quisiera Regar Cuando le toque su derecho severa
Obligado a esperar asta que de Vuelta
Vuelta el Regadillo y le Vuelva a Tocar su derecho
La Repartición de el Agua se hara de dia y
de Noche segun le Valla tocando a cada uno

12 También es Acordado por la Comiscion que
el pago del mayordomo se hara para el dia
30 de Junio a D 1913. Teniendo que pagar Cada
Dueño de dicha Asequia de la Margarita el Dinero
segun le Corresponda por su derecho Oh derechos,
En Manos propias del Tesorero para el dia Referido
y Sacar su Resibo de dicho Tesorera a Razon de-

Reglas y Reglamentos, 1913, Margarita Ditch Journal *(continued)*

dos Pesos y medio ($2.50) Por un derecho entero y un medio Peso $1.25 por medio derecho.

13 Y Qualesquira Dueño de dicha asequia que no tenga para ese tiempo su importe. Su Derecho de usar el agua para su Regadillo le Sera Retenido por orden de la Comircion hasta tanto haga dicho Pago.

14 Por esta Es Combenido que el agua Sea Suelta desde las Dies de la mañana el Domingo asta las seis de la mañana el Lunes, para el uso de los gardines su mas

Firmados Hoy   de   A D 1913

{ Presidente
{ Tesorero
{ Secretario
{ Mayordomo

Reglas y Reglamentos, 1913, Margarita Ditch Journal *(continued)*

Two years later, in 1913, the commissioners of the Margarita Ditch approved a fifteenth rule requiring the *mayordomo* to report the names of all persons who failed to show up for the ditch-cleaning annual event, and to make similar reports on the first day of every month noting delinquent workers who failed to perform their share of work. Along with *mayordomos* of other ditches who were also charged with this typical responsibility, the *mayordomo* of the Margarita Ditch at San Patricio probably began to keep a timebook for his posting of the labor credits and debits. Each *mayordomo* would log information he needed to comply with his duties as the ditch superintendent, to enforce the rules pertaining to labor credit requirements, and to report to the commissioners monthly as to any infractions or *delincuencias* (delinquencies).

Many of the written ditch rules prior to statehood in 1912 probably were not as comprehensive or detailed as those of the Margarita Ditch. For the most part, then and now, ditch rules tend to be expressed in plain and straightforward instructions. In some sections they may appear to be general, while still enumerating specific rules, whether six, sixteen, or more. Even the most general of statements, however, leave little doubt as to the requirements for communal sharing of the physical labor demanded of all irrigators to maintain the diversion dam in the river and to clean the *acequia madre*. Brevity and plain language are the norm. The rules of the Acequia de la Abra de los Cerros in the community of Guadalupe, within the middle Río Puerco valley, for example, were confined to two simple paragraphs and were restated each year from 1916 to 1936 in almost identical form, on a ledger kept by the ditch commissioners.[8] The rules in effect around 1921 serve as an illustration of the clear set of obligations and penalties that applied uniformily to all irrigators:

> It is hereby understood that each one of the workers of the aforementioned irrigation ditch is under obligation to bring with him the necessary tools as specified by the major-domo. It is understood that if a worker fails to appear, he has to pay $1.00 if he was supposed to appear alone and $2.00 a day if he was supposed to come with a wagon and team of horses and fails to do so. It is understood that anyone not arriving at the time specified by the ditch mayor-domo or anyone not able to do the job may be dismissed by said mayor-domo and be subject to a fine as specified above.
>
> It is further understood that if the dam or ditch should suffer any damage all workers are under obligation to offer their services and to give all necessary help toward restoring the said ditch or dam. This is written up and approved by the commission of the above named ditch, and for the record we hereby sign our names.

> Teodoro García, President
> Manuel Jaramillo, Treasurer
> Modesto Gallegos, Secretary
> We were elected December 5, 1921

Rules of the more complex community ditches were also restated yearly, but there was always the likelihood of amending existing rules or adding new ones to handle unexpected problems. In Corrales, for example, the acequia commissioners would often inscribe into their minutes amended or new rules that would remain in force for each particular year. Some items were simply updates or adjustments in rates of pay, amounts set for fees and penalties, or the assignment of labor requirements corresponding to quantity of water rights. The minutes for November 25, 1918, for example, recorded the passage of a resolution described in Spanish as a "regla munisipal para el manejo y gobierno de la . . . acequia" (municipal ordinance for the management and governance of the community ditch). In this resolution, "los dueños de propiedad regable" (the owners of irrigable lands) authorized the level of payment for services at ten dollars to be rendered the commissioners during the subsequent year, 1919.

The Corrales Ditch apparently was large and complex enough that the commissioners had to be provided compensation as opposed to serving voluntarily, as was the case in most other ditches. The irrigators determined that their commissioners for 1919 would be compensated in the amount of ten dollars plus the right to irrigate twelve acres of land. Part of their responsibility would include serving "como ayudantes" (as helpers or assistants) of the *mayordomo*. In addition, the resolution required that the secretary of the commission henceforth maintain a journal to record the quantities of ditch labor and other business transactions.

The rules in force during 1919 also established the labor requirements for Corrales irrigators who did not own frontage on the ditch. In this case, the members would be obligated to provide a minimum of two days of ditch labor, and more than two days depending on the quantity of water-rights acreages. Members who failed to either provide the labor or its equivalent in a cash payment to the *mayordomo* would not be eligible to use acequia waters until their "delincuencia" was paid up. Should the member attempt to take water, meanwhile, the *mayordomo* retained *el derecho de presecutar* (the right to prosecute). Irrigators with ditch frontage, on the other hand, would be required to clean out those particular sections of the ditch, including maintenance of berms, which traversed their properties.[9] Upon completion of this task, members were forewarned that the adequacy of their work would have to meet the standards of the *mayordomo* or risk a fine sufficiently high for him to contract and pay for the work to be done properly by hired laborers.

The procedures in Corrales for maintaining ditch frontage coincide with the Old World customs in Spain and subsequently transplanted to Mexico and New Mexico. In his study of water practices in medieval Valencia, Thomas Glick noted that an irrigator who owned property fronting an irrigation canal was responsible for maintaining that particular stretch; failure to do so would prompt the *cequir* to hire out for the work and charge the owner double the amount.[10] Centuries later in Spain, the practice was still in effect, as reported by Ruth Behar in her study of Santa María del Monte, a traditional farming village in the foothills of the Cantabrian Mountains of northern Spain. Per a 1776 ordinance, the *vecinos* of Santa María were required to clean out their *faceras* (irrigation ditches) the first Thursday of April every year. In addition to attending the collective *hacendera* (the annual cleaning), *vecinos* with *faceras* bordering on their lands had to clean them out themselves by the following Sunday.[11]

In recent times, written acequia rules in New Mexico have become the norm, appearing both in Spanish and in English. A number of govern-

ment financial-assistance programs now require ditch associations to have
written bylaws on file at the State Engineer's Office in order to qualify
for participation in loan and grants-in-aid programs. Undoubtedly, some
standardization of rules has occurred, especially as a result of handbooks
that provide acequia officials with the sample set of bylaws they will need
to qualify for loans or grants.[12] Legal advice on how to protect the water
rights of *parciantes* has also affected the local process of rule making. In
the main, however, the ditch rules continue to reflect local conditions and
adaptations to circumstances unique to each system and the surrounding
community.

Historically, ditch rules have been simple and clear. The fact that they
are not generally posted or handed out to the irrigators with any regularity is testimony to their effectiveness and conformity to the local norms.
In this sense, they easily meet the test for survival as a common-property
regime: the rules are clear to all appropriators; they can easily articulate
and transmit them; the consequences of nonconformance are borne by the
appropriators themselves. Generally, records not only for Corrales but for
many other ditches indicate full enforcement of even the most severe
penalties, such as the denial of water use, without protest from those who
committed the infractions. This result probably stems from the fact that
the acequia irrigators themselves establish the rules, set the penalties, and
elect the officers to enforce the rules. Effectiveness of enforcement is typical of other common-property regimes found throughout the world.[13] In
the upper Río Grande bioregion, the high risk and variable arid environment, coupled with isolation from more distant authorities, produced a
setting ripe for self-government anchored in the democratic principles of
equity, fairness, access, and local control.

Mayordomo Journals and Timebooks

In the Corrales Ditch rules during the 1920s and 1930s, as elsewhere, the job
of enforcement fell on the *mayordomo*. To aid them in keeping track of labor debits and credits, most *mayordomos* have kept journals or other types
of record books. Designed to function as a basic reference ledger, each
mayordomo journal is unique in format, style, and the depth of information
included. A minimal level of precision, however, is present in even the
most simple timebooks. Labor amounts per irrigator, for example, are often calculated to include fractions of days either due or already contributed. The type of work performed is related to a predetermined scale

of values, such as crediting an irrigator with one day of labor if he contributes only his time, but three or more days if he shows up with a team of horses, wagon and an *escrepa* (scoop or fresno). In the larger ditches the quantity of work expected from each irrigator is pro-rated to the number of acres he cultivates and irrigates annually. In the Corrales Ditch Rules for 1932, for example, members with ten acres were required to provide a *carro* (horse or mule-drawn wagon) and *escrepa* during the ditch cleaning, while those with fewer than ten acres would simply have to supply a *peón*. For more routine hand labor, such as clearing the ditch of weeds, the Belen Ditch credited the irrigator in 1949 with one day's worth of annual labor. (See ledger documents at the end of this chapter for more examples.)

Some early journals, probably the majority, were simple timebooks listing the names of the irrigators and the quantity of days each one worked during any particular agricultural season. The larger the ditch system the more elaborate the journal. The timebooks for the Belen Ditch, for example, were detailed and meticulous, as in the case of the ledger that recorded labor credits and debits for the year of 1922. Titled "*Trabajo de La Hasequia* [*sic*] *de Ntra. Sra. De Belén*," this timebook recorded the names of 117 irrigators, the number of acres irrigated per member, and the *taso* or quantity of assessed labor days for ditch work. On a second column, each irrigator was credited with days actually worked during the *limpia* (annual cleaning) and the *faina* (fatigue labor); the last column calculated whether the person was *atras* (ahead/credit) or *adelante* (behind/debit) in the quantity of work assigned versus performed. For the early summer season, the labor requirement (*taso*) was pro-rated at 1.75 day per acre of land irrigated, but this ratio was increased later the same season to 2.0 days per acre.

Equitable sharing of the ditch work, a cardinal principle of any community acequia, was dutifully recorded in subsequent years by the Belen Ditch *mayordomos*. The minutes for the March 23, 1925, meeting of the irrigators recorded only two action items, both of them related to the importance of keeping track of the labor requirements and the maintenance of proper timebooks. The announced purpose of the meeting, called by the president of the commission, was "to determine the amount of work completed on the acequias . . . and to compile reports on the labor performed and the amount of money collected for same." The only other entry was a statement noting that the commission had ordered certain monies for payment to one of the members and that the treasurer would be authorized to purchase "*un belís para guardar los libros de la asequia*" (a suitcase to hold all the books of the acequia).

Unlike many other acequias, the Belen Ditch was sufficiently large in

Mayordomo's Timebook, Belen Ditch, 1922.

Source: Hobson-Huntsinger University Archives, New Mexico State University.

the amount of acreage irrigated and the size of membership that the *mayordomo* was assisted by a *rayador* whose sole function was to mark off the *tareas* (ditch sections) assigned to each laborer for cleaning and to keep track of the total work being performed by each worker. Members who did not contribute their share of the labor would not be allowed to vote in the election of officers. The *rayador* was responsible for issuing daily receipts "to those who ask for same while they are at work, not any earlier than three o'clock in the afternoon nor later than five" (Ditch Rule No. 18, 1939). As the official timekeeper, the Belen Ditch *rayador* was required to maintain an updated and accurate set of books to pass on to the *mayordomo* and the commission after each spring cleaning. By order of the commissioners, he would also report the results of all ongoing work to his superiors:

> The commission has prepared a resolution calling for labor to clean the ditch, whereby each member is obligated to work on the ditch according to the number of water rights each has. The 1941 acequia book and register will be followed. Furthermore, the mayordomo and the secretary will make sure that no one does more labor than they are responsible for. The *rayador* will be careful to keep track of each laborer and report the completion of all work assignments to the mayordomo and [commission] secretary. (Minutes, February 9, 1942)

As in Belen, the *mayordomo* journals maintained by the Acequia de Corrales also quantified the amount of labor to be performed by each irrigator. In the Corrales timebooks from 1919 to 1932 these labor requirements were called *asignaciones*, or assignments. An entry for the year 1919 listed some ninety members along with the corresponding number of their acreages eligible for ditch irrigation, as few as one and as many as fifty acres. Periodically, this list was updated as additional acreages or new irrigators were added. By 1927 some 150 names were included: surnames of dozens of families with longtime association with Corrales, such as Gonzales, Chávez, Gutierres, Perea, Wagner, Tenorio, Salse, Martínez, and Alary. Lists of this type were labeled *"Asignación de La Acequia"* (literally "Ditch Assignments") and were extremely important since the ditch rules in any given year would allocate quantities of ditch work owed by each member based on the number of irrigated acreages listed in the table of names. For example, the rules for 1928 stipulated that the *mayordomo* could order all irrigators with an *"asignación"* of eight or more acres to provide labor plus wagons *"para una entrompe de acequia"* (to remove an obstacle in the acequia canal) whenever this became necessary. Later in 1932, irriga-

Certificado de Derecho de Agua (Water Rights Certificate), Belen Ditch, 1926.
Source: Hobson-Huntsinger University Archives, New Mexico State University.

tors of ten or more acres would have to supply either a wagon or a scraper; those with five to ten would only have to provide a *peón* or laborer; and those with fewer than five acres *"no estarán obligados a trabajar toda su asignación en la limpia"* (would not be obligated to work off all of their assigned days of ditch cleaning) but would be on call to the *mayordomo* to work when and where necessary.

The quantity of a predetermined amount of allocated work did have its positive effects. Other Corrales Ditch Rules made certain that the irrigators with the greatest labor debits also had more voting strength proportionate to their *asignación* or quantity of irrigated acreages:

Regla pasada por la comisión de asequia del Precinto No. 2 de Corrales, N.M. Resuélbase que en una junta tenida hoy este día 12 de Noviembre, año de 1925, dicha regla lea como sige: que en la elección que será tenida en el primer lunes de diciembre, año de 1925, para un mallordomo [sic] y tres comisionados de dicha asequia será legal que cada dueño que tenga derecho en dicha asequia tendrá derecho de votar por los derechos que tenga ante dicha asequia, y nosotros asi[g]namos que cada un acre será un voto legal, y que cada dueño de agua tiene el derecho de votar por los acres que tenga. Así lo firmamos, hoy este día de la fecha arriba mencionada.

> *Octaviano López, Presidente*
>
> *Agustín Wagner, Tesorero*
>
> *Alejandro Gonzales, Secretario*

[Rule adopted by the acequia commission of precinct no. 2 in Corrales, N.M. Resolved that at a meeting held today the 12 of November, 1925, said rule should read as follows: that on the election scheduled for the first Monday of December, 1925, to elect the *mayordomo* and three commissioners of said ditch, it shall be lawful that each proprietor with water rights on said ditch shall have the right to votes according to the number of water rights he holds before said ditch, and we herewith assign that each acre equals one legal vote, and that each proprietor has the right to vote the acres that he owns. We herewith attest to the above, on the date mentioned above.

> Octaviano López, President
>
> Agustín Wagner, Treasurer
>
> Alejandro Gonzales, Secretary]

Treasurers' Ledgers

Other than journals and timebooks maintained principally by the *mayordomo*, community ditches have also kept "*libros del tesorero*," or treasurer's ledgers. The purpose of these books has been to record basic revenues and expenses of ditch operations and maintenance. Annual assessments levied by the commissioners as well as fines collected for infractions of rules or for the payment of delinquencies are the most typical sources of income. Expenses vary from construction materials purchased for the repair of headgates to the payment of attorney fees when acequia officers have to be represented in court proceedings. As with many acequia documents, however, very few examples of these ledgers have survived even though documentation of fiscal transactions has been required by statute since at least 1903.

One exception is an early ledger maintained for an entire year in 1913, and again in 1914, by the Acequia de Sausal, Bolsa y Rincón, a ditch system irrigating three small plaza communities located northeast of Belen. The treasurers who served on the ditch commission during these two years made extra efforts not only to record the most minute financial transactions, but to note the years when the ledger was handed down from the outgoing to the incoming treasurer. The 1913 ledger, kept by treasurer Juan Rey Gabaldón, is scrupulous in its attention to detail, recording the amount of ditch funds expended by date and the variety of purposes; for example:

2/25/13   *Madera para las compuertas en la toma y material.* . . . *$19.90* [Lumber and materials to build headgates]

3/20/13   *Le entregué a Don Juan Chaves y Luna la suma de sinco pesos por un pedaso de ter[r]eno que ocupó la acequia de Sausal.* [I delivered to Mr. Juan Chaves y Luna the sum of five dollars for a piece of property occupied by the Sausal ditch.]

10/13/13   *Por servicios de Abogado en el pleito con don Deciderio . . . Baca y el mayordomo por [h]aber usado el agua en un terreno sin derecho.* . . . *$10.00* [For attorney services in the court case between Mr. Deciderio Baca vs. the *mayordomo* for having irrigated in a property without water-rights.]

By year's end, the ditch had spent as much as it had collected, prompting the incoming treasurer, Mr. Enrique Gabaldón, to advise the irrigators:

Today, January 2, the year of Our Lord 1914, I received this "*Libro del Tesorero*" from the outgoing [treasurer] Juan Rey Gabaldón, and by this act I inform the Pueblo [members] of the *Sausal, Bolsa y Rincón* acequia that there is not one single cent in the treasury, nothing more than the treasurer's book itself. And everyone can review all the information recorded during the past [year], and likewise, all entries from this day forward.

When Mr. Enrique Gabaldón himself closed out the books on December 31, 1914, he recounted how it had been necessary to impose a special tax of twenty-five cents for each day that a member used water. With the coffers replenished, the last entry in the ledger boasts that while he collected a total sum of $79.90 for the year, he paid out only $29.55, leaving a cash balance of $50.35 on hand for use in 1915.

Almost a decade later, in a county further to the north, the treasurer of the Acequia de Corrales, Melquiades Martínez, was equally as meticulous in accounting for ditch funds. His ledger for 1924 was prefaced with a statement concerning the condition of the account when he had assumed responsibility near the close of the previous year: "*Protocolo del dinero e[x]istente de los fondos de La Acequia de Corrales y resibido por Melquiades Martínez, hoy diciembre 6 de 1923, seinto cuarenta y nuebe pesos cuarenta y cinco sentabos $149.45* [Protocol for balance of funds of the Corrales Ditch as received by Melquiades Martínez, December 6, 1923, amounting to one hundred forty dollars and forty-five cents]." The ledger then posts each

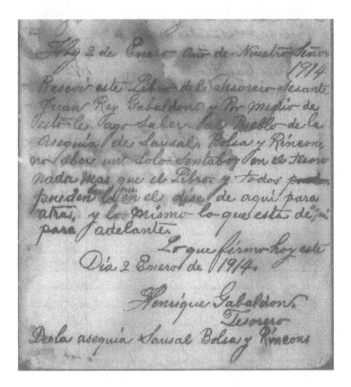

Treasurer's Ledger, Acequia de Sausal, Bolza y Rincón, 1913–1914.
Entry records the transfer of the ledger to incoming
treasurer, Henrique Gabaldon.
Source: Hobson-Huntsinger University Archives,
New Mexico State University.

Sausal de Bolza y Rincón

Sepan todos los Dueños de dicha Asequia

Que los Comisionados de la misma Viendo que la asequia tenia algo de Dependencia desde el año antes que fué de 1913. y haora en este año 1914 se propuso Colectar un impuesto especial de 25 centabos por Cada un Dia de taso que es asi por ejemplo un peon del año se Compone de 6 Dias ymportan $1.50 y asi todo Aproporción. habiendo un total de $66.20 Sesenta y seis con beinte Sentabos y los que han Cuperado con dicho impuesto Son a Saber.

	Pagado	no Pagado
Desiderio Sanches y Baca	6.25	
Pablo Garcia	.85	
Encarnación Chabez	.25	
Jose M.que Sanches de alonso payo	2.25	
Lucas Sanches	4.00	
Latario Castillo	1.75	
Decidorio Sanches y Padilla No	1.85	1.85
Alfredo Sanches	.25	.25
Felistto Sanches	2.85	
Ramon Sanches y Chabes	2.8	.25
Jesus M.rie Sanches	1.10	1.10
Federico Baca y Luna	2.05	2.05
Juan Padia	1.85	
Eulogio Baca	.60	.60
Franseca Romero	.15	
Benito Sanches	.75	.75
Juan Chabes y Luna	.35	
Balentina Chabes	3.00	
Aurelio Sanches		.25
John Becker	3.00	
Jesus Jaramillo y Gallego	.85	
Luis Trujillo	1.25	1.25

Treasurer's Ledger, Acequia del Sausal, Bolza y Rincón, 1913–1914 *(continued)*

	Pagado	Pagado 915
Jose Baca y Rael	1·85	
Ygnacio Aragon y Barreras	·50	
Pablo Gabaldon	1·50	
Julian Tafolla	·60	
Estéban Baca y Rael	2·10	
Miguel Tafolla	1·85	
Marcos Baca	1·60	
Henrique Gabaldon	1·10	
Juaquin Garcia	1·25	
Silbestre Baca	·50	
Enrique Jaramillo	·35	
Isabria Garcia	1·10	
Jesus Tafolla y Trujillo	1·00	
Gavino Tores	·25	
Atanacio Sanches	·25	
Jose Barela	15	·45
Balentin Montaño	·25	
Ana Maria Gallegos	115	
Ruperto Jaramillo	1·00	
Alvino Rael	·25	
Ygnacio Chabes	1·00	
Ramon Jaramillo	35	
Benito Baca	15	·45
Jesus Ma Baca y Montaño	15	·45
Francisco Jaramillo	1·00	
Pablo Gabaldon	2·60	
Dionicio Gabaldon	1·60	
Jose Ma Jaramillo		15
Juan Ry. Gabaldon	1·00	

Aora are saber al Pueblo
de dicha asequia del Sausal bolsa y Rincon
El Dinero que se taso por terminos
Nuebos que entraron para Riego este año
1914, y son a saber.

Treasurer's Ledger, Acequia del Sausal, Bolza y
Rincón, 1913–1914 *(continued)*

Treasurer's Ledger, Acequia del Sausal, Bolza y
Rincón, 1913–1914 *(continued)*

transaction throughout 1924, ending with a positive and increased balance of exactly $275.86. Most of the other entries for this year document the amount of funds collected by the *mayordomo*, which were then deposited with Mr. Martínez as treasurer. The only other source of income was a one-hundred-dollar lump-sum payment from one of the members "*por [l]as sobras de agua por un año* [for the right to use the surplus waters in the ditch for a year]," a practice that continued into subsequent years.

A more recent example of a treasurer's ledger is from the Ensenada Ditch in Río Arriba County. Built in 1862 as a diversion from the Río Brazos, itself a tributary of the Río Chama, the Ensenada Ditch is the oldest active ditch in the area. The acequia lies within the Tierra Amarilla Land Grant and has been identified as a significant physical property because of its historic role in local governance and decision making.[14] Though the earlier ledgers from the Ensenada Ditch have apparently not survived, the 1946 ledger maintained by Treasurer Eduardo Vigil includes entries for the entire calendar year and provides a prototypical view of transactions common to this and other community ditches a half-century ago. The ledger dutifully acknowledges a $83.00 carry-forward balance from the former treasurer during 1945, Julio Archuleta, and an additional $13.60 in 1945 collections received from the outgoing *mayordomo*, Santiago Gonzales. As in the Sausal, Bolsa y Rincón ledger, the Ensenada treasurer recorded all expenditures and purposes, such as the entries made for July 10, 1946:

Money spent from the Ensenada Acequia fund to build a floodgate

Lumber	$19.65
For transporting the lumber	3.00
Nails	1.28
Carpenter	2.40
[Total]	$26.33

Charges paid to Mayordomo and Treasurer	2.00
Costs of this very book	1.50

Entries in subsequent years, 1948 and 1949, round out other typical expenditures and payments: fines, or *delincuencias*, received when water-rights owners did not attend the annual spring cleaning, which would then enable the *mayordomo* to hire other members or laborers to clean out the ditch on behalf of the delinquent members; payments made to members for performing extra work such as installing a culvert by using their own team of horses.

Organizational Minutes

For the most part, early proceedings of commission and membership meetings have not been consistently recorded compared to the relatively more formal keeping of timebooks and financial ledgers. One reason for this comparative lack of consistency has to do with the sporadic and irregular nature of calling meetings, especially in the smaller and more numerous ditch associations. During the territorial period and after statehood, New Mexico statutes required an annual meeting for the election of officers. Since 1987, these elections and general membership meetings are conducted biennially. Beyond that, local ditch officials, once elected, decide when to convene special membership meetings based on need, on pending business each season, on past practices, or on the request of the members. Also, the annual spring cleaning of the ditch often preempts the need for a general meeting. During this event, the officers and irrigators, informally in small groups or as a whole, discuss a broad range of timely acequia issues, such as the condition of the *presa* (dam) in the river, any repairs that will be needed, the amount of expected water flows based on the winter snowmelt in the *sierra* peaks, ditch finances, and other items of importance to the ditch or to the community as a whole.

The larger the ditch system in physical size and membership, the more regular the official meetings and the more likely that formal minutes have been kept. Often, the minutes record only the major action items decided or discussed at any given meeting. Examples of the diverse range of action topics that are more likely to prompt written entries across most ditches include:

- the annual election results;
- a motion to accept the treasurer's report;
- approval of ditch rehabilitation and conservation projects;
- orders to clean the ditch;
- the announcement of the dates when the *mayordomo* will begin the distribution of irrigation water;
- the commissioner's review of labor debits and credits;
- special problems raised by the *mayordomo*;
- fines to be imposed on specific irrigators when shown to be delinquent;

- settlement of disputes within the membership or cases pending in
  the courts;
- legislative intiatives that may impact acequias;
- documentation of special resolutions passed; and
- the adoption of new or amended ditch rules.

Minutes of meetings have been recorded and written in any number of
places, not necessarily in a separate book designed for this purpose. For
example, the Ensenada treasurer's ledger for December 4, 1950, contains
a special entry to document and certify the results of the annual election
meeting called to elect officers for the following year. The entry simply
lists the names of the irrigators and the quantity of water rights held by
each, in this case from one to as many as six. Next, and just as simply, the
names of the candidates for each position are listed with an indication of
the votes each candidate received by use of crosshatch marks and grand
totals. At the bottom, the two election judges, members themselves, an-
nounce the winners and certify the election results. After this, the ledger
continues with the main purpose of this particular journal, that is, to log
revenues and expenses of the ditch.

Sometimes the minutes, or at least particular decisions reached during
a meeting of the membership, are combined with an acequia journal that
also records the changing rules and regulations from year to year. For example, when the irrigators of the Margarita Ditch adopted their set of
rules for 1911, they inserted a lead paragraph in their journal to document
the date and the purpose of the meeting on the day the rules where considered for adoption, that is, January 28. The fourteen enumerated rules
then follow and are certified by the officers at the end of the journal. This
journal of ditch rules was also used to record the minutes from meetings
held for general purposes. An entry later that same year, on December 27,
indicated that the irrigators of the Margarita Ditch met again, this time to
elect officers for 1912, to establish the 1912 rate of pay for the *mayordomo*,
and to amend for 1912 the amount of the fine to be imposed when an irrigator failed to share in the ditch labor.

Organizational minutes were also written into the record when the
officers needed to castigate specific members for violating the more serious ditch rules. The February 27, 1922, minutes for the Acequia de Corrales, for example, describe a complaint filed by the *mayordomo* against
longtime and respected irrigators in the community, prompting the
acequia commissioners to cut off their ditch water without the slightest
hesitation:

14

Estado De N Mex. Condado de Sandoval
hoy Este dia sinco de marzo de 1919
Nosotros los Comisionados de la Asequia
de Abajo Pasamos y Aprobamos la Siguiente
Regla ser como Sige a Saber
que no se Admitira a ninguna Persona a
Trabajar Por mas que una asinasion Cuando
Alguna de eyas no tubiere enfrente que
Sacar Sinpre tendra que trabajar o Pagar
Por dicha asinasion que no tenga enfrente
que Sacar Cuando traga la Limpia de la
asequia

Jacobo Sanchez Presidente
Primitivo Leal Sigurdario
Leopoldo Martinez
Comicionados

Estado De N Mex Condado de Sandoval
hoy Este dia 10 de marzo de   1919
Nosotros los Comisionados de la Asequia de Abajo
Pasamos y Aprobamos la Regla en el modo
de Avisar los Carros para el Trabajo de la
Asequia toda Persona que Tenga de dose Acres
Ariba Estara Obligada de mandar su Carro
a la Asequia Cuando el mayordomo lo
Considere nesesario dicho Carro Sera adisional
amas de su Asinasion Cualquiera Persona que
se lla nombrada Con Carro y faltare el mandar
dicho Carro a la Asequia tendra que Pagar la
Suma de $2.00 Pesos Por dicha falta Aprobado
Este dia 10. de marzo de   1919

Jacobo Sanchez Precidente
Primitivo Leal Sigur.taro
Leopoldo Martinez Tesorero

Corrales Minutes, March 5 and March 10, 1919.
Acequia de Corrales Journal.
Source: Center for Southwest Research, Zimmerman Library,
University of New Mexico

*[El] mayordomo puso queja que los dichos señores, Jesús A. Sandoval, Pablo
Gutiérrez, Federico Gutiérrez, Agustín Wagner, no sacaron su enfrente, el
cual la dicha comisión ordenó que se les notificara a dichos señores, y que no
fueran a usar la agua sin el permiso del mayordomo.*

[The *mayordomo* filed a complaint against *señores* Jesús A. Sandoval,
Pablo Gutiérrez, Federico Gutiérrez, [and] Agustín Wagner; they
did not clean out their ditch frontage; upon which the commission
ordered that these gentlemen be notified that they may not use any
water without permission of the *mayordomo*.]

The most complete and consistent set of minutes have been those kept
by the largest New Mexico ditch, La Acequia de Nuestra Señora de Belén
de la Ladera. Starting in 1905, the Belen Ditch was under construction for
seven years, and by 1934 was twenty-three miles long, serving five very diverse communities: part of the Indian Pueblo of Isleta, Village of Los Lentes, Town of Los Lunas, Village of Los Chavez, the Town of Belen, and
the irrigable lands surrounding these communities. Due to its enormous
size — actually a conglomerate or system of community ditches — plus its
complex and conflictive relationship with the Middle Río Grande Conservancy District during the 1930s, the records for this ditch by far are the
most extensive and best preserved, covering at least a period of time from
1911 to 1955.[15]
The northern portion of the Los Lentes section was actually constructed prior to 1905 by Isleta Pueblo Indians living in the Los Lentes
community at the time. An inspection report in 1910 indicated that the
Los Lentes Ditch was located one and a half miles south of the Isleta
Pueblo and was originally built by Isleta Indians and later extended by
Mexicans:

This ditch was built by the Indians of [Isleta] pueblo (according to
one of them) to irrigate lands on their grant, but during the past 25
years, the Mexicans who own land to the south of the grant and receive water from the ditch, have been doing work in connection with
the maintenance and operation, and claim an interest in it. . . . This
ditch is very old.[16]

After 1911, the records of the ditch labor for the Los Lentes Ditch were
logged into the Belen Ditch journal, following a written agreement to
unify these two ditches. Henceforth, the Los Lentes Ditch would be man-

aged by a joint commission and a principal *mayordomo* from the Belen
Ditch, assisted by a second *mayordomo* from the Los Lentes Ditch.[17] Minutes of a meeting some fifteen years later, March 27, 1926, substantiated
that the agreement to jointly manage the Los Lentes section was still in
effect and, by all appearances, was working out satisfactorily. Minutes of
Belen Ditch meetings continued to be kept throughout the rest of its history, up until the time that the Middle Río Grande Conservancy District
(MRGCD) took over full responsibility for ditch operations, maintenance,
and management not only in the Belen area, but elsewhere within its ju-
risdictional boundaries.

DOCUMENTS

MARGARITA DITCH

Reglas y Reglamentos, Rules and Regulations, 1911

Located in Lincoln County at San Patricio, the Margarita Ditch established a formal set of rules shortly after the turn of the century, when written rules began to be required in the water codes and statutes of the territory of New Mexico. In the preamble to the rules in effect in 1911, the *parcionistas*, as they described themselves, declared that their organizational meeting held on January 28 was convened for the purpose of conforming their rules to the territorial laws of 1903 and 1905. It appears that they may have had rules already adopted, but felt obliged to elaborate them in a manner consistent with the law. Rule number one, for example, requires the placement of a bond for the *mayordomo* and the treasurer with the Territory of New Mexico.

The *parcionistas* of the Margarita Ditch formalized a total of fourteen rules. Most of the rules served to specify customs or requirements of long standing, perhaps with some updating to fit new or changing circumstances. For example, rule seven authorizes the *mayordomo* to fine members who do not contribute the requisite amounts of ditch labor. The fines are set at $1.50 per person each day of delinquency, an amount that would be adjusted in future years. Rule five is significant because of its focus on environmental and public-health concerns: the *mayordomo*'s duty is to monitor the ditch to ensure that no one pollutes the waters with filthy rags, tubs, dirty hides, barrels, or other filth that can endanger the health of the inhabitants who have need to use the water. Rules eight, nine, ten, and eleven together establish the system of water distribution and rotation, ensuring that each irrigator has a turn at the rate of a day and half per water right during each rotation cycle, a practice which has continued to the present day in San Patricio and in other acequia communities. While other ditches began the rotation process at the point farthest upstream at the mouth of the ditch, the Margarita *parcionistas* chose to begin their rotation with the most downstream user taking the first turn. Sundays were exempted from the schedule. On this day, all *parcionistas* were allowed to irrigate their gardens, provided they did not exceed one acre in size. A fifteenth rule was added in 1914, requiring the *mayordomo* to report to the commission all members who failed to share in the spring cleaning of the ditch or in subsequent tasks during other months of the year.

Nosotros los abajo firmados comisionados nombrado[s] por los asociados de la acequia conocida con el nombre Margarita del Pr. No. 2, San Patricio, Condado de Lincoln, y Territorio de New Mexico, teniendo su voca acequia en terreno de G. W. Matsler y su desagüe en terreno de F. V. Hilburn, nos hemos reunido hoy día 28 de Enero A.D. 1911, con el fin de poner nuestros Reglamentos según la ley de 1905.

1. El mayordomo es requerido de dar fianza y el tesorero de dicha Acequia de Margarita al Territorio de Nuevo México en una suma según acordado por la comisión.

2. El mayordomo es requerido por la comisión de dicha acequia de exejir a todos los dueños de terrenos en dicha acequia que tengan su regadillo en la misma de poner sus compuerta[s] en la acequia principal de 5 pies de ancho y cuatro pies de largo, sus tarjellas en sus sangrillas de 2½ de ancho y 5 pies de largo, para que de esta manera se priben las excabaciones del vordo de la acequia. Y el que no lo haga según requerido por el mayordomo, quedará entendido que desde luego quiebra la Ley que autorisa en dichos casos.

3. Que todas las personas que viven en las márjenes de dicha acequia sellan excejidas a un día de trabajo con la limpia general de dicha acequia por el uzo de el agua para sus familias [o] usos domésticos en la misma.

4. El mayordomo es requerido por la comisión de vijilar que no vajen partidos de ganados a vrevar [brebar] en dicha acequia para que no sea obstruída de ninguna manera.

5. Será dever del mayordomo de vijilar que no se echen porquerilla en dicha acequia como son garras, cajetes, puercos cueros, barriles, [u] otras porquerillas que sean en prejuicio de la saludbridad de los havitantes que tengan uso para usar la misma, y la persona o las personas que no cumplan con la orden del mayordomo quedará sujetas a la Ley que [h]alla sobre estas Reglas de Limpiesa.

6. Se hace el dever del mayordomo de imponer multas y de colectar el mismo según la Ley de 1903, y entregar dichas multas al tesorero de dicha acequia y sacar su recibo del tesorero para cuando venga susesor y descargarce él de su responsabilidades y descargarce de tal cargo.

7. El mayordomo es ordenado por la comisión de tasar $1.50, un peso

y sincuenta centabos, por cada día que falte al trabajo en dicha acequia de los trabajadores que estén obligados a trabajar en dicha acequia, y si cualesquiera persona obligada al trabajo en dicha acequia faltare quedará sujeta a los requisitos de la Ley que [h]alla sobre multas por hinfligir la Ley en tal casos.

Ahora es ordenado por la comisión de dicha acequia al mayordomo de comenzar el trabajo general de dicha acequia para el día 30 de Enero A.D. 1911.

Firmado hoy 28 de Enero
A.D. 1911
Juan Maes, Presidente
F. V. Hilburn, Tesorero
Higenio Lucero, Secretario

8. Ahora es acordado por dicha comisión de la Acequia de la Margarita que para el día 6 de Febrero, 1911, comiense el mayordomo de la Acequia Margarita a repartir la por derechos, dándole a cada dueño [o] a autoris[a]do a dicha agua, un día y medio (1½) por cado derecho. Entre y se hace el dever del mayordomo de vijilar la acequia y la agua que entre en buena orden para que comienze con dichos regadillos.

9. Comenzando del primer regadillo abajo ques es en terreno de F. V. Hilburn, y de allí para arriva por su orden [h]asta el terreno de G. W. Matsler, que es la voca acequia.

10. Si alguna persona de los parcionistas no quiere regar cuando le toque su derecho se verá obligado a esperar [h]asta que de vuelta el regadillo y le vuelva a tocar su derecho.

11. La repartición de el agua se [h]ará de día y de noche según le valla tocando a cada uno.

12. También es acordado por la comisión que el pago del mayordomo es ahora para el día 30 de Julio A.D. 1911, teniendo que pagar cada dueño de dicha acequia de la Margarita el diario según le corresponda por su derecho, [o] derechos en mano propias del tesorero para el día requerido. Y sacar su resibo de dicho tesorero a razón de cuatro pesos ($4.00) por cada un derecho entero y dos pesos par cada medio derecho. Y cualesquiera dueño de dicha acequia que no tenga para ese tiempo su importe, su derecho de usar el agua para regadillo le será retenida por orden de la comisión [h]asta tanto haga dicho pago.

14. Ahora es acordado y combenido que el agua para uso de gardines sea suelta el sábado a las seis de la trade [h]asta el lunes a las seis de la ma-

ñana, cada semana, para uso de cada derechosa de dicha acequia para regar solamente gardines que no sea más de un acre, por cada dueño [o] autorisado asegún sea el caso.

Firmados hoy día [28?]
de Enero A.D. 1911
Juan Maes, Presidente
F. V. Hilburn, Tesorero
Higenio Lucero, Secretario

[Rule 15 added in 1914]:

15. Por esta la comisión de dicha acequia está en acuerdo y requiere al mayordomo que de reporte a dicha comisión tan pron[to] que acabe de [h]aser la limpia general de todas las personas que falten de [h]aser tal trabajo. Y de acuerdo que cada primer día de cada mes [h]aga un reporte de los trabajadores y los que falten [h]aser dicho trabajo.

Minutes, December 27, 1911

Se llamó una junta para votar por 3 comisionados y un mayordomo, y para votar por siertas reglas y Reglamentos a según sige.

Primero: John Cole, un comisionado

Segun[do]: Martín Sedillos, un comisionado, Damián Gutiérrez

Tersero: G. W. Matsler, un comisionado, Oscar Anderson

Cuarto: Frank Randolph, mayordomo

Quinto: Se votó por el Reglamento para el pago del mayordomo. El voto es pagar al mayordomo $4.00 por cada un derecho por el periodo de un año y dos pesos por cada medio derecho por el año.

Sexto: Regla por el pago de los que faltaran en al trabajo de la asequia y en la limpia general for cada falta, un peso y ventecinco centavos $1.25 por cada día.

Septimo: Los Reglamentos del año 1911 quedan en plena fuerza y Reglas por este año 1912.

Oscar Anderson   Presidente
John Cole   Tesorero
Damián Gutiérrez   Secretario

[A meeting was called to elect three commissioners and a *mayordomo*, and to vote on certain proposed rules and regulations per the following.

First: John Cole, a commissioner

Second: Martín Sedillos, a commissioner, Damián Gutiérrez

Third: G. W. Matsler, a commissioner, Oscar Anderson

Fourth: Frank Randolph, *mayordomo*

Fifth: Voting took place for the regulation pertaining to the *mayordomo*'s salary. It was voted to pay the *mayordomo* $4 for each water right for a period of one year and two dollars for each half of a water right for the year.

Sixth: Rule for the payment to be provided by those who do not participate in working on the ditch and during the general cleaning, for each absence, one dollar and twenty five cents per day.

Seventh: The regulations for 1911 remain in full force in addition to the rules for the coming year 1912.

> *Oscar Anderson, President*
> *John Cole, Treasurer*
> *Damián Gutiérrez, Secretary]*

Water Schedule, 1947 Irrigation Season

Watson	March 10–11–12 Beginning 6 A.M. 72 hours
Ease Pena Herrera	March 13–14–15 "
	" "
Sparkman	March 17–18–19 "
	" "
Allen	March 20
Gardner	March 21–22–24–25th till noon
Lara	March 25 at noon till 26 at 6 A.M.
Chavez	March 26 at 6 A.M. till midnight
Randolph	March 26 after midnight till 27 6 P.M.
Russell	March 27 6 P.M.
	28–29 6 P.M.
	31–1st 6 A.M.
Coe	April 1st 6 A.M. [April] 2–3
Babers	April 4 6 A.M. [April] 5 till 6 P.M.
Olguín	April 7 6 A.M. till midnight

Chavez	April 8
Warner	April 8 6 P.M. [April] 9–10–11 at 6 P.M.
Watson	April 12–14–15
E.P.H.	April 16–17–18
Sparkman	April 19–21–22
Allen	April 23
Gardner	April 24–25–26
Lara	April 28
Chavez	April 29
Randolph	April 30
Russell	May 1–2–3
Coe	May 5–6–7
Babers	May 8 6 P.M.–[May] 9 to 6 P.M.
Olguín	May 9 6 P.M. to [May] 10 noon
Chavez	May 12 6 P.M.
Warner	May 13 6 P.M. to [May] 16 6 A.M.

[Rotations repeated for rest of irrigation season, until Nov. 5.]

ACEQUIA DE SAUSAL, BOLSA Y RINCÓN

The Acequia de Sausal, Bolsa y Rincón no longer operates as a community ditch in the traditional manner. Along with scores of acequia systems, this ditch has been subsumed by the Middle Río Grande Conservancy District, headquartered in Albuquerque. In comparison to other, much larger systems also absorbed by the mega-conservancy district, the Acequia de Sausal, Bolsa y Rincón was much smaller, irrigating three plaza communities northeast of Belen in Valencia County. Their Treasurer's Ledger for the year 1914 survived and is archived at the Río Grande Collection of the Branson Library, New Mexico State University. The ledger is scrupulous in its attention to detail. Though not many early ledgers are known to have been preserved, the few that are archived share this latter characteristic, indicative of the serious purpose of the acequia institution as well as that of the officers and the members who elected them and to whom they were accountable.

Treasurer's Ledger 1914

Sepan todos los dueños de dicha asequia que los comisionados de la misma viendo que la asequia tenía algo de dependencia desde el año antes que es de 1913 y ahora en este año 1914 se propuso colectar un impuesto especial de 25 centavos por cada un día de taso que es así por ejemplo un peón del año se compone de 6 días [i]mportan $1.50 y así todo a proporción [h]aciendo un total de $66.20, sesenta y seis con veinte sentabos.

Y los que han cuperado con dicho impuesto son a saber:

	Pagado	No Pagado
Deciderio Sanches y Baca	6.25	
Pablo García	.85	
Encarnación Chábez	.25	
José Miguel Sanches		
Lucas Sanches	4.00	
Latario Castillo	1.75	
Deciderio Sanches y Padilla	1.85	
Alfredo Sanches	.25	
Felisita Sanches	2.85	
Ramón Sanches y Chabes	.25	
Jesus Mria. Sanches	1.10	
Federico Baca y Luna	2.00	
[thirty nine more names follow]		

Ahora [h]aré saber al Pueblo de dicha asequia del Sausal, Bolsa y Rincón el dinero que se tasó por terrenos nuebos que entraron para riego este año 1914 y son a saber:

	Pagado	No Pagado
John Becker	4.50	
José Baca Rael	.50	
Luis Trujillo	1.50	

Ademas [h]aré saber al Pueblo que he resevido como tesorero de dicha asequia dinero atrasado de impuestos por el año de 1913 y es a saber:

Desiderio Sanches y Baca	9.35
Felisita Sanches	2.90
Lucas Sanches	4.25
Lucas Sanches	.25

Resevido como tesorero por este año de 1914:

La suma total de $79.90. Lo que doy Fé hoy este día 31 de Diciembre 1914.

Henrique Gabaldón
Tesorero

Hora [h]aré saber al Pueblo lo que a salido de mí como tesorero en 1914:

A Marcos Baca por colectar $59.15 a rasón de un 10. x 100.	5.90
Una cuenta que se devía a Becker según resibo.	6.45
Los costos en el pleito de Lucas y Desiderio Sanches y	
Felisita Sanches y según espeseficado en el Libro.	17.00
Tinta, papel, y una pluma.	.20
Total de lo que salió	29.55
Queda un total en mano $50.35 para 1915.	50.35

H[enrique] G[abaldón]

[Be it known by all owners of the ditch that the commissioners, recognizing that the ditch had fallen somewhat in arrears in the previous year, 1913, has proposed for this year, 1914, that we collect a special tax of 25 cents for each day of assessment, as in the example of a peón worker for the year consists of six days contributing $1.50 and this all in proportion resulting in a total of $66.20.

And those who have complied with said tax include:

	Paid	Not Paid
Deciderio Sanches y Baca	6.25	
Pablo García	.85	
Encarnación Chábez	.25	
José Miguel Sanches		
Lucas Sanches	4.00	
Latario Castillo	1.75	
Deciderio Sanches y Padilla	1.85	
Alfredo Sanches	.25	
Felisita Sanches	2.85	
Ramón Sanches y Chabes	.25	
Jesus Mria. Sanches	1.10	
Federico Baca y Luna	2.00	
[thirty nine more names follow]		

Now let it be known to the community, in regard to the Acequia del Sausal, Bolsa and Rincón, the dollar amounts that were assessed for new irrigated lands entering in the year 1914 include:

	Paid	Not Paid
John Becker	4.50	
José Baca Rael	.50	
Luis Trujillo	1.50	

In addition, I inform the community that I have received, as treasurer of said acequia, past due assessments paid for the year 1913 as follows:

Desiderio Sanches y Baca	9.35
Felisita Sanches	2.90
Lucas Sanches	4.25
Lucas Sanches	.25

As treasurer I collected for this year, 1914:
The grand total of $79.90. This I state in good faith this day, the 31st of December, 1914.

Henrique Gabaldón
Treasurer

At this time I inform the community the outgoing expenditures I authorized as treasurer in 1914:

To Marcos Baca for collecting $59.15 at 10. x 100	5.90
A debt owed to Becker per receipt	6.45
The costs of litigation of Lucas and Desiderio Sanches and	
Felisita Sanches as specified in the Book	17.00
Ink, paper, and one pen	.20
Total Outgoing	29.55
Leaving a total balance in hand for 1915 $50.35	50.35

H.G.]

ACEQUIA DE CORRALES

As with scores of other ditches located in the Middle Río Grande Valley, the Acequia de Corrales was crafted by the original settlers to function as a community-based institution. The ditch is still very much in use, but is now operated, maintained, and managed by the Middle Río Grande Conservancy District headquartered in Albuquerque. The papers in this selection, from 1918 to 1932, capture the heyday of Corrales Ditch self-government before this unique element was usurped by the conservancy district. During this period, the Corrales Valley was almost entirely a farming area well outside the city of Albuquerque. Almost everyone was a "*dueño de propiedad regable*," (owner of irrigable land), the essential criteria to become a voting member of the Acequia de Corrales. Notwithstanding the diversity of ethnic backgrounds evident in Corrales since its early history, the agricultural economy dominated all other aspects of social life, underscoring the need to maintain the acequia system for mutual benefit of the entire community.

The excerpted minutes, rules, and treasurer's ledger, below, convey a stong sense of unity, order, and common purpose, despite the inherent complexities of democratic participation in a relatively large community ditch. The commissioners of this large ditch, unlike most others, received compensation during the 1919 irrigation season by way of a minor salary (ten dollars annually) and exemption from ditch taxes (up to twelve irrigated acres each). Other items of special interest included: the reference to the ditch rules as a *"regla munisipal"* (municipal ordinance) and to the ditch itself as *"la asequia mancomún"* (commons ditch); the requirement that all irrigators with an *"enfrente"* (property bordering the ditch itself) must clean and maintain that section of the ditch themselves; the local practice, by the association, of selling off the rights to all surplus or unused water, *"sobrantías de agua,"* every season for a lump sum payment (one hundred dollars); the pro-rated, progressive levels of obligation for ditch repairs and maintenance based on the size of irrigated acreages; and the predetermined system of ditch-labor obligations quantified in *"asignaciones"* (days of ditch assignments).

Due to the sheer size of this ditch and the large number of irrigators who participated in its operations and governance, the insitutional arrangements for the Corrales Ditch were detailed and relatively complex. At the same time, equity was preserved, since the distribution of ditch-labor requirements was tied directly to the amount of benefits received. The *"Asignación de la Acequia,"* for example, allocated the amount of labor expected yearly based on the number of irrigated acreages listed in a table of names. By the same token, those members with the greatest amount of labor debits also were entitled to a higher quantity of votes in the same proportion.

Minutes and Rules, November 25, 1918

Estado de Nuevo México, Condado de Sandoval

Hoy este día 25 de Nobiembre de 1918, los cuidadanos y asociados de la Asequia de Abajo del Presinto No. 2 del Condado de Sandoval y Estado de Nuebo México, en junta reunido, [h]emos combenidos en pasar una resulución o regla munisipal para el manejo y gobierno de la arriba mencionada asequia.

Artículo Primero 1. Es conbenido por el pueblo, dueños de propiedad regable en dicha asequia, que los comisionados de asequia sean los que ayudarán a el mallordomo principal como ayudantes y el secretario de la comisión tendrá que llebar el registro del trabajo y demás negosios de la asequia consenientes.

Artículo 2. Es conbenido por los dueños de propiedad regable en dicha asequia que al los comisionados de asequia se les pagará por sus servicios comisionados la suma de $10.00 diez pesos, de los fondos de la asequia y se les consederá regar 12 acres de tierra con la agua de dicha asequia. Con esto se les pagarán sus serbicios como ayudantes del mallordomo, por el año. Entendidos que si alguno de los ayudantes no tiene regadío por 12 acres como se les libra por sus serbicios, se les pagará la suma de $2.00 dos pesos por cada un acre [h]asta acabalales el número de 12 acres de los mismos fondos de la acequia.

Artículo 3. Esta resulución o regla munisipal tomará efecto el 1 de enero año de 1919. Permaneserá en [fuerza] ha[s]ta que sea alterada o modificada por los dueños de propiedad regable en dicha asequia arriba mencionada. Es entendido además que dichos ayudantes no tendrían derecho de bender días a ninguna perzona.

[State of New Mexico, Sandoval County

On November 25, 1918, the residents and associates of the Lower Ditch of Precinct No. 2, Sandoval County and State of New Mexico, at a regular meeting, we have agreed to adopt a resolution or municipal ordinance for the management and governance of the above mentioned ditch.

Article 1. It is agreed by the community, the owners of irrigated property within said ditch, that the ditch commissioners shall serve as assistants to the principal *mayordomo*, and the secretary of the commission shall maintain a timebook of labor and other current business of the ditch.

Article 2. It is agreed by the owners of irrigable property at said ditch that the ditch commissioners shall be paid for their services the sum of $10, from the ditch treasury, plus they shall be allowed to irrigated 12 acres of land with water from the ditch. With this they shall be paid for their services as assistants to the *mayordomo*, for the year. It is understood that if one of the assistants does not have 12 acres to irrigate as payment for his services, he shall be paid the sum of $2 for each acre until he makes up for the 12 acres, from the same ditch funds.

Article 3. This resolution or municipal ordinance shall take effect January 1, 1919. It shall remain in force until it is amended or modified by the owners of irrigable property within said ditch mentioned above. It is understood, moreover, that said assistants shall not be permitted to sell off any of their days to any person.]

Minutes, February 27, 1922

Febrero 27, 1922

En un junta tenida el día arriba mencionado por la comisión y el mayordomo, fue puesto en mosión por Salomé García y secundada por Secundino Sandoval, que J. M. Sandoval Jr. sea puesto como el comisionado de dicha comisión siendo sido vacante por la muerte de Don Higinio Córdova.

Dicho mayordomo puso queja que los dichos señores Jesús A. Sandoval, Pablo Gutiérrez, Federico Gutiérrez, Agustín Wagner, no sacaron su enfrente, el cual la dicha comisión ordenó que se les notificarle a dichos señores, y que no fueran a usar la agua sin el permiso del mayordomo.

Se presentó en dicha junta Napoleón Gutiérrez pidiendo que se le pagará por de su sueldo como ayudante y lo que pertenecía a Don Higinio Córdova como comisionado, y la dicha comision le dió diez ($10.00) pesos, parte de su sueldo y ocho ($8.00) pesos por Don Higinio Córdova.

Cristobal Gonzales, Presidente
Salomé García, Tesorero
J. M. S., Sec.

[*February 27, 1922*

At a meeting held on the above date by the commission and the *mayordomo*, a motion was made by Salomé García and seconded by Secundino Sandoval that J. M. Sandoval Jr. should be named as a commissioner of the ditch due to the vacancy caused by the death of Don Higinio Córdova.

The *mayordomo* filed a complaint that Jesús A. Sandoval, Pablo Gutiérrez, Federico Gutiérrez, Agustín Wagner, did not clean out their ditch frontages, upon which the ditch commission ordered that said gentlemen be notified that they should not use any water without the permission of the *mayordomo*.

At said meeting, Napoleon Gutiérrez made a presentation requesting that he receive payment for his salary as an assistant plus the amount that was due to Don Higinio Córdova as commissioner, and said commission gave him $10, part of this for his salary and $8 for Don Higinio Córdova.

Cristobal Gonzales, President
Salomé García, Treasurer
J. M. S., Sec.]

Treasurer's Ledger, 1923

Estado de N.M., Condado de Sandobal

Protocolo del dinero esistente de los fondos de La Acequia de
    Corrales y resebido por Melquiades Martínez, tesorero, hoy
    Diciembre 6 de 1923, siento cuarenta y nuebe pesos cuarenta
    y cinco sentabos $149.45
    . . .

Marso 6 resibió Melquiades Martínez, tesorero, sien pesos
    $100.00 pagados por MacMillen por la[s] sobras de agua
    por un año $100.00
Marso 4 resibió Melquiades Martínez, tesorero, catorse
    pesos viente sentabos, dinero coletado por el mayordomo,
    Pablo Griego $14.20
Junio 19 resibió Melaquiades Martínez, tesorero, nuebe pesos,
    dinero coletado por el mayordomo, Pablo Griego $9.00
Octubre 8 resibió Melquiades Martínez, tesorero, ochenta y
    sinco pesos, $85.00
Dinero coletado por el mayordomo, Pablo Griego $357.70
Nobiembre 27 recibió Melquiades Martínez y Griego seis
    pesos, dinero de los fondos que a entrado $6.00
Octobre 20 de 1923 resibió Melaquiades Martínez y Griego
    trese pesos cincuenta centabos, dinero coletado por el mayor
    domo, Pablo Griego   13.50
Entradas   377.00
Dinero que debía Cándido G. Gonzales por trabajo a la acequia,
    dinero usado para gastos en la acequia, siento un peso, treinta
    y siete sentabos
Salidos $101.37
Balance $275.86

Hoy 1 de enero de 1924, el dinero que hay esistente en manos del tesorero, Melaquiades Martínez y Griego, es la suma de docientos setenta y sinco pesos ochenta y seis sentabos, $275.86.

Enero 1. Fondos de acequia esistentes por el año de 1924
balance $275.86c

Julio Martínez
Secretario

Ditch Rules, 1928

Estado de Nuevo Mex.   Condado de Sandoval

Hoy este día 15 de enero de 1928 se reunió la comición de la acequia de Corrales del Presinto No. 2 con el fin de pasar las reglas como nos pareció mejor.

Regla 1. Que cuando el mayordomo nesesite car[r]os para una entrompe de acequia, podrá llamar a los de 8 acres. También eso quiere decir que cuando se [h]alle obli[gad]o a llamar esos de 8 acres para un apuro, y si no serán llamados de 10 acres para ar[r]iba.

Regla 2. Que cuando el mayordomo mande a sus ayudantes para avisar a la gente cuando los nesesite y aque[ll]a persona que llame el ayudante falte al trabajo no estando enfermo, tendrá que pagar los $1.50 por cada día que falte a la acequia, y el mayordomo tendrá derecho de quitarles la agua [h]asta que pagen los días que [h]an faltado; y por los car[r]os que falten serán $3.00 por cada día que falten a la acequia cuando los mande a llamar el mayordomo.

Regla 3. Y además, el mayordomo no será el colector ni la comición ni los ayudantes. La persona que falte los días cuando los mande a llamar el mayordomo tienen ellos mismos que llevarle el dinero al mayordomo. Y si la persona sea llamada por el mayordomo no va al trabajo o no paga, no tendrá derecho de usar la agua [h]asta al tanto que ar[r]egle con el mayordomo. Y si usa la agua de la acequia sin pagar con su trabajo o con dinero, será multado según la ley.

Regla 4. Nadién tendrá derecho de destruir los bordos de la acequia madre a modo que [haiga] peligro de que se rompa la acequia [h]acerse perjuición a si mismo o al vecino. Y nadién tendrá derecho de usar la agua de la acequia afuera de siembra, diremos que cuando esté escasa la agua, diremos los que es para anivelar ter[r]ones cuando esté escasa la agua, o si viene la agua revuelta, pueden usarla para lo que qu[i]eren.

Presidente, Melaquides Martínez
Secretario, Louis De[bante?]

Ditch Rules, 1929

Estado de Nuevo México Condado de Sandoval

Hoy este día 11 de Febrero año de 1929, se reunió la comisión de la Asequia del Precinto No. 2 de Corrales, Condado de Sandoval, con el fin de organisarse, y [h]emos convenido, y botado y Julián Silva para presidente, Leopoldo Martínez, tesorero, Clory Tenorio, secretario. Y [h]an pasado los sigientes reglamentos a saber el manejo de la asequia por el año de 1929. Y es como sigue, por cuanto que la comisión a propuesto, que ellos sostendrán al mayordomo en cuanto sea nesesario, en beneficio de todo este público de Corrales, P. No. 2.

[S. 1] Que toda persona que no tenga enfrente que sacar en la limpia de la asequia, tendrá que sacar en donde quiera que el mayordomo le ordene o pagar por ello, para que así tenga su derecho desde el día que se comiense el trabajo, en el tiempo que se trabaje.

S. 2. Y que dicho mayordomo tenga el derecho de colectar el pago por trabajo echo tan pronto como se [h]aya.

S. 3. Ninguna persona tendrá derecho de usar agua [h]asta que [haiga] pagado su delinquencia.

S. 4. El mayordomo tendrá derecho de presecutar por dicho pago.

S. 5. Además, la comisión de asequia [h]a pasado las reglas en el modo de abisar los dueños de terreno o ar[r]endatarios. Que pasará el ayudante a la casa y dejará el abiso a qualquiera miembro de la familia, o abisarlo en donde lo encuentre.

S. 6. Y también pasamos la regla, toda persona dueño y ar[r]endatario que sea ausente de dicha Plaza de Corrales por más de tres días, no será excusado del trabajo de la acequia. Si en este tiempo se estubiera dando trabajo a la asequia, estará obligado de pagar dicho trabajo bajo esta regla. Estas reglas estarán en plena fuerza desde el día once 11 de Febrero, 1929.

S. 7. Además, una regla pasada sobre el modo de abisar la jente sobre el trabajo de las fainas. Y es como sigue. Una persona que tiene diez acres estará obligada a trabajar con un pión [peón] y carro cuando el mayordomo lo nesesite. La comisión considera que de otro modo no [h]abrá sufisientes carros para jalar el material que se nesesita, como es terrón y rama a la presa.

Julián Silva, P[residente]
Clory Tenorio
S[ecretario]

Minutes, Election Results, and Rules, 1932

Oficiales del año 1932

Los oficiales de la asequia mancomún del presinto número 2 de Corrales por el año de 1932 son los siguientes.

Abenicio Perea, Mayordomo

Comisionados, Clory Tenorio, Leopoldo Martínez, Joseph Alary

Estado de Nuevo México, Condado de Sandoval

Hoy este día 10 de Feb. 1932, reunió la comisión del ante dicho presinto y condado, y por lo tanto hemos convenido y votado a

Clory Tenorio, Presidente
Leopoldo Martínez, Tesorero
Joseph Alary, Secretario

Y por lo tanto hemos aprovado las siguientes reglas.

Reglas de la Asequia por el Año de 1932

Artículo 1. Regla para abisar la jente. El ayudante irá la casa del dueño de terreno o arrendatario y abisará a un miembro de la familia como es el hom[b]re o la mujer, y con esta será suficiente abiso. O abisarlo en donde lo encuentre.

Artículo 2. Que ellos sostendrán al mayordomo en cuanto sea nesesario en cosas justas, o sea [desechios?] y [i]guales para todos [pribilyia?] especiales para [miaguiso?] en beneficio de todo el Pueblo de Corrales.

Artículo 3. Que toda perzona que tenga 10 acres tendrá que [trabajar] con un carro o escrepa según sea nesesario. Perzonas que tenga[n] abajo de 10 acres tendrán que trabajar con un pión [peón]. Entendido que no se le quitará a ninguna perzona abajo de 10 acres de asignación derecho de trabajar con su tiro o carro si así el desea [h]aserlo, o el mayordomo lo nesesite.

Artículo 4. Perzonas que tengan abajo de 5 acres no estarán obligados a trabajar toda su asignación en la limpia. Pero siempre tendrán que dar algún trabajo en dicha limpia si es nesesario para que así puedan entrar y adquerer sus derechos en el agua.

Artículo 5. Todas perzonas que no tengan enfrente que sacar en la limpia de la asequia tendrán que ayudar a limpiar los descanzos o en donde el mayordomo considere que es nesesario.

Artículo 6. Toda perzona que falte a la asequia con un pión [peón] y carro tendrá que pagar la suma de $3.00 por cada un día que falte. La perzona que tenga que trabajar con un pión [peón] y falte a trabajar, tendrá que pagar la suma de $1.50 por cada un día que falte al dicho trabajo. Dicho pago tendrá que ser colectado por el mayordomo el día que se [h]aga el trabajo. Y al faltar en pagar, no tendrá derecho a usar el agua hasta que halla pagado dicha delincuencia.

Artículo 7. Que el mayordomo tendrá que [h]aser su reporte a la comición de la dicha asequia cada día 1 primero de cada mes de todos los dineros colectados por el dicho trabajo y obtener un recibo del tesorero de la ante dicha comición. También el mayordomo tendrá que dar un resibo a cada una perzona que colectó dinero de ella y guardará todos sus tacones de sus libros de recibos para así poder la dicha comición dar su reporte en tiempo nesesario. Es entendido además que toda perzonas que tenga[n] enfrente que sacar y no desea sacar su enfrente o componer los bordos o limpiar las yierbas o jaral a gusto del mayordomo, el mayordomo tendrá derecho de haser dicho trabajo, y el dueño dicho o arrendatario estará obligado a pagar por dicho trabajo conforme su asignación. Además, es entendido que toda perzona que se ausentare por más que 3 tres días no será escusado del trabajo de la asequia si en este tiempo de su ausencia se estubi[era] dando trabajo a la asequia. Estará obligado a pagar por dicho trabajo en la asequia según su asignación.

Artículo 8. También pasamos la regla que toda perzona o perzonas que deseen arrentar agua o sobrantías de agua, tendrá que pagar por dicha renta de agua o sobrantías el día que comienze a usuarla o antes.

Clory Tenorio, Comicionado
Joseph Alary, Comicionado
Leopoldo Martínez, Comicionado

BELEN DITCH

Prior to the establishment of the MRGCD in 1928, the largest and most complex of all community acequia systems was the Belen Ditch, also known by its more formal name in Spanish: La Acequia de Nuestra Señora de Belén de la Ladera. Like the Corrales Ditch and others, the systems that once comprised the Belen Ditch are now operated and maintained by the conservancy district. During its heyday, the Belen Ditch was actually a conglomerate of several ditches and branches, from the Isleta Pueblo on the north to the town of Belen on the south. The ditch was twenty-three miles in length, serving the irrigation needs of the Indian Pueblo of Isleta, the Village of Los Lentes, the Town of Los Lunas, the Village of Los Chavez, the Town of Belen, plus the land located between and around these communities.

The organizational papers below represent only a fraction of the records archived in the Río Grande Collection, Branson Library, New Mexico State University. Additional records are on file at the MRGCD headquarters in Albuquerque. Many of these latter papers relate to the continuous attempts on the part of the ditch officials and the MRGCD to share in the management of the system by way of formal agreements outlining their mutual responsibilities from the 1930s to the 1950s. Most often, however, the relationship was conflictive, as evidenced by the letter written by the ditch commissioners to President Franklin D. Roosevelt in 1934. Local area newspapers reported on the escalated nature of the failing relationship, referring to it as "the Belen Ditch War."

Meanwhile, the sheer size of the Belen Ditch necessitated a more formal process of decision making and documentation compared with most other small-scale acequias of the region. As early as 1925, for example, the minutes of the meeting held on March 23 indicate that the treasurer of the association was ordered by the commissioners "to purchase a suitcase to hold all the books" of the acequia. Record books, from at least 1911 to 1955, were kept on all the essential transactions mandated by the Belen Ditch Rules: labor debits and credits, collections received from membership dues and fines, financial ledgers on expenditures, and more general business items such as resolutions, election results, minutes of meetings, and other deliberations. The ditch also issued numbered shareholder certificates to keep track of the growing membership. (See p. 90.)

The Belen ditch rules required a strict accounting of time contributed to ditch cleaning and repairs. The 1949 *mayordomo* timebook, below, provides an index of fifty irrigators at the start of the ledger and then allocates a page for crediting of work for each irrigator during the busy months of February and March. Page one of the ledger displays the dates credited to Lorenzo Sánchez for his work as a commissioner at the time as well as his other specific contributions, as noted. The ditch rules credited the number of days worked according to an established schedule. In the entry for Lorenzo Sánchez, his time and effort serving as a commissioner counted for two days every day except Sundays. Plowing time per day was worth three days, while providing a team of horses with a scraper was counted as two days. Hired labor, in this case Carlos Córdova, was counted as an even exchange at one day's credit. The timebook also credits the other two commissioners, Carlos P. Sánchez and Gile Sánchez, the *mayordomo*, Juan P. Sánchez, and the *rayador*, Heginio Mirabal, for their services as officers. Clearing weeds or "weeding work" by individual members or *peones* appears frequently and counts for one day on each occurrence. The detailed and complete timebook for 1949 underscored and helped to enforce a resolution passed by the ditch commissioners in May of 1948: "in the future, no person shall be allowed to vote if he has not worked at least 5 days on the ditch during the year in which any election is held for the election of new officers."

Minutes, March 23, 1925

The meeting was called to order by the President of the Commission of Our Lady of Belen Acequia. The purpose of the meeting was to determine the amount of work which was done on the acequias of Los Lentes and Belen, and to compile reports on the labor which was performed and the amount of money collected for same:

Selso Trujillo reported to the Treasurer $126.22
Antonio García reported to the Treasurer $20.00

At the same time, the commission ordered that the money owed Don Simón Hurtado be paid, and the Treasurer was ordered to purchase a suitcase to hold all the books to said acequia. Everything was concluded and with no further business, the meeting was closed.

Selso Trujillo, Secretary

Minutes, March 27, 1926

Junta tenida hoy 27 de Marzo de 1926 entre la comisión de Belén y Los Lentes para ar[r]eglar negocios de la Asequia de Nuestra Señora de Belén de la Ladera.

Una mosión echa pro J. X. Tondre que Salomón Gabaldón sea presidente por las dos partes. Segundada por Selso Trujillo y fue aprobado por los comisionados de Belén y Los Lentes que sea Presidente Salomón Gabaldón.

1. Que el trabajo que se yso [hizo] en la asequia de Nuestra Señora de

Belén de Ladera. En la limpia este el día 17 de Marzo. El día que se [h]echó el agua sea____. En la última junta que es en Noviembre de 1926.

2. El rallador [rayador] y los ayudantes se contaron al fin del año o es desir poco antes de día 1o de Disiembre de 1926. Cuando se buelba a juntar la comisión de Belén y Lentes para [h]aser el último ar[r]eglo para saber como está uno y otro para el año de 1927.

3. Que la comisión de Belén resibirá cada uno 15 días por su comisión y los de Los Lentes cada un comisionado resibirá 5 días por su comisión según estaba en año de 1925.

4. El número de acres de un lado y otro se contarán en Julio no más tarde que el día 1o de agosto.

5. Esta es para saber cuanto nos toca a Belén a Los Lentes por simento y madera que se compró para [h]acer la compuerta. A Belén le importan $55.52, a Los Lentes les importa por simento y madera $10.92. Pagados hoy a la comisión de Belén por H. Sichler en el lado sur de la casa de Seferino Balensuela. Se propuso de ver si sease por la comisión de Belén y Lentes en considerasión para lo de adelante.

Salomón Gabaldón, Presidente y
Francisco X. Tondre, Secretario

Después siguió la comisión de Belén transando negosios sobre negosios que tocar el ____ de abajos y abiendo echando balanze de los fondos de la Asequia de Nuestra Señora de Belén de la Ladera. El tesorero Lorenzo Sánchez dió su reporte como sigue.

Entrados de dinero $492.74. Salidas de dinero $302.46. Balanse que queda después de pagar todas las cuentas de dicha asequia $78.46.

Aprobado por la comisión de Belén día de la fecha ar[r]iba.

Comisión Salomón Gabaldón
Lorenzo Sanches
Selso Trujillo

[Meeting held today, March 27, 1926, by the commission of Belen and Los Lentes to settle concerns of Our Lady of Belen of La Ladera Acequia.

A motion was made by J. Tondre that Salomón Gabaldón be the president for both parts [the two acequia commissions]. It was seconded by Selso Trujillo and approved by the commissioners of Belen and Los Lentes that Salomón Gabaldón serve as president. [Other motions approved]:

1. That the work already completed in the acequia, Our Lady of Belen of la Ladera, during the cleaning of March 17, when the water was released be [unclear word] on the last meeting to be held in November, 1926.

2. The *rayador* [marker] and his helpers will be included at the end of the year, or just before December, 1926. This will occur when the Belen and Lentes [joint] commission meets again to review their books and see how they stand for 1927.

3. That the members of the Belen commission each receive fifteen days for serving on the commission, and that each commissioner from Los Lentes receive five days, the same as in 1925.

4. The number of acres from one end to the next will be counted in July, no later than the first day in August.

5. This is to inform us about our responsibility for the cement and lumber which was purchased to make the headgate. Belen owes $55.52 and Los Lentes, for cement and wood, $10.92, paid today to the Belen commission by H. Sichler, at the south side of Seferino Valenzuela's house. It was proposed by the Belen and Lentes [joint] commission to approve the foregoing.

Salomón Gabaldón, President and
Francisco X. Tondre, Secretario

Afterward, the Belen commission [by itself] continued with other business. They determined what the balance of funds on hand was. The balance for Our Lady of Belen and La Ladera Acequia was reported by Treasurer Lorenzo Sánchez to be as follows:

Money coming in: $492.74. Money paid out: $302.46.
Balance remaining after all debts for said acequia have been paid: $78.46.

Approved by the Belen commission on the above mentioned date.

Commission: Salomón Gabaldón
Lorenzo Sánchez
Selso Trujillo]

Minutes, February 9, 1942

Regular meeting of the Commissioners of Our Lady of Belen Acequia, the following being present: Francisco Chábez, President; Nester B. Sánchez, Secretary; Ignacio Aragón y García, Treasurer.

The commission has prepared a resolution calling for labor to clean the ditch, whereby each member is obligated to work on the ditch according to the number of water rights each has. The 1941 acequia book and register will be followed. Furthermore, the *mayordomo* and the secretary will make sure that no one does more labor than they are responsible for. The *rayador* [marker] will be careful to keep track of each worker and report the completion of their work assignments to the *mayordomo* and secretary.

The treasurer's report was received and scrupulously examined. We found it to be correct and satisfactory. The amount of money which has been received and the expenses paid by the commission are as follows:

Money received for the year 1941	$145.17
Money paid	$161.45
Balance held by the Treasurer	$16.45

And further, $25.00 is owed to the attorney Tibo J. Chávez for services during the year 1941.

Minutes, May 22, 1948

A meeting was held on this day mentioned above, by us, as commissioners of Our Lady of Belen acequia. In the meeting held on this day, we proposed and adopted the following resolutions as will be stipulated further on. Said resolutions passed under our sane judgment are considered to be of major importance for all acequia members in that they must lend their services and all must work together in the maintenance and cleaning of said acequia in the future. They read as follows:

We the undersigned, being duly elected, by those having voting rights in said election, to serve as commissioners of Our Lady of Belen acequia, and acting in such capacity, we will perform our duties in conformity with the 1941 Law on Community Acequias, and we therefore pass the following resolutions to conduct the next election at which time new officers will be elected, that day being December 6, 1948.

Resolutions

1. Any person not working three days in said acequia, or who does not provide a paid peon, during the year 1948, shall not be allowed to vote in said election.

2. Those persons who wish to vote through proxies can do so if such proxies are certified by a notary public.

3. Further, we also pass a resolution that in the future, anyone who has not worked at least five days in the acequia during the year will not be allowed to vote in any election. This includes elections in which new officials are to be elected.

To make this binding, we affix our hand and seal on all the aforementioned.

> *Commission*
> *Lorenzo Sánchez, President*
> *Ignacio Aragón y García, Treasurer*
> *Carlos P. Sánchez, Secretary*

Mayordomo Timebook 1949

Lorenzo Sánchez

Feb. 14	Comisionado	2 days	Feb. 21	Plow	3 [days]
15		2	22	Plow [3 days]	
16		2	22	By Carlos Córdova, escrepas [scraper]	1 [day]
17		2	23	Team [of horses]	2
18		2	23	By C. Córdova	1
19		2	24	Team	2
21		2	24	By C. Córdova	1
22		2			
23		2	25	Teams	2
24		2	25	By C. Córdova	1
25		2			
26		2	26	Teams	2
28		2	26	C. Córdova	1
Mar. 1			Mar. 7	3 Teams	6
to			Mar. 8	3 Teams	6
Mar. 17		30			

Petition to President Roosevelt

February 6, 1934
Belen, New Mexico

His Excellency, Franklin D. Roosevelt
President of the United States of America
Washington, D.C.

Esteemed and Honored Sir:

As you are the head of this country, the guiding wheel of our Ship of State, elected to lead our country out of chaos into which it had fallen, we are appealing to you with the same trust and confidence that the voters of America had in the election of 1932 when they turned to you for guidance. Therefore we, the undersigned, knowing your integrity, your fairness, and your honesty, especially with regard to the rights of the common people, are calling to your attention, in the form of a petition, a matter which affects every property owner and taxpayer in the Río Grande Valley.

This matter, the Middle Río Grande Conservancy Project, was passed as a law unexpectedly and while the people were not aware of what it consisted. At least 95% of the property owners and taxpayers in our vicinity, who will be directly affected by the law, are opposed to it because instead of being a beneficial law it is more or less a process of confiscation of property and of driving out the poor farmers who are unable to meet the high assessments required by the Conservancy and who have lived on their poor small farms all of their lives, as did their fathers, grandfathers, great-grandfathers, and other ancestors before them.

Now the conservancy wishes to take our local ditches and make them a part of their system and then compell [*sic*] us to pay them approximately $2.00 per year per acre for the use of the water, regardless of whether the land is farming land, alkali land, pasture, grazing land, or hills. Our main ditch, called La Acequia de Nuestra Señora de Belén de la Ladera, has been rendering satisfactory service for more than seventy years and was reconstructed and enlarged at a cost of approximately $53,600.00 (not including the annual maintenance cost), or an individual cost of $13.40 per acre on 4000 acres which it serves. The work was begun in 1905 and finished in 1912 after much labor, difficulty and cost on our part. This ditch is twenty-three miles long and serves several communities, to-wit: part of Indian Pueblo of Isleta, Village of Los Lentes, Town of Los Lunas, Village of Los Chávez, and Town of Belen, including the land located between, and around, these communities. The Conservancy is now attempting to take this ditch and use it as part of their system without reimbursing us for our cost of reconstructing the ditch or for the right-of-way (actual land covered by the ditch), which amounts to 197.575 acres, and valued at a reasonable figure ($50.00 per acre) would amount to $9878.75. Without paying us for any of the above, the Conservancy would then force us to pay them for the use of the water carried in our ditch which we built, maintained, and used all these years.

The Conservancy is constructing a canal approximately the entire length of our ditch which will be almost parallel to our ditch, being only from 100 feet to 100 yards west of our ditch. Much unnecessary work and expense could have been saved if the Conservancy had paid us for the ditch, deepened, enlarged, and improved same and then used it instead of duplicating it a few yards away and then using our ditch as a branch.

We are calling this matter to your attention in the hope that you can do something to assist us in this difficulty. We know of the good that you have done for the country at large, especially for the poor unfortunate people who were in danger of losing their homes or farms, so we are placing our case in your hands and know that you will not disappoint us.

Respectfully,

INDIAN PUEBLO OF ISLETA
*By Faustín Lente * his mark*
ACEQUIA DE NUESTRA SEÑORA DE
BELEN DE LA LADERA
(Northern Section)

By Eutimio Carrosco, Commissioner
Carlos Lobato, Commissioner
F. X. Tond[re], Commissioner
ACEQUIA DE NUESTRA SEÑORA DE
BELEN DE LA LADERA
(Southern Section)

By José M. García, Commissioner
Ignacio Aragón Y García, Commissioner
Juan Luna, Commissioner,
Maximiliano Sánchez, Chief Ditch
Foreman

P.S. If you find it possible, we would appreciate it very much if you could send someone here to investigate the matter from all angles and assure you of our appreciation and gratitude for anything that you can do in our behalf.

ENSENADA DITCH

The Ensenada Ditch is the oldest acequia diverted from the Río Brazos near Tierra Amarilla, in Río Arriba County. In 1946 Eduardo Vigil served as treasurer. Like others before and after him, his ledger consists of simple but clear entries recording expenditures and receipts on the exact days of the year when they occurred. The itemized purchases for July 10, for example, indicate the list of materials he bought for the construction of a *desagüe*, along with the costs of each item: lumber, transportation costs to obtain the lumber, nails, and the carpenter's labor charge, for a total cost of $26.33. Subsequent treasurers who made entries in the ledger through 1957 included Max Velasques, Manuel G. Martínez, Gomisindo F. Durán, George Valdez, and Hayden Gaylor. As a common practice with ledgers of this type, each incoming treasurer would record the date of his receipt of the ledger, the name of the outgoing treasurer, and the fund balance at the time of the transfer. The last treasurer to have maintained the 1946 to 1957 book was Hayden Gaylor. On January 7, 1957, he noted that $138.60 was available in the account at the time the treasurer's book was turned over to him by George Valdez, the preceding treasurer. Previous to Gaylor, the ledger entries had all been recorded in Spanish, as shown below. Though intended as the treasurer's notebook, other miscellaneous entries were inscribed as needed, such as the minutes and certification documenting the results of the election of officers on December 4, 1950.]

Treasurer's Ledger
Entries, 1946

Ensenada, New Mexico Enero 18, 1946
Eduardo Vigil, Tesorero de La Acequia de Ensenada, N.M.

Recibíd de Julio Archuleta anterior comicionado y tesorero
    de La Acequia de Ensenada, la suma de $83.00
Enero 26 de 1946: Recibíd de Perfecto Valdez, entregados por
    Santiago Gonzales, mayordomo por el año de 1945   13.60
Junio 1 de 1946: Recibíd de Don Frank Durán, mayordomo   71.50
Julio 8 de 1946: Recibíd de Don Frank Durán, dinero entrado
    por durante el año de 1946   6.50
                      $174.60

Julio 10, 1946: Dinero del fondo de La Asequia de Ensenada
  que se [h]a gastado en lo siguiente para [h]aser un *desagüe:*

Madera	$19.65
Por traller [traer] La Madera	3.00
Clavos	1.28
Carpintero	2.40
	26.33

Se pagó por fiansas de mayordomo y tesorero	$2.00
Por este mismo Libro	1.50

12/12/46: Se le pagó a Perfecto Valdez por cuatro vigas para un
  puente   4.00
12/12/46: Se le pagó a George Valdez por jalar 1873 pies de madera 8.00
12/12/46: Se le pagó a Manuel Sánchez por 1873 pies de madera   85.90
12/14/46: Por clavos, 35 libras   4.28 + 134.01
Dic. 8, 1946: Dinero entrado al fondo ____ depósito de la
  Acequia de Ensenada en mano recibido por el tesorero,
  es la siguiente suma $174.60

Desenbolso [h]asta hoy de Dic. 8, 1946	29.83
Depósito	144.77

Eduardo Vigil, Tesorero

Ledger Entry, 1947

Junio 1, 1947: Se le pagó a Gomisindo Durán y a Gavino Velarde
  por [h]aser cuatro *desagües*, . . . compuertas y jalar la madera $18.00
Oct. 30, 1947: Se le pagó a Perfecto Valdez por medio barril de
  clavos para puentes   6.25
Abril 25, 1948: Recivíd de Gomisindo Durán la suma de $26.00 por
  delinquencia que se pagó por el año de 1947, Colectados por
  él como mayordomo de la Acequia de Ensenada, New Mexico   26.00
Abril 27, 1948: Recibíd de Don Luciano Rodella [mayordomo]
  la suma de $6.00 que fueron pagados por Atilano Suazo por
  el Rancho de Doña Isavel S. Valdez, pagados por delincuencia
  del año 1947 $6.00
Junio 22, 1948: Recibíd de Luciano Rodella, mayordomo, trienta
  y cuarto pesos. Pagados por delinquencia de travajo a la
  Acequia de Ensenada   34.00

Ledger Entry, 1949, Max Velasques, Treasurer

Dinero que resibíd yo Max Velasques como tesorero, $50.32, sincuenta pesos y treinta y dos sentabos, fondo de la asequia de la comunidad de Ensenada, N.M.

6/3/49: Se le pagó a George Valdez por trabajo por poner un
caño con su tiro $5.00
Se le pagó a Bidal Valdez por trabajo por poner el mismo caño $3.50

Embolsos Por el Año de 1949

5/03/49	Pagó	Perfecto Valdez	Por tareas	$6.00
5/03/49	Pagó	Miguel Chábez	Por tareas	.50c
5/22/49	Pagó	Manuel Sánchez	Por tareas	2.00
5/22/49	Pagó	Gomisindo Durán	Por tareas	.50c
5/22/49	Pagó	Rossana Romero	Por tareas	.50c
5/25/49	Pagó	Frank Luna	Por tareas	4.00
5/30/49	Pagó	Esperidión Velásquez	Por tareas	2.00
5/30/49	Pagó	Manuel Montoya	Por tareas	2.00
6/03/49	Pagó	Eloy Durán	Por tareas	4.00
6/03/49	Pagó	Manuel Martínez	Por tareas	10.00
6/03/49	Pagó	José Benabidez	Por tareas	2.00
6/03/49	Pagó	Isabel Valdez	Por tareas	2.00

Jan. 9, 1950: Colecta especial para canios   71.50

Max Velásquez, tesorero /s/

Ledger Entry, 1950, Manuel G. Martínez, Treasurer

[January 9, 1950]: Yo Manuel G. Martínez, receví de el anterior
tesorero, Max Velasques, la suma de $2.00, fondo de la
Acequia de Ensenada. M. G. Martínez /s/
Junio 20, 1950: receví de Ubaldo Martínez, mayordomo,
(por tareas, 1950) $45.00
Dec. 4, 1950: Por f[a]ina José Leandro Redela   2.00
                                                                  ‾‾‾‾‾
                                                                  49.00
August 13, 1950: Por trabajo [h]echo en la acequia . . .
a G. F. Durán, 2.40   2.40
                                                                  ‾‾‾‾‾
                                                                  46.60

Dec. 3, 1950: Receví de Ubaldo Martínez por tareas	47.00
	93.60
January 5, 1951: Gastos 2.00 para la fianza de mayordomo y	
tesorero	2.00
Bal.	$91.60

Ledger Entry, 1951, G. F. Durán, Treasurer

Enero 6, 1951: Receví de Manuel G. Martínez	$88.60
Gastos de la Asequia de Ensenada por semento y caños	$86.22
Se le pagó [a] José A. Benavídez por clavos	.59
Se le pagó a Miguel Chávez [y] José Rascón por trabajo en la	
puente de el acequia que va para la Escuela	2.50
6/28/51: Papel de escribir para eleción	.30
Dinero por fainas de la acequia	5.00

Ledger Entry, 1955, George Valdez, Treasurer

[January 20, 1955]: Dinero que receví yo como tesorero,	
George Valdez,	$148.00
Pertenciente a la Asequia Madre y sus Benas [Venas]	

Ledger Entry, 1957, Hayden Gaylor, Treasurer

[January 7, 1957]: Hayden Gaylor (Tres) received from George Valdez preceding (Tres), the Treasurer's book and the ditch funds amounting to $138.60.

Minutes of Election Meeting, December 4, 1950

Eleción tenida en Ensenada N.M. el día 4 de Dicembre 1950 para ele-jir Comisión y Mayordomo de la Acequia de Ensenada

[Parciantes]	[Derechos]
George Valdez	2
Luciano Rodela	2
Faustín Trujillo	1
Perfecto Valdez	1

[Parciantes]	[Derechos]
Manuel G. Martínez	6
Eduardo Vigil	4
Cornelia Martínez por José A. Benavídez	1
Hayden Gaylor	5

[Twenty seven other names follow]

Resultados de Elesión de la Asequia de Ensenada tenida el día 4 de Dic. 1950

Comisionados	
Ubaldo Martínez	33
Gomicendo Durán	56
Manuel V. Valdez	31
Max Velásquez	49
Mayordomo	
Manuel G. Martínez	42
José Leandro Rodela	18

Ensenada N.M.
Dic. 4, 1950

Nosotros abajo firmados Juezes de eleción Certificamos que los siguientes Comicionados fueron Elejidos:

Ubaldo Martínez
Gomicindo Durán
Max Velásquez

Y Mayordomo para la Acequia de Comunidad de Ensenada fue Elejido:

Manuel G. Martínez
Juezes de eleción:
Manuel G. Martínez
Ubaldo Martínez

ALGODONES DITCH RULES, C. 1920S

Undated, these ditch rules for the Asequia de Algodones north of Bernalillo appear to have been in effect sometime during the 1920s, prior to the establishment of the Middle Río Grande Conservancy District. Other than the provision made for the collection of dues to pay the *mayordomo* and a few other details, most of the rules have to do with the allocation of labor to conduct the annual cleaning and to perform other work during the course of the irrigation season, upon the call of the *mayordomo*. The tone of these particular rules is somewhat stern, reflecting perhaps the seriousness of the task at hand: the common ditch and the individual headgates must be maintained at all times; all irrigators must contribute labor in proportion to the acreages they farm and irrigate; the *mayordomo* must impose fines on any and all delinquent members, otherwise, the amount in question will be deducted from his own salary.

Nosotros los abajo firmados como comisionados de la Asequia de Algodones imponemos estas reglas.

Regla 1ra. Por esta se le impone la suma de $1.50 a toda persona que falte en hacer su trabajo durante la limpia cada un día que faltare.

Regla 2nda. Por esto se le impone la suma de $1.50 a toda persona que faltare en hacer su trabajo durante el año en dicha acequia.

Regla 3ra. Cuando el mayordomo nombre a la asequia y si alguien faltare de no ir a la asequia no se le dará la agua hasta el tanto no page el impuesto ejecutado el mayordomo de ir el mismo día a cobrar el impuesto. Si el mayordomo faltare en ejecutar dicha regla se le desquitará de su pago al mayordomo.

Regla 4ta. En caso de alguna grave necesidad como es una quiebra o entrampe de asequia el mayordomo tendrá el derecho de nombrar a la jente asegún la necesite y vea el paso mas prudente, también se le requiere al mayordomo de dejar el uso de agua de dicha asequia libremente para regar jardines y huertas los siguientes días de la semana a saber sabado y domingos. No se interrumpirá la agua en otra clase de sembrados durante estos días a no ser de que [h]aiga agua suficiente o sobrante, entonces el mayordomo tendrá el derecho de disponer de las sobrantillas. El resto de la semana el agua será usado en otros sembrados como el mayodomo disponga de ellos asegún baya [vaya] tocando.

Regla. 5ta. Se le advierte al mayordomo que ejecute el trabajo a los que tienen 12 acres y días como a los que tienen 24 acres a saber. Si el que tiene 12 acres se nombra con un carro, el que tiene 24 acres tendrá que ser nombrado con dos carros. Las personas que tengan 1.02 acres de terreno no serán nombrados al trabajo hasta que los que tengan más terreno [h]aigan trabajado una tercera parte de su trabajo y trabajarán en proposición a todos los dueños de terreno. Se les advierte de tener buenas compuertas en los regadíos que sean suficiente anchas. De otra manera si se rompe la asequia en su compuertas ellos serán responsables por tales perjuicios. Y el mayordomo y la comisión no serán responsables por tales perjuicios. Si siguiera una lista de las personas que están sujetas y obligadas al trabajo en dicha acequia. Como también a los impuestos del mayordomo. También en esta se les notifica que el pago del mayordomo será cole[c]tado por el mayordomo todo [colectado para] el día 15 de Julio y si alguno no paga su parte del pago no se le dará la agua hasta que no page el dinero del mayordomo y si el mayordomo dire el agua sin pagarle, nosotros los comisionados no seremos responsables [crossed out: "y la segunda mitad será cole(c)tada para el día 15 de Sept[i]embre."] Y si alguna persona o personas se opusiere en hacer tales pagos serán presecutados por la dicha comisión. Sigue la lista de las personas que están sujetas al trabajo. También se le impone ha toda persona la suma de $3.00 por cada día de trabajo con carro o tiro como el mayordomo los mande con carro o tiro.

Alberto Griego, Presidente
Casimiro Lovato, Secretario
Andrés Armijo, Tesorero

[We the undersigned, as commissioners of the Algodones Acequia, hereby impose these rules:

Rule No. 1. Through this, any person who neglects to work during the annual cleaning shall be fined $1.50 for each day of work missed.

Rule No. 2. Through this, any person who fails to do any work throughout the course of the year will be fined in the amount of $1.50.

Rule No. 3. Whenever the mayordomo calls out the members to work on the acequia, those persons who do not respond to the work call shall not receive their water until they have paid their fine imposed by the mayordomo. If the mayordomo fails to impose such fines, they will be deducted from his own salary.

Rule No. 4. During times of emergency or dire need, such as a break or blockage of the acequia, the mayordomo will have the authority to recruit workers as he might need them in a prudent manner. The mayordomo will also allow the people to have free and liberal use of the water for their gardens on Saturdays and Sundays. Water for other types of irrigation will not be interrupted during these days, unless there is sufficient excess water. In such case, the mayordomo will be allowed to distribute the excess waters. During the remainder of the week, water will be used in other planted fields under the direction of the mayordomo in accordance to the people's rights.

Rule No. 5. The mayordomo is advised to require work from all persons owning 12 acres and days as well as those owning 24 acres, to wit. If the person having 12 acres provides one wagon, the person having 24 acres must provide two wagons. Persons having 1.02 acres of land will not be asked to work until those persons having more land have completed one-third of their work, and they will work in proportion to the land owned by the others. People are hereby advised to have good, wide headgates in their irrigated lands. If the acequia and headgates break along their lands, they will be responsible for those damages. The mayordomo and commission will not be responsible for those damages. When required, a list of those persons owing work and/or being delinquent in their fines will be prepared by the mayordomo. Also, through this, everyone is notified that the mayordomo's salary will be collected by himself, and all money will be collected by July 15. If an acequia member has not paid his share of the mayordomo's salary, he will not receive any water until his share has been paid. If the mayordomo gives out water before he has been paid, we the commissioners are not responsible. [Crossed out: The second half of the mayordomo's salary shall be paid by September 15.] If a person or persons are opposed to making such payments, they will be prosecuted by said commission. The list of all persons obligated to work follows. Every person failing to provide a wagon or team of horses shall pay $3.00 per day as so directed by the mayordomo.

> *Alberto Griego, President*
> *Casimiro Lovato, Secretary*
> *Andrés Armijo, Treasurer]*

Rebalse y Cuchilla Ditches

Ditch Rules, 1941

This simple list of six rules sufficed to govern the two ditches mentioned in the rules: the Asequia del Rebalse and Asequia de la Cuchilla on the Río Hondo in Taos County. As noted in rule number four, a single commission established the assessment rates for both ditches and probably decided all other matters in the same fashion. At various points, the members are referred to as "[h]ortaliseros," "dueños de propiedad," and "regador[es]." Later, the Rebalse and the Cuchilla ditches each organized separate commissions. The practice of a single commission governing the affairs of two or more acequias continues elsewhere. For example, the commissioners of the Questa Citizens Ditch Association manage the affairs of four acequias. In the Arroyo Seco area twelve ditches are considered one system, and are managed by one *mayordomo* and one set of commissioners through the Acequia Madre del Río Lucero y Arroyo Seco.

1. Se tasará por [h]ortaliseros medio día por la Asequia del Rebalse y un día por la Cuchilla.

2. También de un acre a tres, se tasará un día en el Rebalse y dos días en la Asequia de la Cuchilla.

3. De tres acres para arriva, se tasará en lleno.

4. También se tasará $3.00 pesos al día en la Asequia del Rebalse y $3.00 por la Asequia de la Cuchilla o asegún la opinión de la comisión.

5. También se require que cada dueño de propiedad por cada veinte acres le conviene un peón y sujeto a un surco de agua.

6. También el Mayordomo negará el surco de agua a cualquier dueño de propiedad o regador que no page cualquier delincuencia que se deva a la asequia.

En junta abierta hoy día 13 de Abril, 1941. Una mosión por Salvador Rendón que las reglas fueran apovadas según leídas, y las mismas quedaron aprovadas.

Comision Presidente, Leocadio Montaño
Sec. Wilfredo Pacheco

[1. Farmers will be assessed one-half day for the Acequia del Rebalse and a full day for the Acequia de la Cuchilla.

2. Also, from one to three acres, one day shall be assessed to el Rebalse and two days for the Acequia de la Cuchilla.

3. Three acres and over will be assessed in full.

4. Also, $3.00 per day will be assessed to the Acequia del Rebalse and $3.00 for the Acequia de la Cuchilla, or whatever amount the commission might determine.

5. It will also be required of property owners to have a *peón* assigned to irrigate each twenty acres of land.

6. Also, the *mayordomo* shall deny the water to any property owner or irrigator who is delinquent to the acequia.

In an open meeting held today, April 13, 1941. A motion made by Salvador Rendón that the rules be approved as read, and the same stood approved.

Commission: President,
Leocadio Montaño
Sec., Wilfredo Pacheco]

SAN AUGUSTÍN DITCH

Community Ditch Bylaws, n.d.

These rules were found in English and were undated, but note the clarity, directness, and economy of expression in this language as well, whether adopted in original form or translated later by the irrigators. In five very brief sections, the rules manage to cover all of the essentials that these local irrigators believed they needed: elections and voting rights, annual reports, labor and financial obligations of the irrigators, the *mayordomo's* explict duties, water rotation schedule and process, and penalties for failure to contribute the requisite share of ditch labor. The ditch is located in San Miguel County.

I. On the first month of every year, the water rights owners of the San Augustín community ditch elect commissioners and a *mayordomo*. And each year the commissioners give their report on the work that has been done on the ditch and on any members that are delinquent.

II. Each water right owner is obligated to contribute to the construction of the ditch every year and also to contribute funds for material needed on the ditch whenever necessary. The amount needed for materials must be equally contributed from each water right.

III. These are the *mayordomo's* duties:

1. He takes his orders from the commissioners.
2. The ditch is under his care.
3. He will guide the work being done on the ditch.
4. He will keep a work record for each water right owner.
5. He must not let any member accumulate more than (2) days of work.
6. He will divide the water among the members.

7. He will give his annual report on the work that has been
done.

If the mayordomo cannot be present, then one of the commissioners
must be in charge.

IV. Each member may vote according to the number of water rights
that he has. Each water right has 24 hours in which he can use the water.
These 24 hours begin at 8:00 A.M. and end on the following morning at
8:00 A.M. The irrigation commences at the 1st property owner at the
headgate and alternates until all the members have had their water rights.

V. If a water right owner does not give the required labor on the ditch
for a year, his water right will be suspended. He will then have (1) one year
in which to pay up his delinquency in full in labor.

SAN ANTONIO DITCH

In a single journal, the *parciantes* of the San Antonio Ditch at Valdez recorded the business and proceedings important to them during the period
1949–1971: minutes of meetings, *relgamentos* or rules, lists of delinquent
members, and, as shown below, a notarized statement that the incoming
officers for 1949 took as their oath of office, swearing to conduct their
work as commissioners with "Honesty, Justice and Impartiality."

Oath of Office, Ditch Commissioners, 1949

Valdez, Condado de Taos, N.M.
Abril 20 de 1949

Hoy este día comparecieron ante mí la comisión de la Acequia de San
Antonio

Sinforoso Ortega
Max B. Maes
Bautista Córdoba

y fueron devidamente juramentados que ellos obraran con Honestidad,
Justicia y Imparcialidad con sus deberes como comisión.

Alex S. Martínez, Notario Público
My Commission Expires March 6, 1951
SEAL

Reglamento por 1949

Todos los dueños de terreno de regadío por la Acequia de San Antonio tienen que trabajar al tiempo de limpiarla desde el *desagüe* hasta la presa. Si alguno faltare en el trabajo pagará la cuota de un peso y medio por día [y] los de hortalisas setenta y cinco centavos por día.

Delinquentes por el año 1952

Trinidad Martínez	$2.50
Luis D. García	2.50
Rod[o]lfo Sanches	5.00
Marcos Espinoza	2.50
Carl Schosier [Schlosser]	6.25
Pedro Durán	2.50
Mardoqueo Herrera	.50
Telésforo Salazar	.50
Santiago Valdez	paid 1.25

[All owners of irrigated land within the Acequia of San Antonio are obligated to provide labor during the cleaning time from the return channel to the diversion dam. Should a person fail to participate in the labor, he shall pay a fine of one dollar and a half per day (and) those with gardens (shall pay) seventy-five cents per day.

Delinquencies for 1952

Trinidad Martínez	$2.50
Luis D. García	2.50
Rod[o]lfo Sanches	5.00
Marcos Espinoza	2.50
Carl Schosier [Schlosser]	6.25
Pedro Durán	2.50
Mardoqueo Herrera	.50
Telésforo Salazar	.50
Santiago Valdez	paid 1.25]

Minutes May 10, 1971

. . . También fue descutido y votado de que cuando una regla nueva se ponga, que sea escrita en el libro de reglas y se abrogue la regla vieja para que quede en fuerza la regla nueva nomás.

[. . . It was also discussed and voted that when a new rule is proposed, it must be written into the rule book and the previous rule deleted so that only the new rule remains in force.]

El Prado Middle Ditch

Ditch Rules, 1957

The rules in effect during 1957 in the community of El Prado, just north of Taos, were available to members in both the Spanish and the English languages, signaling a permanent state of bilingualism in this and most other acequia communities in the region. Both versions were approved by the members at a meeting held on April 28, 1957. While retaining their penchant for clarity, as in the rules of earlier periods, the rules and regulations for the Asequia del Medio at El Prado nevertheless appear to have been developed with a somewhat more formal tone and approach, perhaps due to the assistance of a lawyer or another professional familiar with the style of modern-day bylaws and regulations of comparable agencies. The clear but strident tone might also reflect the maturity of the irrigation institution after hundreds of years of evolution. The 1957 rules for the El Prado Middle Ditch exude confidence in the ability of the irrigators to promulgate rules for their continued self-government during the more businesslike climate of the modern era.

Regla Numero 1
Que el salario del mayordomo de la Asequia del Medio será regulado por la comisión de la Asequia del Medio de El Prado, New Mexico. Se colectará la suma de 25 centavos por cada un acre de todos los dueños de propiedad de regadío bajo la Asequia del Medio para el pago del mayordomo, y todos los dueños de propiedad que tengan de tres acres o menos que tres acres se les colectará la suma de $1.00 al año para el pago del mayordomo. Y a los que tengan hortalizas se les colectará la suma de $1.00 al año para el mismo propósito.

Regla Numero 2
Que la destribución del agua quedará a la descripción del mayordomo exepto en caso de [alguna] dificultad entre uno o más de los regadores; entonces y en tal caso, será el dever del mayordomo de consultar con la comisión de la asequia, para que la comisión arregle la dificultad entre los litigantes.

Regla Numero 3

El Mayordomo: tendrá que atender al desempeño de sus deveres como mayordomo, con toda atención y usando la autoridad vestida en él por los patrones de la Asequia del Medio. Desde la limpia de la asequia temprano en la primavera hasta que su sucesor sea electo y calificado.

Regla Numero 4

Que el trabajo para la limpia de la Asequia del Medio queda establesido como sigue a saber, que todos los dueños de propiedad de regadío tendrán que mandar peones para la limpia de la dicha asequia. Como Sigue: Los dueños de propiedad que tengan menos que tres acres mandarán un peón a la asequia por medio día, y los dueños de propiedad de regadío bajo la Asequia del Medio que tengan de 3, ha[sta] 10 acres mandarán un peón por un día. Y los que tengan de 10 ha[sta] 13, o mas o de días a 20 tendrán que mandar 2 peones por todo el día, o hasta que la limpia de a asequia sea terminada.

Regla Numero 5

El Mayordomo: tendrá la responsavilidad de limpiar la asequia tan pronto como sea posible temprano en la primavera. Todo dueño de propiedad de regadío bajo la dicha asequia tendrá que cumplir con el trabajo de la misma, cuando sea notificado por el mayordomo. Para la limpia de la asequia si uno o mas dueños de propiedad bajo la antedicha asequia faltare en poner trabajo él mismo o mandar uno o mas peones según la regla lo ordena, tendrán que pagarle el Tesorero de la Asequia del Medio, J. E. Flores, la suma de $4.00 por cada un día que faltaren de poner trabajo.

Regla Numero 6

El mayordomo colectará su pago de todos los dueños de propiedad de regadío bajo la Asequia del Medio, durante el tiempo del regadío. Si alguna persona o personas de los interesados en el regadío de la Asequia del Medio se opusiere en pagar lo que las reglas proveyen o faltare en poner o rendir trabajo, será el dever del mayordomo de reportarlo o reportarlos a la comisión de la Asequia del Medio, para que sea tratado o tratados según la Ley lo ordena. El mayordomo queda por medio de estas reglas autorizado de reportar todo dinero colectado por él por multas o por trabajo que no halla [haya] sido rendido por alguno o más dueños de propiedad bajo la Asequia del Medio. La Fianza del Tesorero y la del Mayordomo sera en la Suma de $100.00 por el Ano por Ambos Dos Oficiales.

Regla Numero 7

A ninguna persona o personas, dueños de propiedad de regadío, bajo la Asequia del Medio, le es permitido cortar el agua cuando otra persona la esté usando, y hacer uso de la agua sin el consentimiento del mayordomo. Y cualquier persona o personas que violasen esta regla tan sustancial será el dever del mayordomo de multar a persona o personas por primera vez en la suma de $5.00; por la segunda ofenza será o serán multados en la suma de $10.00. El mayordomo queda revestido con esta autoridad, según la Ley lo ordena; la persona o personas que cometieren tal violación y fueren multados por el mayordomo y no quederen satisfechos con el fallo del mayordomo apelarán a la comisión de la dicha asequia. Quienes darán su decisión según Ley. Si todavía no quedaren satisfechos con la decisión de la comisión, tienen el derecho de apelar al Juez de Paz del Presinto en donde la ofenza fue cometida. En caso que no huviere Juez de Paz en el Presinto donde se cometió la ofenza, entonces pueden presentar su apelación al presinto del vecino presinto. El mayordomo y la comisión tienen autoridad para demandar al culpable ante un Juez de Paz, y al fallo que sea dado por el Juez de Paz que oiga la causa será final.

Regla Numero 8

El Mayordomo: Queda autorizado por medio de estas reglas de negar el agua de regadío a qualquier persona o personas dueños de propiedad de regadío bajo la Asequia del Medio que estén delinquentes en los derechos de la asequia o en el trabajo de la misma hasta tal tiempo que las dichas personas se cuadren en el trabajo y derechos de la Asequia del Medio. Tienen que arreglar sus delincuencias con el Tesorero de la comisión de la dicha asequia.

Regla Numero 9

El Mayordomo: es el encargado de la repartición de el agua de la Asequia del Medio, de El Prado, New Mexico, y se inforsará en hacer una repartición igual y será imparcial con todos los interezados. Queda entendido además que el mayordomo [tiene el] derecho y autoridad de nombrar uno o más de los dueños de propiedad para que le ayuden cuando haiga nesesidad de hacerlo, para hacer algún trabajo en la asequia o en la compuerta en el Río de Lucero. Los nombrados tendrán que obedecer la orden del mayordomo.

Regla Numero 10

Será el dever de todos y cada uno de los dueños de propiedad de regadío bajo la Asequia del Medio de cooperar con la comisión de la Asequia del Medio y con el mayordomo de la asequia arriva mencionada, para el mejoramiento de todos los constituyentes del arriva mencionado regadío.

Regla Numero 11

El mayordomo podrá usar el dinero que él colecte de los dueños de propiedad bajo la Asequia del Medio, de los que faltaren de rendir trabajo durante la limpia de la dicha asequia, tendrán que pagar la suma de $4.00 por cada un día que falten. El dinero colectado por falta de rendir trabajo o por multas impuestas por el mayordomo a los que violaren estas reglas será usado para reparar la asequia en donde sea necesario hacerlo. El mayordomo tiene autoridad de nombrar los peones que necesite para la reparación de la asequia. Concluído el trabajo, el mayordomo les pagará del Fondo que el haiga colectado.

> *Juramentados y Subcriptos ante mí*
> *Un Notario Público por el Condado*
> *de Taos, Estado de Nuevo Méjico,*
> *Hoy Día 28 de Abril de 1957. Mí*
> *Comisión Expira 3/12/61*
> *[Signature of Notary Public]*

[Rules and Regulations for the Management of the Work on the Middle Ditch and for the Distribution of Water of the Said Ditch. These rules and regulations were read at a meeting of the patrons and owners of land under the Middle Ditch at the School House at El Prado, New Mexico, on the 28th day of April, A.D., 1957. The same were approved by the majority of the owners of land under the Middle Ditch, and they took effect immediately after their approval.

RULE NUMBER 1
That the salary of the mayordomo shall be determined by the Commission of the Acequia del Medio de El Prado, New Mexico. [The commission] shall collect the sum of $ .25 per acre from all owners of irrigation lands within the Middle Ditch for the salary of the mayordomo. And property owners with three acres or less shall pay $1.00 per year toward the mayordomo's pay. And those with gardens shall pay $1.00 per year for the same purpose. Owners with more than three acres shall pay the sum of $ .25 per acre.

RULE NUMBER 2
That the distribution of water is at the discretion of the mayordomo except when a difficulty arises between two or more irrigators using the water without the consent of the mayordomo. In that case it shall be the duty of the mayordomo to consult with the ditch commissioners so that they can resolve the difficulty between the litigants. The three commissioners shall be the judges of the guilt or innocence of the violator, and if he is found guilty as charged by the mayordomo, the commissioners shall im-

pose on him a fine not to exceed the sum of $10.00, and the violator shall be ordered by the ditch commissioners to pay his fine to the secretary-treasurer immediately after the fine is imposed.

RULE NUMBER 3

The mayordomo shall attend to his duties with care, attention and impartiality, utilizing the authority vested in him by these rules and regulations approved by the majority of the patrons of the Middle Ditch and by the three commissioners. The mayordomo shall serve for a term of one year beginning with the ditch cleaning in the early spring until the time for election of officers the first Monday of December or until his successor is elected and qualified.

RULE NUMBER 4

That the labor for cleaning of the Middle Ditch shall be provided in the spring, shall be performed by the owners of irrigation property or by a peón whom they might send as follows. Property owners with fewer than three acres shall furnish a peón for half a day; owners of irrigated property with more than three acres and up to 10 acres shall furnish a peón for a full day; and [thereafter] one man each day for every 10 acres until the cleaning of the ditch is completed.

RULE NUMBER 5

The mayordomo shall be responsible for the cleaning of the ditch as early as possible, weather permitting, in the spring of every year. All owners of irrigated property shall comply with the ditch work when notified by the mayordomo. If one or more owners of property fails to render work or to send a peón in his place, they shall pay the treasurer of the Middle Ditch, J. E. Flores, the sum of $4.00 for each day that they failed to perform work. If any person refuses to pay what the rules and regulations provide for, or fail to render work on the ditch, then it will be the duty of the mayordomo to report such person to the ditch commissioners to be treated according to Law.

RULE NUMBER 6

The bond for the mayordomo and the secretary-treasurer shall be in the sum of $100.00 for both officials.

RULE NUMBER 7

No owner of irrigated property shall be permitted to take water from the ditch when another owner is using it or without the consent of the mayordomo. Whosoever violates this so substantial a rule shall be fined by the mayordomo the sum of $5.00 for the first offense and $10.00 for the second. The mayordomo is vested with this authority, as the law orders him.

Should a violator not remain satisfied with the mayordomo's actions, he can appeal to the ditch commissioners who shall render their decision according to the law. Should the violator not be satisfied with the decision of the commission, he has the right to appeal to the Justice of the Peace in the precinct where the violation was committed; the decision of the Justice of Peace shall be final. It is also provided by the rules and regulations that the ditch commission has the authority to file against such violators before the Justice of the Peace.

RULE NUMBER 8

By virtue of these rules and regulations, the mayordomo is authorized to deny irrigation waters to any person who is delinquent in the payment of the mayordomo or the labor on the ditch until such time that the person so delinquent pays the delinquency in full to the treasurer.

RULE NUMBER 9

The mayordomo is authorized to apportion the ditch waters in an impartial manner to all interested parties. It is understood that the mayordomo has the right and authority to name one or more property owners to assist with the repair of the ditch as needed or to perform work on the headgate at the Río de Lucero. Such named persons shall obey the orders of the mayordomo.

RULE NUMBER 10

It shall be the duty of each owner of irrigated property to cooperate with the ditch commissioners and with the mayordomo for the betterment of all constituents of the ditch.

RULE NUMBER 11

The mayordomo may utilize funds he collects from the property owners, from those who fail to render labor during the ditch cleaning, and from any fines imposed, for the purpose of repairing the ditch whereever necessary. The mayordomo has authority to name as many workers as are necessary to repair the ditch and to pay them from the funds collected.

Salomón Cisneros, Mayordomo
J. E. Flores, Secretary-Treasurer]

FIVE

Contemporary Status of Acequias:

Development vs. Sustainability

During the colonial period of Nuevo México, only a handful of the irrigation settlements ever achieved the status of municipalities. The great majority of settlements were loosely grouped *ranchos* located in the narrow valleys on or near the major rivers. Land grants issued to petitioners by the republic of Mexico from 1821 to 1846 increased the number of new settlements well beyond the confines of the Río Grande, but in the vast majority of cases, acequia communities have remained unincorporated even into the contemporary period. In these communities the acequia associations are the only form of local government at the subcounty level, and for this reason they perform political and social functions outside of their main purpose as irrigation institutions. For example, the annual cleaning of the acequia not only marks the beginning of the agricultural season in early spring; it is also an occasion for the *vecinos* to address other local issues, reconfirming the sense of traditions that undergird the social and political life of the community.

In the acequia culture, connections with a geographic locale are an integral part of individual as well as collective identity. Everyone is "from a place." When two persons introduce themselves, invariably the next question of mutual interest is: *"De dónde eres?"* ("Where are you from?") The acequia delineates the physical boundaries of the community; thus, many acequias bear the name of the locality itself, as in *"La Acequia de Corrales."* Others pinpoint an interesting natural feature, such as *"La Acequia del Monte,"* at Talpa, *"La Acequia del Bosque"* at Embudo, the *"Acequia de los Ojos de la Agua Caliente"* at Agua Caliente Canyon, and the *"Acequia Madre del Llano Largo"* on the Río Santa Barbara, near Peñasco. Still others identify

family surnames with longtime connection to the ditch and the community: "*Acequia de los Chavez*," "*Acequia El Llano de Abeyta*," "*Acequia de los
Duranes*," "*Acequia de Tío Borrego*," and scores of others. At the time of the
annual acequia cleaning, the *parciantes* renew their strong attachment to
the locality, assuring the continuance of place for yet another cycle of irrigation and community antiquity.

Acequias as Political Subdivisions

The political role of the acequia is more than just symbolic and not simply a matter of historical accident. Numerous state supreme court cases
and attorney general opinions have conceded that ditch associations hold
special standing as political subdivisions of the state of New Mexico. This
special domain was recognized by the state supreme court in a 1914 case
wherein the court considered the history and nature of the ditches. Among
other acknowledgments, the court made note of the significant fact that
the arid conditions in the region required settlers to assure the availability
of water to irrigate crops at the needed times.[1] In an earlier case in 1905,
Candelaria v. Vallejos, the court determined the public status of acequia associations as similar in class to other public, involuntary quasi-corpora-
tions such as counties, townships, and school districts.[2] Later, in 1912 at
the time of statehood, the state constitution included community ditches
in the list of governmental units that would be exempted from ad valorem
taxation.[3]

Since statehood, at least two attorney-general opinions have considered
the question as to whether community ditches are political subdivisions of
the state of New Mexico.[4] In 1940, the then–attorney general noted that
the ditches had functioned for hundreds of years as rural water systems
providing benefits to farmers similar to those that municipal waterworks
provide to city dwellers, "both being of a benefit to the public and a necessity for the maintenance of health and life by the distribution of a publicly
owned commodity, to-wit: water." Later, in 1963, a subsequent attorney
general was asked for a ruling on the specific question: "are acequia association ditches political subdivisions?" His reply was unequivocal:

> Most certainly. . . . It is no exaggeration to state that community
> acequias have been serving as "political subdivisions" in the area that
> now comprises the State of New Mexico since at least 1851. Statutes
> enacted by the New Mexico territorial legislature, and subsequently
> the State Legislature, have merely confirmed this status.[5]

To remove any doubt, perhaps for all time, the state legislature enacted an acequia law in 1965 declaring that "[a]cequia and community ditch associations are hereby declared to be political subdivisions of this state."[6] In the same session the legislature expanded acequia financial powers. In chapter 183 of the laws of 1965, acequia associations were authorized to contract indebtedness and specifically to borrow money and accept grants from the United States government or its agencies, to issue notes or obligations, and to secure payment thereof by mortgage, pledge, or deed of trust.[7] More recently, the federal government has taken a step of its own and recognized acequia associations as public entities. In Public Law 99-662, the Water Resources Development Act of 1986, the U.S. Congress directed the Army Corps of Engineers "to consider the historic Acequia systems (community ditches) of the southwestern United States as public entities [allowing them] to enter into agreements and serve as local sponsors of water-related projects . . ."[8] The text of Public Law 99-662 continues:

The Congress finds that . . . these early engineering works have significance in the settlement and development of the western portion of the United States . . . [and therefore] declares that the restoration and preservation of the Acequia systems has cultural and historic values to the region. . . . The Secretary [of the Army] is authorized and directed to undertake, without regard to economic analysis, such measures as are necessary to protect and restore the river diversion structures and associated canals attendant to the operations of the community ditch and Acequia systems in New Mexico.[9]

Two years later, acequia associations gained additional political standing when the governor of New Mexico issued an Executive Order[10] creating a new advisory unit that he called the "Acequia Commission." The initial purpose of this commission would be to advise state government, the Interstate Stream Commission, and the U.S. Army Corps of Engineers on criteria for the joint federal and state funding of acequia-rehabilitation projects authorized under the Water Resources Development Act of 1986. By 1996 these cooperation agreements had resulted in fifty-two contracts with local acequias for the construction of forty-nine construction projects amounting to 14.2 million dollars in federal funds.[11] An additional function of the ten-member Acequia Commission would be to advise the governor, by way of review and comment, on any plans or legislation at the state level affecting New Mexico acequias. Toward the end of the decade, the Acequia Commission was still in place, meeting on a regular basis in Santa Fe and advising the executive branch from one governor to the next, Republicans and Democrats.[12]

Water Markets and a Changing Political Economy

Acequia associations have benefited from their status as political subdivisions in many ways, especially with their direct access to federal and state funds for ditch rehabilitation, soil conservation, and other construction projects.[13] Together, these grants-in-aid, low-interest loans, and contracts have enabled acequia officers to shore up the canal and diversion-dam infrastructure with each passing generation of users. Thus, for much of the period following World War II, the acequia tradition, with its localized agricultural practices, continued much in the same manner as before. The late 1960s and 1970s, however, began a period of change, challenges, and new opportunities for the water-based communities of the upper Río Grande and its tributaries. Activity in the water markets, adjudication suits in the major river streams, an emerging conservation ethos in the general society, and land-development pressures converged in the region, destined to impact state water planning and the myriad of stakeholder institutions well into the closing years of the twentieth century.

On the surface, the acequia institution appears to have enjoyed many points of strategic advantage. Compared to other water-use groups, the acequias have represented the single largest constituency, numbering more than a thousand associations. Other than water resources protected under federal reserved rights, such as tribal and other land reservations under United States jurisdiction, acequias often hold the oldest rights in most streams. In the face of mounting pressures caused by expanding water markets, the "first in time, first in right" principle embodied in the doctrine of prior appropriation seemingly should provide the centuries-old institution with a margin of protection and long-term security. But compared to most other stakeholder groups, acequia associations have been the least organized and poorest equipped in terms of technical, financial, and legal resources. When pitted against the most powerful interests, the playing field, at least in the early rounds, has been decidedly uneven.

Until the 1960s, the water markets in New Mexico had not been strong enough to pose any systemic threat to traditional agricultural uses. The business of managing the acequia waters had continued much as before: the local ditch rules, based mostly on custom and tradition, carried the force of law.[14] From the time of settlement, water resources and the land base had remained whole. Through native engineering, trial and error, and sheer tenacity in making permanent settlements sustainable, these first appropriators had crafted an institution that had withstood the test of time over successive generations of heirs. Economic change and water-transfer cases outside the control of acequias, however, began to pose a series of concerns to traditional water users, accustomed as they were to local autonomy.

In the late sixties, land and water-rights values began to increase in parts of the Río Grande bioregion at faster rates than had been the custom. Municipal growth, an expanding industrial sector, mineral extraction, timbering, increased agribusiness, tourism and recreation development, and other demands converged in the 1960s and 1970s and began to test the longevity of acequia agriculture in new ways. Local impacts were felt directly when acequia irrigators and other villagers observed marked increases in real estate values for their ancestral farmlands. In the Río Hondo watershed of Taos County, for example, the demand for second homes, condominiums, lodges, and an expansion of recreational facilities increased land values from one thousand dollars per acre in 1965 to twenty-five thousand dollars or higher by 1986.[15] By 1997, in the same vicinity, land values had risen to forty thousand dollars per acre and higher. Water rights could be transferred for five thousand dollars per acre foot.[16] New projects of this type often rely on water-rights transfers from area acequias or from underground wells that are hydrologically connected to the streams supplying the ditches with surface irrigation waters. Either way, local water rights and the acequia as an irrigation institution are threatened.

Without the benefit of municipal water infrastructure, new subdivisions in the rural portions of Taos and other counties invariably require a central deep well or a series of private wells on each property. The stresses precipitated by these higher-density development projects have brought to the surface a latent clash of values and diametrically opposed perspectives concerning the relationships of land, water, and culture. The traditional belief that water was the "lifeblood" of the community became juxtaposed against a legal system that classified water rights as a commodity that could be sold and severed from previous historic uses by a simple market transaction. The so-called "lower-value uses," such as those practiced by the majority of acequia water users, became the most vulnerable to potential water transfers to nonagricultural uses, as depicted in some of the following case illustrations concerning five north-central counties of New Mexico.

El Llano Unit and Indian Camp Dam

The project proposal for the El Llano Unit was initiated by the federal Bureau of Reclamation, with subsequent participation by the city of Española in north-central New Mexico. The Bureau sought to construct a dam, scheduled to commence in mid-1976, just north of the acequia village of Velarde, the heart of the largest and most productive fruit-orchard valley irrigated by acequia waters in the entire upper Río Grande basin. Authorized by federal legislation in 1962 as a segment of the much larger San Juan-Chama Reclamation Project, the El Llano Unit involved eighteen miles of properties with water rights, potentially impacting twenty-two communities in the counties of Santa Fe and Río Arriba. If completed, the dam would divert fifteen thousand acre-feet per year from the Río Grande just north of Velarde and deliver it to the Santa Cruz River, via a canal to be built paralleling the Río Grande to the east.[17]

Among other objectives, the project would enable the municipality of Española, fourteen miles downstream from Velarde, to acquire water for its future growth through the creation of a conservancy district, pending approval of the necessary water-rights permits from the Interstate Streams Commission. Purportedly, agricultural beneficiaries included the San Juan Indian Pueblo and the other acequia communities throughout the Velarde valley. However, the irrigators knew nothing about the eminent construction of the dam until the summer of 1974, when they noticed that survey stakes were being placed on the ground marking the location for the digging of the canal. Though they had been aware of the 1962 and earlier plans connecting the El Llano Unit to the San Juan-Chama project, they had been led to believe that the El Llano portion was not going to be built, at least not without further public notice and input.[18]

The project had moved this far along without much public participation partly because, years earlier, the city of Española had taken advantage of a legal procedure that allowed it to petition the District Court for the formation of a conservancy district and then to sign the petition on behalf of all landowners within the city of Española. The municipality claimed that it needed to augment its water supply in order to fill the domestic water requirements of its current and increasing population plus the service needs of adjacent smaller communities it was planning to annex. Without much fanfare, the conservancy district had been formed at a special meeting of the Española City Council in 1970. Anticipating access to the new sources of water from the San Juan-Chama Reclamation Project and the El Llano Unit, the city subsequently entered into agreements with the

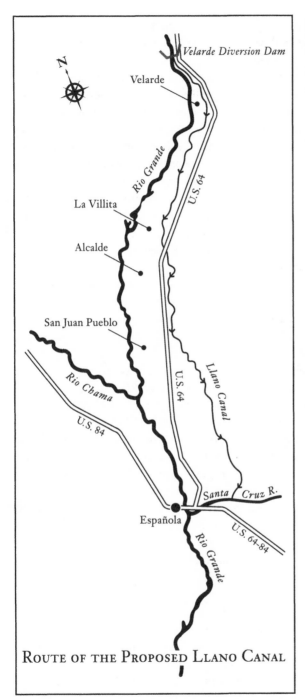

Route of Proposed El
Llano Canal from
Velarde Dam to the
Santa Cruz River.
Source: La Confluencia
*(1976). Map courtesy of
U.S. Bureau of
Reclamation.*

Velarde Diversion Dam

Velarde

N

Rio Grande

U.S. 64

La Villita

Alcalde

San Juan Pueblo

Llano Canal

Rio Chama

U.S. 64

U.S. 84

Santa Cruz R.

Española

U.S. 64-84

Rio Grande

ROUTE OF THE PROPOSED LLANO CANAL

Bureau of Reclamation in support of the construction of the canal. In 1974 the nascent conservancy district began to assess mill tax levies on properties within the district's boundaries.[19]

When the plans for the actual construction of the dam and canal became more widely known during the fall of 1974, the valley residents and acequia irrigators began to mount an intensive campaign against the project. To publicize their concerns, they formed an association of valley communities to protect the Río Grande, *La Asociación de Comunidades Unidas para Proteger el Río Grande*, and began distributing their monthly newsletter, *La Voz del Río* (The Voice of the River). With broad-based membership representing the communities of Velarde, Alcalde, El Llano, Española, La Mesilla, and Santa Cruz, the association conducted fact-finding research, collected reports and data, wrote petitions against the project, and attended countless meetings and hearings.[20]

One of the most important meetings was held on June 4, 1975, when officials from the Bureau of Reclamation and the State Engineer's Office met with association members and other residents from the valley communities. Also participating were acequia *mayordomos* respresenting the eight ditches that would be impacted directly by the project. The *mayordomos* at the meeting were especially concerned when the agency officials confirmed one of their most grave suspicions: with its proposed system of interconnecting canals, the project would divert Río Grande waters for delivery to the Santa Cruz River, resulting in lower and reduced water flows downstream from the proposed dam north of Velarde.[21]

Acequia irrigators below the proposed dam envisioned the possibility of drastic impacts on their ditches, especially during dry or otherwise low-flow summer months when volume and gravity flow are most needed to irrigate their extensive fruit orchards and fields. They were also wary of the ecological impact of reduced flows in the river itself, especially on fishlife habitats and the foilage along the banks.[22] On matters of administration, they were fearful that the conservancy district would usurp their traditional system of water distribution replaced by district control over the headgates of the diversion canal, a crucial point stated during the June 4 public meeting:

> Several of the mayordomos expressed grave concern for future equitable distribution of water if they lose their authority over water usage in the communitites granted to them by New Mexico statute. If this authority is, in fact, taken from the mayordomos, then one of the strongest mechanisms of local government in the Spanish American communities will be lost.[23]

The weight of these and other potential impacts caused anthropologist Sue-Ellen Jacobs, a participant-observer and author of a social impact study contracted to her by the Bureau of Reclamation, to conclude that "significant adverse impacts were likely to occur in a majority of the sociocultural categories required for the analysis by federal regulations if the dam was built"; and additional time should be allotted for more in-depth assessments and consideration of other alternatives in consultation with the irrigation communities.[24] This preliminary finding was issued in August 1975, but the Bureau of Reclamation nonetheless proceeded with its intentions of constructing the dam and the canal.

The association members intensified their campaign and complained directly to the governor, the state engineer, and the congressional delegation from New Mexico, culminating in a public hearing that convinced the Congress to stop the project from going ahead absent resolution of the local problems. At this juncture, the House-Senate Joint Conference Committee directed the Bureau of Reclamation to attempt a compromise or to propose other alternatives that would be satisfactory to all parties. If no solution was agreed upon, the Congress would have to reevaluate the political feasibility of the project.[25] A final meeting was held in mid-January 1976, even though both sides acknowledged beforehand the futility of such an event. Opposition to the project continued and, in fact, gained momentum a month later, when both the board of the controversial conservancy district and the Tribal Council of San Juan Pueblo publicly expressed their own dissatisfactions with the project and withdrew their support. On February 27, 1976, the Bureau of Reclamation commissioner announced that any further work on the project would be terminated due to the overwhelming desire of the area citizens "to retain their life style to the maximum extent possible."[26]

The victory of the protest campaign to block the El Llano Unit in 1976 inspired other acequia communities confronted with similar projects being planned for their watersheds. Upstream from Velarde a year later, a coalition of acequia associations, the Tres Ríos Association, cited the defects of El Llano Unit as evidence for their own opposition to the proposed Indian Camp Dam slated for construction by the Bureau of Reclamation on the Río Grande del Rancho near Talpa and the Ranchos de Taos area.[27] Initially proposed in 1971 as part of the San Juan-Chama Reclamation Project, the sixteen-million-dollar dam would supply water to a proposed irrigation district to be called the Rancho del Río Grande Conservancy District, ostensibly to benefit local farmers and, in the process, "save a dying [acequia] culture."[28]

The cost-sharing arrangements called for the federal government to pay

for 96.5 percent of construction costs; the irrigators and the other intended beneficiaries residing within the service boundaries of the district
would pay the remaining 3.5 percent.[29] According to the Bureau, the reservoir would increase and stabilize the water supply needed by the acequia
users in the area, enabling them to transform their subsistence, marginal
agriculture to more productive levels with higher-yield crops. The average
annual shortage of water at 28.2 percent per annum would be reduced substantially to a mere 2.9 percent.[30]

To be cost-effective, however, the dam would also create a reservoir lake
holding more than nine thousand acre-feet of water as a permanent pool
to attract fishing, tourism, and related recreational uses, features that drew
the unabashed support of business owners, real estate brokers, developers,
bankers, and other commercial interests from nearby Taos. Farther down-
range, even industrial and municipal uses were contemplated by the Bureau of Reclamation. Though the reservoir would be located on property
owned by the U.S. Forest Service and would be managed by that agency,
half of the maintenance costs of the facility would have to be borne by the
acequia farmers and the remaining beneficiaries of the proposed conservancy district.[31]

In order to pay off their share of taxes to the district, acequia farmers
were being encouraged to convert their cropping patterns from traditional forage crops of hay and pasture to vegetables, fruits, and other
truck-farming produce. To achieve the needed economies of scale, however, most of the irrigators would either have to consolidate their small
parcels into larger and more efficient units or open up new, previously unused lands. These conversions would require varying amounts of capital
for equipment, machinery, supplies, storage facilities, and more intensive
agricultural production. Most farmers would have to take out loans with
liens against their properties in order to participate in this high-risk
experiment.[32]

After a period of initial interest by some of the farmers, the Tres Ríos
Association, a coalition of acequias from the three affected streams, studied the implications of the project designed supposedly to benefit them as
the principal irrigators. The more they analyzed the likely costs and
benefits, the more they began to view the project as a threat to their customary land and water-mangagement practices and as a boon, instead, for
urban tourists and area real estate developers. They reasoned that acequia
irrigators, in the main, would not gain income or other benefits from the
projected recreational uses, and instead would be impacted adversely by
the higher land valuations and taxes that development would bring to the

area. Additionally, not only would acequia self-government be circumvented by a superimposed board from the conservancy district, but the economic risks could bankrupt the irrigators individually, as had happened after the construction of Elephant Butte Dam in southern New Mexico, the Middle Río Grande Conservancy District in central New Mexico, and other reclamation projects on the Río Grande. "To put it simply, the small farmers in the area felt the project was so large it would tax them severely, and they would lose control over their own acequias."[33]

Armed with reports of how conservancy districts had contributed to land losses of New Mexican *parciantes* in other parts of the state, the Tres Ríos Association fought the project for five years at an endless series of public meetings and court hearings. They were convinced that the proposed Indian Camp Dam would erode the agropastoral economies of the area and undermine the historic acequia institutions in their communities. The effects of the project would be permanent and irreversible, as they graphically depicted in a widely circulated position paper against the formation of the conservancy district:

> [C]onservancy districts in New Mexico have advanced the causes of agribusinessmen and urban growth and progress without considering the needs of small farmers and poor people. In fact, they have usually destroyed marginal farmers and subsistence ranchers by forcing them into high pressure cash economies where they cannot compete. Thus they go bankrupt, losing their land and water, and also their roots.[34]

The acequia irrigators were especially concerned with the extraordinary, sweeping powers that a conservancy district, with its five-member board, would have at the expense of the acequia associations. The acequia tradition, its purpose, its autonomy, and its very existence were at stake, with dire consequences at virtually all levels of acequia administration. As with the acequia irrigators who opposed the El Llano Unit, the Tres Ríos Association feared that the Indian Camp Dam Project and the proposed Rancho del Río Grande Conservancy District would centralize control over the distribution and management of ditch irrigation waters:

> If a conservancy is formed in Taos, the board will have the power to plan and regulate all water development and conservation activities throughout the district; foreclose on land and dispose of it for non-payment of conservancy taxes; alter water allocations and distribu-

tion in times of shortage without regard to legal water rights or priorities . . . ; change the course of . . . watercourse[s], including ponds, ditches, lakes and arroyos; divert the flow of water *out* of the district; [and] take over the ancient community ditches and change their locations.[35]

Curiously, the scores of meetings, court hearings, public demonstrations, and other events where the acequia irrigators presented the adverse findings of their own cost-benefit evaluations did not stop the project from moving forward. At a final public hearing in district court, the legal team for the proponents, aided by the expert water lawyer representing the State Engineer, actually convinced the presiding judge to approve the formation of the conservancy district and the appointment of the board to run its affairs. According to author John Nichols, who observed the event, the judge had amended the district boundaries illegally while taking steps to form the conservancy district: "And, in an appeal to the State Supreme Court based on that technicality, the Tres Ríos Association won a reversal of the district court decision: the conservancy was dissolved some five years after it first became a major issue."[36]

By the time of the reversal, the Tres Ríos Association had attracted the support of a much wider group of community-based institutions such as the local land grant, other acequia associations, and the rural domestic water-supply cooperatives in the vicinity. The triumph of this alliance and the many lessons the acequia irrigators learned in the process did not end with this particular case. As noted by anthropologist Sylvia Rodríguez, who herself chronicled the Valdez "Condo War" some years later, the struggle over the Indian Camp Dam proposal, coupled with a growing capacity for the mobilization of acequia-based opposition, "marked the beginning of a new kind of protest activity in Taos."[37]

Water Transfer Cases

The defeat of the two dam construction projects in north-central New Mexico coincided with the reduction of large-scale waterworks projects financed by the Bureau of Reclamation and other federal water agencies. A new water ethic was taking hold in the West, emphasizing conservation, regeneration, and sustainability of resource use. With the prospects of new water-development projects fading, perhaps for the very long term, the growing demand for water would have to be satisfied through a process of reallocation in the water marketplace. Proponents of growth, especially municipalities and industry, began to advocate the transfer of water rights from lower-value uses to sectors producing higher economic benefits. In states with prior appropriation water laws, this meant that some water uses might become "more beneficial" relative to others. The emerging water markets began to place acequia water rights held individually by the irrigators at risk for purchase and transfer to other uses outside the community.

During the 1980s, acequia associations rallied again in other streams and watersheds when proposed developments sought to disturb the delicate watershed ecosystem that acequia villagers depended on, as illustrated by the Valdez "Condo War" in Taos County. Anthropolgist, and participant-observer of the events, Sylvia Rodríguez recorded the community's alarm when a developer businessman from Taos, Pete Crandall (a pseudonym), proposed to transfer water from a parcel of farmland irrigated by La Acequia de San Antonio to an underground well needed to supply domestic water for a planned condominium project between the *placita* of Valdez and the world-class Taos Ski Valley nine miles upstream.[38] By January of 1982 the water transfer had already been approved by the State Engineer without knowledge of the residents of Valdez. The legal notice in the local newspaper had gone undetected. So the users of the San Antonio Ditch and the majority of their neighbors decided to protest the impending construction of the condos along several fronts.

Their initial objections were hydrological or physical in nature: the much deeper well needed for the multi-unit condominium would cause a "draw-down" of the single household wells already existing; sewage from the project would pollute either the groundwater in the community or the river, depending on the point of discharge; the higher-density development would increase traffic along the narrow, winding road, endangering both children and livestock accustomed to a much more relaxed pace of village life.[39] Rodríguez's account makes clear that Valdez's direct-action protest against the project took place within the context of growing local alarm over accelerated secondary development caused by resort expansion of the ski industry in the upper Río Hondo watershed. The proposed condominium project was merely the latest in a series of recent developments that involved water-rights transfers as well as sewage-discharge permits. Her analysis, based on ethnographic fieldwork in the region, spells out the cumulative impact that water-rights transfers will have on the survival of the time-tested acequia system of communal labor and maintenance:

each time a parcel loses its water rights, a proportional amount of labor and ditch fees is also lost to the system as a whole, thereby increasing the burden of maintenance upon the remaining parciantes. Each member is a link in the chain of community water use and control, and each time a member and his quota of water and labor are lost, the overall chain is weakened.[40]

With regard to the condo project, the residents of Valdez filed a petition with the State Engineer, belatedly protesting the water transfer. Additionally, they sought a moratorium from the county commission on further development within the Río Hondo watershed, and they petitioned the county clerk to form a special zoning district of their own that would curtail luxury residential and commercial development.[41] As it became clear that these administrative initiatives would probably not succeed in blocking the imminent construction of the units, the residents of Valdez, visibly including officers of the community acequia, the domestic water association, and the land grant, pressed on with more dramatic expressions of opposition. For a period of many months during the summer and fall of 1982, a stream of public-event protests, such as parades, marches, boycotts, and pickets against Mr. Crandall preoccupied virtually all segments of the greater Taos Valley. These public dramas were epitomized by ingenious anti-condo signs with powerful messages and ominous warnings:

"Nuestro Pueblo no se Vende" ["Our Village Is Not for Sale"]

"Condos Kill Raza [the Race]"

"Commandments Against Condos: Thou shall not build condos . . . pollute our water . . . disrespect our way of life . . . pollute our land . . . covet our land and water . . . steal what belongs to our children. Thou shall not kill our valley."

"Pete Crandall: the Blood of Valdez is on Your Hands . . . Give Up and Get Out."[42]

Faced with a barrage of negative publicity brought on by the very tight alliance of opponents, coupled with a rapid loss of support from his contractors, employees, and financial backers, Mr. Crandall finally quit. In early November of 1982 he published an article in the Taos newspaper announcing that he was leaving town. By the end of the following summer he had filed for bankrupcy; the local bank had initiated foreclosure proceedings for a mortgage on the land, resulting in the eventual sale of the property to another party.[43]

Another much-publicized case occurred in neighboring Río Arriba County, where District Court Judge Art Encinias denied an application that would have transfered water rights from the Ensenada Ditch near Tierra Amarilla to a proposed lake development project. In this case, the applicant, Tierra Grande Corporation, requested a diversion in 1982 of 61.32 acre-feet of water from the Nutrias Creek to create a recreational lake for use by a planned subdivision housing complex. After its creation, the lake project, if approved, would require annual diversions of 13.32 acre-feet, permanently retiring 14.02 acres of acequia farmland irrigated with waters diverted from Nutrias Creek. Once severed from the ditch waters, the land and the landowners selling the water rights would no longer form part of the acequia system and its procedures for upkeep and maintenance. The applicant, however, contended in state district court that the subdivision project and lake would support the public interest in terms of jobs created for a new tourism economy. Not convinced, the acequia members argued a contrary public-interest position. They claimed that the retirement of a portion of the agricultural lands and appurtenant water rights would burden the remaining association members with increased responsibilities for ditch maintenance, due to the loss of the participation by the two property owners contracted for the sale of water rights.[44]

Though reversed later by the New Mexico Court of Appeals, Judge Encinias's ruling in the Ensenada case continues to be cited by acequia officials and other advocates as a potent argument for the preservation of acequia-based culture:

> The second main line of agrument pits economic values against cultural values. Here, it is simply assumed by the Applicants that greater economic benefits are more desirable than the preservation of a cultural identity. This is clearly not so. Northern New Mexicans possess a fierce pride over their history, traditions and culture. . . . I am persuaded that to transfer water rights, devoted for more than a century to agricultural purposes, in order to construct a playground for those who can pay is a poor trade indeed.[45]

At the time of the ruling by District Judge Art Encinias, the state legislature had not yet implemented the conservation and public-welfare statute. This far-reaching statute was enacted in 1985 as an addition to the New Mexico water-transfer statute and could have strengthened the ruling by Judge Encinias, had it been in force. Under this new provision, henceforth the State Engineer would be instructed to endorse and approve permit applications only if the proposed transfers would not impair existing water users "and are not contrary to conservation of water within the state and not detrimental to the public welfare of the state."[46]

Though "the public welfare" was not defined in the 1985 statute, acequias and other political subdivisions of the state were provided standing to protest water-transfer applications and to present testimony and other evidence of negative public-welfare impacts should the transfers be permitted.[47] A decade after its enactment, no court proceeding or legal hearing had fully tested the ability of the statute to protect acequia water rights against the onslaught of permit applications to transfer agricultural water uses to other higher economic values. In preparation for these eventualities, acequia associations began to marshal arguments in order to bolster the statute and give it the meaning they hoped would stand up to closer scrutiny in cases likely to materialize under the development scenarios projected into the late 1990s and the turn of the century.

Under a high water-transfer scenario, the resource base protected under the traditional acequia practices will disappear or be reduced substantially. The open-space pastures will lie fallow and village life itself could possibly wither away. Increased development will drive up property values, further contributing to the demise of the acequia-based culture. More and more water will be transferred to fill the spas and swimming pools of the rich. By the early 1990s, condominiums, multifamily dwellings, gated luxury communities, and other commercial subdivisions had already replaced parts of rural Santa Fe and Taos counties and, on occasion, had threatened communities in Río Arriba, Guadalupe, and San Miguel counties. The conservation and public-welfare statute held out some promise – absent other tighter measures – of preventing the transfer of acequia community waters, a point made by the acequia communities located within the historic Anton Chico Land Grant.

The Anton Chico Land Grant

An opportune time for acequias to advance public-welfare arguments occurred in 1991, when an executive and training corporation, the Pecos River Learning Center (PRLC), applied to the Office of the State Engineer for the purchase and transfer of 45.35 acre-feet of surface water rights from one of the acequia landowners on the historic Anton Chico Land Grant.[48] Located in Santa Fe, PRLC owned and operated the Pecos River Ranch and

Conference Center, forty-five miles outside Santa Fe, where the training activities took place. Occupying some sixteen hundred acres nestled in the foothills of the Sangre de Cristo mountain range, the ranch compound included conference rooms and facilities, a restaurant, and hotel accomodations for fifty guests.

To supply the needs of its guests and clients, the ranch drew groundwater from two wells on-site that were hydrologically connected to the Río Pecos. Since the summer of 1987, however, these two wells had not kept up with the actual consumption requirements at the PRLC ranch, forcing the PRLC to lease water rights from two property owners in the neighboring farm village of San José. Three or so months before the expiration of those leases, PRLC decided to acquire permanent water rights downstream from the ranch through outright purchase and transfer from an acequia landowner in the community of Dilia, one of the villages located on the largest, still functioning land grant, the Nuestra Señora y Sangre de Cristo (Our Lady and Blood of Christ) grant at Anton Chico.

When word of this potential transfer reached the acequia communities on the land grant, the commissioners, *mayordomos,* and other *parciantes* rose in protest. From their perspective, this sale would be unprecedented. For over 160 years of continuous occupation, water and land uses within the grant had remained whole and intact. At stake were more than the 45.35 acres of farmland that would lie fallow permanently. The entire landgrant economy was threatened. If the transfer was approved and the sale went through, perhaps other water-rights owners in need, now or later, would sell out. At a public meeting held in April 1992, they presented a series of concerns they viewed as critical to the survival of the acequiabased culture of the land grant: the severing of water rights from ancestral farmlands goes against local customs and cultural values; the transfer would hamper the gravity-flow techniques of acequia irrigation, which require sufficient flow and head from the river; the transfer from one parcel would break the link in the chain, creating a domino effect of other sales and threatening the social fabric of the community.[49]

Though PRLC temporarily withdrew its application a short time after the community meeting, the corporation resurrected its efforts in 1993, this time for thirty acre-feet of water. The refiling of the application served only to prolong the controversy. Ditch officials and other users would not accept any arrangement that would sever water rights from properties within the land grant. From the time of settlement, the land base and the availability of water had been essential to the land-grant economy. The raising of livestock, for example, requires not only access to the common grazing lands in the summer, but during the winter months the livestock are fed bales of hay harvested on the irrigated parcels owned by the individual heirs along the frontage of the Río Pecos. The acequia members and the other residents were not opposed to the landowner excercising his right to sell, if only he sold the land along with the water rights.

Ultimately, their unrelenting campaign against the proposed transfer resulted in a compromise solution. In August 1994, the State Engineer denied the request for the transfer; instead, he approved the continuation of the former leasing agreement that had been in place. Appropriately for the protestants, the newspaper byline reporting the final outcome read: "State nixes water-rights sale: Move protects Anton Chico."[50]

In the upper Río Pecos case, the thirty to forty-five acres of land that would have gone fallow might not seem significant to the outside observer, but within the acequia system, custom and tradition require that all water users participate in the upkeep and maintenance of the entire system. These practices are reinforced by way of simple ditch rules that are based on cooperation, reciprocity, and when necessary, sanctions. The annual cleaning of the ditch, for example, requires all water users to help or to hire *peones* to take their places. To lose one of the acequia members results in a greater burden on the rest of the association, both in labor and in the more costly repairs that are needed from time to time.

The Adjudication of Customs and Traditions

The potential loss of water rights through market transfers was a major concern of acequia associations throughout the 1980s and well into the 1990s. Equally important, however, were the numerous adjudication suits also under way during this period. In the adjudication process, the State Engineer seeks to have the court determine the nature, ownership, and priority dates of all water rights in a stream or groundwater basin. The hydrographic reports that result from the process can affect the quantity of surface waters available for diversion at the acequia headgates in the immediate and long-term future. By 1997, at a time when most of the state's surface water had been appropriated, the State Engineer had initiated legal proceedings to adjudicate the streams most crucial to the greatest number of community acequias in north-central New Mexico: the Río Pojoaque, Río Santa Cruz, Río de Truchas, Río Chama, Jemez River, Río Hondo, Río Pueblo de Taos, Red River, and the Río Gallinas Basin.[51]

From the acequia perspective, the adjudications in theory afforded them with an opportunity to document their historic rights to the stream waters by virtue of their relatively early priority dates. Most acequia *parciantes* enjoy "vested rights," meaning that their historic uses of water predate the New Mexico Water Code of 1907 and are among the oldest non-Indian water rights in the state. To finance the research and technical studies that would be necessary, they sought the assistance of the state legislature, resulting in the Acequia and Community Ditch Fund Act of 1988.[52] The Acequia and Community Ditch Fund Act provides exactly what the acequias had anxiously awaited for many years: direct public monies to ditches located in rivers and streams undergoing adjudication. Small grants have been made available to pay for hydrological studies, historic and legal research, economic impact and technical reports, expert-witness fees, and other services that help acequia associations conserve and protect their water rights beyond the adjudication process and into the future.

Since its inception in 1988, the small grant program authorized by the Acequia and Community Ditch Fund Act has been highly popular with acequia associations in streams undergoing adjudication. By 1997, fifteen associations had received grants, totaling some 2,750,000 dollars in state funds. In addition to contracting with legal and technical experts, many of the applicants have utilized the grant funds to conduct historical and ethnographic studies that help document local acequia traditions, providing the acequia irrigators with a forum to assert the importance of historic and cultural values in the adjudication process.[53] Stream by stream, the adjudication hearings have required that *parciantes* and their expert witnesses recover scores of archival documents for presentation as evidence of their historic priority dates compared to most other water rights, excepting aboriginal Indian and federally reserved rights that are the most senior. Supplemented with family genealogies, oral community histories, maps, technical reports, and other data, these documentary records and other court exhibits have produced a wealth of interdisciplinary material for use in research into acequia studies.

Acequia officials have become increasingly expert in gathering and then incorporating a wide array of evidence to defend the antiquity of their customs and traditions and to protect their pre-1907 water rights. By requirement, all evidence presented at adjudication hearings is incorporated into the transcripts as direct testimony or as exhibits, or both, as exemplified in the report of the Special Master Frank Zinn issued in 1993.[54] The report by Special Master Zinn resulted from the adjudication proceedings within the Río Pueblo de Taos and the Río Hondo, when, in 1990 and 1991, most of the acequias in those streams claimed priority dates earlier than those recommended to the court by the state of New Mexico. Affected tributaries included the Río Chiquito, Río Fernando, Río Pueblo, Río Lucero, and the Río Grande del Rancho.

Some 4,300 claimants were named as landowner-defendants in this complex adjudication suit, along with the town of Taos, the Taos Indian Pueblo, and the United States government. Sensing an opportunity to incorporate local practices into the adjudication decree, a coalition of community acequia associations filed a motion with an affidavit before the federal district court on March 18, 1991, seeking legal recognition of "time immemorial" customs and traditions. They claimed that customary usage permitted the sharing of stream and ditch waters in times of need, irrespective of the more strict system of priority dates stipulated in state water law.[55] Application of the priority system quantifies and defines the basis of individual water rights. This procedure, they feared, could erode the communal basis that made settlement in their semiarid lands possible in the first place. In this traditional philosophy, the common welfare has always dominated local water administration.

Since enactment of the surface water code of 1907, adjudication proceedings in New Mexico had considered only technical hydrographic data to identify water-rights owners; to quantify water rights of all legal owners; and to assign priority dates across all owners in a stream, with the oldest right having the priority call. On the other hand, the commissioners who filed the motion argued that the custom of *repartimiento* was in effect prior to the Treaty of Guadalupe Hidalgo of 1848, when the Provincia del Nuevo México fell into U.S. jurisdiction. Furthermore, the first water code of the new territory, the Kearny Code, recognized and protected acequia traditions as did the territorial laws of 1851–52: watercourses in place at the time prior to U.S. jurisdiction "shall not be disturbed" and the "laws heretofore in force concerning water courses . . . shall continue in force."[56]

The affidavit itself was a historic first: the doctrine of prior appropriation and its use of the priority date system for allocating water would be voluntarily suspended by the community ditch commissioners who had filed the affivadit. Instead, the commissioners declared they would follow the *"repartimiento"* system of dividing water according to local customs and traditions, where water is shared by all, regardless of priority dates:

> the aforesaid acequias by and through their duly elected commissioners agree that they will continue to follow and be bound by their customary divisions and allocations of water and agree that they will not make calls or demands for water between and among themselves based upon priority dates.[57]

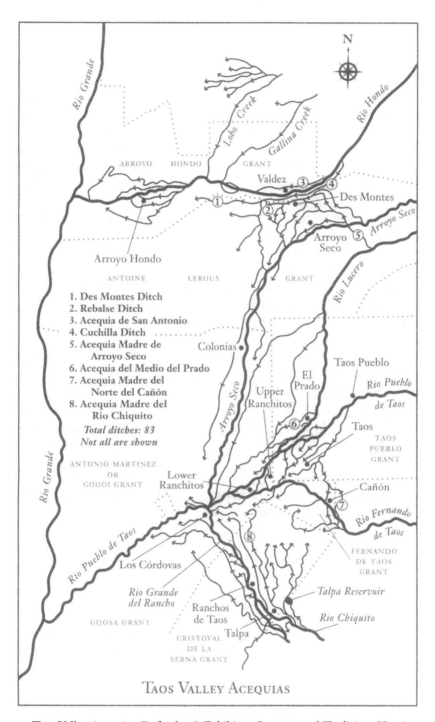

Taos Valley Acequias

1. Des Montes Ditch
2. Rebalse Ditch
3. Acequia de San Antonio
4. Cuchilla Ditch
5. Acequia Madre de Arroyo Seco
6. Acequia del Medio del Prado
7. Acequia Madre del Norte del Cañón
8. Acequia Madre del Rio Chiquito

Total ditches: 83
Not all are shown

Taos Valley Acequias, Defendant's Exhibit 2, Customs and Traditions Hearings.
Source: Report of the Special Master, Frank B. Zinn (July 23, 1993).
Based on map provided by the Taos Valley Acequia Association.

With supporting testimony from expert witnesses, the commissioners attempted to convince the court that the practices and traditions of the *repartimiento* system met all of the definitions of customary law that should now be recognized and incorporated into the adjudication decree. On their behalf, historian Daniel Tyler pointed out that isolation and the lack of access to attorneys had resulted in a usage and distribution of water specific to each locality that over time had acquired the force of law. To Tyler and the acequia commissioners present at the hearings, acequia water affairs had long since met the acceptable definitions of customary law: customs vary from place to place, are locally accepted and obeyed, and for officials to enforce them, the customs must be clear, contain reasonable and immemorial practices not contradictory to each other, and lastly, they must be continuous and remain undisputed.[58] In his written report, Tyler emphasized to the court that *alcaldes* and other government officials had been aware of how customs operated on local ditches; and in the case of disputes, water administration and enforcement depended more on the process of conciliation than on statutory rules from outside the community.[59]

The commissioners themselves presented testimony before the Special Master to verify the practice of dividing acequia waters according to the local customs of sharing and the need to provide *auxilio* (emergency mutual aid). Typical arrangements noted in the hearing transcripts included a variety of practices based strongly on values of mutualism and conservation:

> We share the water . . . based on need. If we feel that a field needs some water, we can help that person . . . those are customs that were developed and used by our ancestors.[60]

> The *auxilio* means to help somebody in need. If any of the ditch[es] come and ask for help, we already [are ready] — our ancestors built the ditch to give this auxiliary water to the people that [weren't] getting any.[61]

> When [the flow is] low, nobody has any. When it's high, everybody has some. That's the way it was too. If there's a cup of water there, we will share it.[62]

Apart from the desire to maintain the time-honored tradition of reciprocal assistance, the commissioners also doubted the ability of the acequia institution to administer and enforce water distribution under a strict system of priority calls. In cases where two or sometimes five ditches share a stream yet do not hold the same priority dates, implementation of the adjudication decree would not be administratively practical. As stated by Palemón Martínez of Taos County: "If you end up with different priority dates, I think we'd have a nightmare trying to run water through all kinds of ditches at different points."[63]

From the viewpoint of the commissioners and their witnesses, the postadjudication scenario potentially could violate the very foundation of acequia community welfare. The process of settlement along the rivers and streams in the region had allowed the more junior acequia systems to partake of irrigation water on the basis of *repartimiento*, where available waters, especially in times of drought, were divided among older and more junior ditch systems alike. Were it not for these essential arrangements worked out long ago, the communities with junior rights would not have prospered and survived, or perhaps they would not have been founded in the first place. The economic survival of acequia communities, according to the testimony and research conducted by Carlos Miera, was dependent on the common thread of shared irrigation. From the crucial point of first settlement, Miera explained, the custom of sharing water across all ditches provided the families with a social structure based on their commonalities rather than differences.[64] The commissioners feared that prior appropriation might force a system of hierarchy among acequias, especially in times of low flows or drought. If ditches holding senior rights exercised their rights to the entire flow, the centuries-old tradition of mutual aid would be broken, removing the foundation of community interdependence.[65]

At one point in the hearings before Special Master Zinn, one of the acequia commissioners plainly stated that the acequia communities from his area had not adhered to the rules of prior appropriation, despite the water laws in effect.[66] To the petitioners before the court, legal recognition of *repartimiento* and *auxilio* now would be in the best interests of their communities. If land or water rights were to be sold anytime in the near future, they feared new owners might not continue the custom on their own, imperiling communities with the junior rights. The adjudication decree forthcoming from the court, on the other hand, could ensure the long-term security of ditches sharing a watershed stream by incorporating the traditional customs of water sharing and mutual aid.

At the end of the hearings, the acequia commissioners were partially successful in convincing Special Master Zinn that the court should incorporate the declaration of local acequia customs in the final adjudication decree. Of broad significance was the finding by the Special Master that it was proper for adjudications to incorporate traditional customs of *reparti-miento*. Specifically, he recommended for inclusion those customs which complied with state statute 72-9-2 NMSA 1978 "as customs, rules or regulations *adopted and in force by local users* of a distribution system [emphasis added]."[67] He also recommended the inclusion of inter-acequia customs founded on previous court decrees. His findings, however, exclude claimed customs in some communities that did not meet these criteria. Customs that were not specifically quantifiable, that remained in dispute, or that were permissive, such as the sharing of surplus irrigation waters, were excluded. Fewer than half of the claims were accepted by the Special Master, but the coalition of acequias did manage to get the attorney for the office of the State Engineer to concede three important stipulations, read into the record:

> 1. Article 8 of the Treaty of Guadalupe Hidalgo protects water rights which were valid under the prior sovereigns of Spain and Mexico as of 1846; 2. Under Spanish and Mexican law, water allocations or *repartimiento de aguas*, were [based] on equity, common good, need, noninjury to [third] parties and earlier use, not on first use alone; and 3. In northern New Mexico water has traditionally been shared in times of shortage so that every acequia would have some water.[68]

After Special Master Zinn filed his report to the district judge, on July 23, 1993, the attorney for the acequias, Fred J. Waltz, appealed the portion of the Special Master's recommendations that had excluded a large number of claimed customs in some of the acequia communities, permissive uses such as the sharing of surplus water and various forms of *auxilio* during periods of extreme drought or other emergencies. Through a process of negotiation, the state of New Mexico ultimately entered into a stipulated agreement with the acequias to recognize these and all the remaining claimed customs for incorporation in the final adjudication decree. (In effect, the only remaining exclusions would be cases where the ditch associations themselves disputed any of the claimed customs or that involved Pueblo Indian water rights.) The district judge, Santiago Campos, agreed with a joint motion to adopt the stipulation and so ordered in December 1993.[69] Though the route was torturous, the acequia commissioners who initiated the customs hearings through the motion and affidavit they had filed back in March 18, 1991, finally succeeded. To date, the judge's order still stands, requiring the court to recognize the acequia customs as binding and lawful.[70]

The strategy employed by the coalition of acequia associations in this adjudication suit demonstrates the lengths to which acequia officials will go to retain and maintain water rights in the community. Whereas the system of priority dates isolates each water right and therefore facilitates the transfer for development or other uses, the relinquishing of specific priority dates in favor of a shared water supply will probably discourage the sale of water rights outside the community when these practices are incorporated within the applicable adjudication decrees. The call for local control over the resource base in the bioregion of the upper Río Grande, as is the case in many other parts of the world, is emerging as an avenue for the achievement of sustainable communities.[71]

Sustainable Communities

Water markets and the demographic forces behind them, such as popula-. tion growth, in-migration, and land development pressures, have placed acequia communities at great risk during the last quarter of the twentieth century. No one disputes the potential of the emerging water markets, if left unchecked, to sever water from the traditional agricultural uses in the region and, in doing so, place rural villages in conditions of significant economic stress. With increasing development pressures and the emergence of new water markets, transfers of water use from agricultural to municipal and industrial uses in New Mexico threaten to dry up the farmlands of the state, as has happened elsewhere in the West, most notably in Arizona and Colorado.

Many experts who have conducted field work in the acequia communities of the upper Río Grande conclude that the agricultural practices and irrigation methods of the *parciantes* have provided cultural and practical as well as ecological solutions of adaptation to the natural environment.[72] To acequia villagers, water is essential to continued economic subsistence. To sever water rights from the land is tantamount to extinguishing all life forms in the ecosystem. Historically, the rural villages of New Mexico and southern Colorado have provided a community safety net for individuals and families in times of need. The extended family structure and the subsistence-based agriculture many times have buffered economic downturns in the outside economy.

By any measure, it is clear that the resource base of land and water have knitted the community together, enabling it to provide mutual support and a system of reciprocal assistance. For many generations, especially during and since the Great Depression of the 1930s, the family *ranchos* have served as economic havens for young people who migrated to the urban employment centers, but returned when jobs ran out, or when the regional mines closed down.[73] The security of *"el país,"* as they call it, beckons them to return from one economic cycle to another. In more modern times, often *el rancho*, mortgage free, is the only place where youth can expect to build affordable housing and somehow earn a livelihood by staying in or returning to the area.

The acequia associations consitute the oldest water-management institution in the region and probably in the entire United States. They have operated with a few basic rules and procedures based on customs and traditions embedded in the local culture. They long ago proved their sustainability as resource-conservation and water-management entities. Arid conditions make for a very fragile ecology. Life and settlement have been maintained through a delicate balance of controls, water conservation rotations, and stewardship of communal resources by a water-management institution that is democratic and a model of resource sustainability with global implications.

In the future, acequia officials and advocates likely will continue to assert the community value of water in other forums and with other refined strategies. As market pressures to transfer water to other uses continue to increase, we can expect a concomitant rise in efforts and actions by the traditional water users to assert their historic claims, customs, and rights. The value systems are fundamentally at odds and cannot be expected to go away — conflict will no doubt continue. It is important for the discourse to be open and informed as to all sides of the issue. Perhaps then the diverse set of values can be accommodated and costly litigation avoided. As a starting point, water-based planning needs to incorporate the social infrastructure and cultural ecology of the region alongside the technical and economic components of planning. Sustainable cultural communities and people's institutions foster rather than hinder other forms of economic development. The final chapter of this book presents a case for the preservation of the acequia-based culture of the upper Río Grande into the twenty-first century and beyond. To realize this future, a combination of state policies and action strategies by the acequia associations themselves will probably be necessary and are recommended.

DOCUMENTS

Judge Encinias Decision, Ensenada
Ditch Case, 1985

Though reversed on appeal, the ruling by New Mexico District Court Judge Art Encinias in 1985 continues to be cited as a landmark in the attempts by acequia *parciantes* to seek judicial protection of their history, traditions, and culture. At the time of his decision, Judge Encinias did not have the public welfare statute to strengthen his basis for rejecting the Tierra Grande Corporation water-transfer application. His denial nevertheless raised many points central to public-welfare arguments, for use at a later time by acequia communities and their advocates.

April 16, 1985

Re: In the Matter of Howard Sleeper, et al.
 Rio Arriba County Cause No. RA 84-53 (C)

Dear Counsel:
. . . On the public interest question, the evidence follows two main lines. First, economic development in the Ensenada area would bring jobs to the local inhabitants because construction would be generated by creation of a central resort project, like a ski area. In the Ensenada area, that construction would take the form of the building of second homes. Over the longer run, more jobs in the associated tourist economy would become available. In this fashion, the previously poverty-stricken populace would be able to shift from a subsistence economy based on agriculture to an economy based on tourism.

This first agrument is not so one-sided. The evidence plainly suggests that such development creates few jobs for local inhabitants, except as [at] menial levels. Over the long run, the local inhabitants lose management level jobs to outsiders and are relegated to service jobs, such as waiters and maids. Other locals survive on the fringes of the tourist industry by becoming professional "natives." Most other locals never realize any particular benefit from the resort economy.

The second main line of argument pits economic values against cultural values. Here, it is simply assumed by the Applicants that greater economic benefits are more desirable than the preservation of a cultural identity. This is clearly not so. Northern New Mexicans possess a fierce pride over their history, traditions and culture. This region of northern New Mexico and its living culture are recognized at the state and federal levels as possessing significant cultural value, not measurable in dollars and cents. The deep-felt and tradition-bound ties of northern New Mexico families to the land and water are central to the maintenance of that culture.

While these questions seem, at first, far removed from the simple question of the transfer of a few acre feet of water, the evidence discloses a distinct pattern of destruction of the local culture by development which begins with small, seemingly insignificant steps. I am persuaded that to transfer water rights, devoted for more than a century to agricultural purposes, in order to construct a playground for those who can pay is a poor trade, indeed. I find that the proposed transfer of water rights is clearly contrary to the public interest and, on that separate basis, the Application should be denied. . . .

> *Art Encinias*
> *District Judge*
> *Division V/First Judicial District*

Acequias Declaration of Concerns, 1985

On September 9–11, 1985, some fifty participants troubled by the water-rights issues confronting acequia and Pueblo Indian communities gathered for a symposium at the Ghost Ranch Conference Center near Abiquiu, New Mexico. The majority of the delegates were representatives of local acequia associations and tribal governments from throughout the upper Río Grande region, one of the few occasions where these two groups were able to articulate their common concerns as traditional water users. A few months after this unique confab, the steering committee that had planned and coordinated the event published a report based on the written proceedings and recorded minutes. Following is an excerpt of the report dealing with one of the five broad issues identified by the participants, the question of development versus preservation. For the complete text, see Research Report No. 003, "The Course of Upper Río Grande Waters: A Declaration of Concerns," Conference Proceedings of the Upper Río Grande Working Group, Southwest Hispanic Research Institute, University of New Mexico, December 1985.

The Challenge of Development

The Upper Río Grande region is a unique and fragile environment. Within the region, there is substantial opposition to economic development which threatens or damages indigenous and traditional communities. However, the communities recognize a need for continued economic development. The task is to encourage the economic activities that will enhance rather than disrupt regional economies. The value of rural areas needs to be preserved and carefully maintained.

Development affects traditional water users in two ways. First, the opportunities for water-dependent local development are quite limited. There is a need for development options which are consistent with traditional values and at the same time which allow for the retention of precious water rights. Second, there is a need to limit and control the adverse impacts which result from non-traditional economic development within the region. Of course, we do not oppose the growth and diversification of the regional economy, but we feel strongly that unplanned growth poses significant threats to traditional water users' water rights and supplies which in turn threatens the region's traditional communities. . . .

Specific . . . concerns include: (a) the lack of incentives for innovative uses of water, (b) the need for more targeted technical assistance, especially in the area of agricultual marketing, and (c) the increasing pressure on traditional communities to sell their water rights in the open marketplace. [We, therefore advance] a corresponding set of solutions and action agendas:

1. A comprehensive rural policy at the state level should be developed and implemented in order to balance the needs of rural and urban areas;

2. The productivity of irrigated agriculture within the traditional communities should be improved taking into account key factors such as crop selection, scale and size of farms, marketing, and government policies;

3. In particular, the marketing of the region's agricultural goods should be improved through the use of cooperatives and with the support of a state agricultural marketing company;

4. Technical assistance services should be developed which will enhance self-reliance at a scale appropriate to community and tribal agricultural enterprizes;

5. Other self-reliance enterprizes such as cottage industries and local tourism businesses should be studied for their development potential.

Stanley Crawford's Chronicle, *Mayordomo*, 1988

Stanley Crawford's published chronicle is a documentary record of a one-year period during the late 1980s when he served as an acequia *mayordomo*. The names of the ditches, places, and personages are fictional, but the events and conditions depicted in the book purportedly took place in real life. In this excerpt, the chronicle illustrates that the principles of equity and the values in support of water conservation have continued into contemporary history as major strands of acequia philosophy and practice. Reminiscent of the instructions issued in the 1789 Plan de Pitic, the commissioners of the Acequia de la Jara devise a list and schedule of water use, during times of shortage, where each irrigator is assigned a block of time proportionate to the quantity of property shares the irrigator owns. See Stanley Crawford, *Mayordomo* (University of New Mexico Press, 1988).

> During the month of August the Río de la Jara has been known to dry up completely. . . .
>
> In a dry season, however, as soon as there is no longer enough water to go around, the commission will put all of the *parciantes* on a ditch "on hours," . . .
>
> Each *parciante's* hours will be determined not only by where his property lies on the ditch but also by how many shares or *piones* his property counts as a portion of the whole ditch. The Acequia de la Jara numbers about thirty *parciantes* whose shares range from one-half to two *piones* each, with a total of about thirty *piones* for the whole ditch. . . .
>
> In order to go on hours, the commission has to draw up a schedule matching the list of *parciantes'* shares to the time period in question, usually a week. A longer period risks running afoul of changing weather. Once a schedule is drawn up, the commission or the *mayordomo* writes out *papelitos* [slips of paper] for each *parciante*, giving the day and the inclusive hours during which the *parciante* may irrigate; the *mayordomo* then distributes the *papelitos* up and down the ditch. . . . [I]n really difficult times it is considered prudent for each *parciante* to have in hand a *papelito* — in order to resolve disputes, correct errors, or to assure that the commission is assigning hours in an equitable manner. Since customs vary widely from area to area, what I am reporting here holds only more or less for the nine ditches of the valley and more certainly for the two ditches I irrigate from, the Jara and the Juntas. [pp. 141–44]

Adjudication Hearing on Customs and Traditions, 1991

During the early and middle 1990s, many important streams were being adjudicated throughout north-central New Mexico. In the adjudication process affecting the Río Pueblo de Taos, its five tributaries, and the Río Hondo, a coalition of acequia associations petitioned the federal district court in the spring of 1991 to incorporate customary usages of water sharing in the Final Decree rather than limiting the adjudication findings to a system of priority dates, "first in time, first in right." The joint affidavit and other excerpts of direct testimony below illustrate the major points advanced by the commissioners.

State of New Mexico vs. Eduardo Abeyta and Celso Arellano, et al., United States District Court for the District of New Mexico, Transcript, May 20, 21, and June 11, 1991.

Affidavit of Commissioners

[The Commissioners] . . . depose and state: . . . That through custom and tradition, from time immemorial, the aforesaid community acequias have shared the water in order to maximize the benefit to individual members to the greatest extent possible. The spirit of sharing available water is part of the "repartimiento" system and local custom. . . . That the aforesaid acequias by and through their duly elected commissioners agree that they will continue to follow and be bound by their customary divisions and allocations of water and agree that they will not make calls or demands for water between and among themselves based upon priority dates. [Signed by sixteen Commissioners]

Testimony of Juan I. Valerio, Former Commissioner and Mayordomo, Acequia del Río Chiquito, Ranchos de Taos, New Mexico

We still keep our own custom and tradition. This is where our custom and tradition comes into play in our system is that if it's real dry that we don't have too much water, instead of having a little bit each ditch, we then put the water in one ditch certain days, and where there's more land — well, like we say two days in the del Monte, four days in the Río Chiquito so they could have the full amount of water that's coming in the river. QUESTION: So then when it's really short, they take turns; is that what you're saying? ANSWER: Yes. Well again that goes on our ancestors showing us to share whatever we have. If we have a lot, we use a lot. If we have little, we share with what we have. . . . my great grandfather passed it on to my father, and my father passed it on to me and so forth. It did come down the generations, I guess, because what I was taught by my father was to share what we had equally with our neighbors, and that's the way we run the ditch system. . . . The *auxilio* means to help somebody in need. If any of the ditch come and ask for help, we already [are ready] — our ancestors built the ditch to give this auxiliary water to the people that wasn't getting any. [Transcript, May 20, 1991, pp. 118–19]

Testimony of Elías Espinosa, Commissioner, San Antonio Ditch, Valdez, New Mexico

Well, when there's a shortage, that's when we exercise the one-third practice, and usually Arroyo Hondo complains that they're not getting their third, so we'll get together and divide it. And eventually it seems like it satisfies the need, and we get our third. . . . Well, we come to the concept of the one-third tradition, so we try to make adjustments so that each community gets the one third, as close as possible. QUESTION: And are you familiar with the strict prior appropriation system that supposedly governs the way waters are divided in New Mexico between water-rights owners, having to do with the rights of one person whose water rights have a better priority date than another? Have you heard of the prior appropriation system? ANSWER: I've heard about it, but it hasn't been a practice in our ditch. We've always maintained the tradition, the one third. There's never been a problem in our — any ditches. We haven't been called — you know, priority. [Transcript, June 11, 1991, pp. 25–26]

Agreement to Divide
Irrigation Waters, 1895

Acequia Madre del Cerro and the Latir Ditch

The custom of *repartimiento* sometimes led to relatively complex arrangements to share or somehow rotate the use of waters among participating acequias. Some localities divide the water according to fractions where each ditch is entitled to its prorated amount of water, such as one-third in the case of three acequias sharing the water in equal parts. Other arrangements divide the water based on a scheduled time rotation, as in the example below. The document is a decree issued on October 23, 1895, by H. B. Hamilton, Judge of the Fifth Judicial District, where he orders a weekly schedule of water allocation to be followed in Precincts 11 and 24 of Taos County. The community ditches in these two precincts were to share irrigation waters taken from four streams in their area: Latir, Jaroso, Rito del Medio, and Rito Primero. The fact that judicial intervention was necessary demonstrates that the more complex arrangements of *repartimiento* were not without the potential for conflicts or misunderstandings from time to time. In fact, the ditches from these two precincts, the Acequia Madre del Cerro and the Latir Ditch, returned to court in 1946. The 1895 document was attached as an exhibit to the Final Judgment decreed in the 1946 case.

Plaintiff's Exhibit A

At Santa Fe, New Mexico, October 23rd, 1895

Present as of October 7th, 1895
John H. Young, et als., vs. Juan N. Gomez, et. als.

Decree

. . . It is further ordered, adjudged and decreed by the Court that during the time devoted to the cultivation and irrigation of the crops in said Precincts numbered 11 and 24, in said [Taos] County, or when there is a scarcity of water, in the streams hereinafter named, that the people herein above named as residents of said Precinct No. 24, shall take the water flowing in the four streams, known as the Latir, Jaroso, Rito del Medio and Rito Primero, for their exclusive use and benefit, for the purpose of irrigating their crops such as grain, vegetables, and cultivated lands of all kinds, diverting said waters of said four streams into their ditches, during such times for said purposes, as follows: to-wit: Beginning Friday of each week at sunset in the evening and continue it on the same exclusively, up and until the following Sunday at twelve o'clock noon; and at that time, the parties in charge of said ditch shall divert the waters of said four streams into the ditch or ditches, belonging to the people of said Precinct No. 11, and the people of said Precinct No. 11, who are entitled to said waters shall have and enjoy the exclusive use and benefit of said waters from the hour of twelve o'clock, noon, on Sunday of each week, until the next following Friday at sunset in the evening. That is, the people of Precinct No. 24 shall have and enjoy the exclusive use and benefit of said waters from said four

streams for the period of forty-two hours of each [and] every week, during the irrigation season of each and every year hereafter for the purposes
above specified; and the people of Precinct No. 11, shall have and enjoy the
exclusive use and benefit of said waters from said four streams for the remaining period of one hundred and twenty-six hours of each and every
week, during the irigation season of each and every year for the purposes
above specified, and according to the times above set out herein, and by
the agreement of all parties in interest hereto. . . .

> *H. B. Hamilton, Associate Justice, etc., and*
> *Judge of the Fifth Judicial District thereof,*
> *acting for and in place of Hon. N. B. Laughlin,*
> *disqualified by reason of having been of counsel in the case.*

ORAL HISTORY TESTIMONIES

During the *Acequias y Sangrías* Project, researchers from the University of
New Mexico conducted a number of oral history interviews with key, life-
long acequia *parciantes*. Below are a sample of the histories illustrating the
specific themes of ditch construction and some details concerning the annual cleaning ritual. The interviews were conducted by Tomás Atencio
and David Luján.

Ben Talache, Ranchitos near San Juan Pueblo, 1985

Construction of an early ditch at Ranchitos

Bueno, no la hicieron toda de una ves porque en ese tiempo a según dicen
ellos, los viejos, que tenían que usar palas de palo, con palas de palo saltaron
[sacaron] esta acequia. Pero tenían/usaban unos palos como postes con
punta y con eso iban aflojando la tierra y lo con estas palas de palo tiraban
para afuera la tierra y hacina iban haciendo [la acequia]. . . .Y se tardaron
años, pero que cada año hacían un tanto, ves? Y luego de hay cuando tenían
tiempo comenzaban otra vez alargarla para agarar más terreno. . . . (El palo
de madera) lo usaban como bara, no tenían fierro en, poquito fierro nomás
que tuvieron los españoles, pero no eran baras eran otra cosa. No trujeron
palas de fierro ni nada. Eso platicó un indio.

[They didn't build it all at once. At that time, according to them, the 'old
ones,' they had to use wooden shovels. With wooden shovels they dug this
ditch. But they had some poles, like posts with a sharp point. And with

those they would go ahead loosening the soil. Then with the wooden shovels, they would remove the soil along the ditch bank. And thus they built their trench for the ditch. And they took years because each year they would dig so much. And from there, when they had time, they would begin again to lengthen it, to acquire more land to irrigate. . . . The pointed stick was used in the same manner one uses a drill to break the soil, because they had no iron tools. The little iron brought by the Spaniards was used for other things. They didn't even bring metal shovels or any such tools. This is what I heard from an [San Juan] Indian.]

Eloy Durán, Ensenada, 1985

Route and Gravity Flow

Venían y echaban agua, una poquita, y se venían adelante poniendo el palito en donde se detenía la agua — en lugar de correr para acá adelante, corría para atrás.

[They would run the water on the ground, and then they would place a stick where the water would settle — the point where the water would recede instead of continuing forward.]

Antonio Durán, Llano Largo, near Peñasco, 1985

Construction of Flume/Las Trampas

The people came and they cut pine trees which were the trees they used the most . . . and they had to be hollow. And they were cleaned real good inside, very good until they were very clean. From these they would make a flume, see. And here they would cut joints . . . to connect one with the other, see. And in this way they would made a flume and it would remain. You have seen the one here at Las Trampas, right? . . . In the beginning, when it was first put in place, the water would leak, see, because it would not form a good seal until the wood would become thoroughly soaked.

Wooden tools

[For] the earliest tools . . . they had to cut *encino*, thick oak, to make the shovels and picks. . . . They had to treat the oak a certain way to harden it for the shovels, picks and other tools, and with those they dug. And when they came upon rocks, there were times it became very difficult, and they did not have the means to buy dynamite and other things. They would build some supports, or gangplanks they called them. They would dig below the rock, and then the men, with these gangplanks would move the rocks.

Folklore Story, Woman Who Built the Ditch

From there, this place which they called Hodges. From there they started this ditch which goes to Llano de la Yegua, see. And when they started this ditch, see, well the hillside where they have the ditch was very rocky and there were many narrow canyons and arroyos. And thus it was very difficult to dig the ditch, see, and they did not have the proper tools, the proper things like dynamite to break the rock. . . . And thus they say that there was a woman who lived there in the same place. She began by telling the people, 'Good, we are going to begin here, and we are going to dig here, and we are going to take the water from there, and as we progress every day, the same water will be trickling right behind us. It will tell us how much we have to dig and how much rock we will have to remove.' And the same was repeated when they would reach an arroyo or a narrow canyon.

Phil Lovato, 1985, former Mayor of Taos

Folklore Story, Woman Who Built the Ditch

I have heard, the Rincón, it's an *ojito* [a spring]. An *ojito*, you know, this little village, it's part of Chamisal, but it's to the east about a mile or so, but it's part of the whole Chamisal Valley. What I have heard is: this woman used to either live by herself or her family, and what she did, she needed to get some water to irrigate her garden, to feed, or to water her cows, her sheep, or whatever she was holding there. And what she did was she began developing an acequia, Acequia Madre de Ojito, by running a little trickle of water down the slope. . . . And by gosh, the story is folklore, I mean, but I imagine there's a lot of truth to it. . . . I used to hear it [from my grandfolks] when I was a little kid. I've heard it since then. How true and how well pinpointed, I don't know. . . . There has to be a lot of truth in there. Somebody did it and took the leadership, maybe to get the rest of the people to complete it.

Cleofas Vigil, Mayordomo, San Cristobal, 1985

Tareas or Cleaning Assignments

The old people from before would clean out [the ditch] by *tareas*. They would order one member to mark off each person's assignment with a stick. A *tarea* or cleaning assignment would consist of six feet, or between six and eight feet, no more than eight feet. . . . The custom in those days was that if you owned land, you had a cleaning assignment or *tarea*, your own *tarea*.

Andrés Martínez, Cañón de Fernández, 1985

Ditch Cleaning, Rayador *and* Tareas

Each year, the month before the new year begins, we hold meetings to designate when the ditches will be cleaned. The commission and the acequia members meet and designate a day, two or three, which will be needed depending on the condition of the ditch. The days are determined, and the directive is passed on to the *mayordomo* that when the established day arrives, he will have the responsibility of directing the work and making sure that each acequia member performs his work task. The work site is determined, for example, and a member is appointed [as the *rayador*] before cleaning and repairs on the ditch are commenced. The *rayador* is usually an elderly member who cannot work too hard anymore. He is sent ahead to mark off each *peón*'s *tarea* or work assignment. Every three steps or three yards, that is a *tarea*. Each worker gets a *tarea*, and the work continues thus as he marks off each *tarea*. The cleaning and repairs of the acequia are carried out in that fashion.

RECORD OF HEARING ON NEW MEXICO ACEQUIAS BY U.S. SENATOR PETE V. DOMENICI, SANTA FE, N.M., JAN. 7, 1980

Off and on, major public officials conduct public hearings on issues important to acequia communities, often at the instigation of the *parciantes* or their officers. Excerpted below are remarks addressed to Senator Domenici in 1980 by three individuals associated with the concerns of the acequias: Andrés Martínez from Cañón de Fernández in Taos County, Wilfred Gutiérrez from Velarde, and former Taos mayor and author of *Las Acequias del Norte*, Phil Lovato. Together, the testimonials illustrate the many frustrations and deep-rooted conflicts that *parciantes* share with and appeal to the higher authorities who may help to resolve their concerns. With increased pressures on rural and agricultural use of water rights, petitions to elected officials and another actions in the public policy arena will likely intensify toward the close of the century and beyond.

Testimony of Andrés Martínez, Tres Ríos Association

On Indian Camp Dam

During the past decade, in matters pertaining to the acequias and water rights, the Taos Valley has experienced similar problems to the rest of Northern New Mexico. These problems were symbolized by the struggle for and against the implementation of the Indian Camp Dam east of Talpa, a part of the San Juan-Chama Diversion Project. During the almost decade-long struggle, many farmers and members of the Tres Ríos Association found themselves pitted against the Bureau of Reclamation, the State Engineer's Office, and much of the Taos business community. At great cost of time and money to themselves, the people finally managed to defeat a conservancy district and the dam, which they felt would contribute to the end of land-based culture in the area, rather than help it survive.

To put it simply, the small farmers in the area felt the project was so large it would tax them severely, and they would lose local control over their own acequias. Farmers believed that if the Government organizations were willing to help finance *smaller* irrigation projects which would not require a conservancy taxation district for their implementation, they would be all for it. Yet, state and federal agencies replied that San Juan-Chama water was an 'all-or-nothing' proposition for *Taoseños*. So we had to reject it. . . . [This] points out a real problem in the north. The priorities of local irrigators, and the priorities of Government organizations set up to theoreticaly help them, often clash bitterly. This leads to suspicions that both groups hold for each other, and makes it difficult for good work to be done.

On Loss of Water Rights

On a more general plane, there is a feeling of desperation among some Taos farmers and irrigators that they are being done out of their just water rights at an ever accelerating pace. Some people lose their water rights through the adjudication process, and because there seem to be no state agencies genuinely concerned with aiding them in protecting those rights. . . . [O]ver the past twenty years, Cañón farmers in Taos have gone to court several times to protect the headwaters of the Río Fernando in the Valle Escondido from developers in the high valley during the peak irrigation season. [I]t is becoming increasingly apparent that state laws may favor the water withdrawal rights of part-time recreation visitors up in the valley instead of the rights of long-time year-round New Mexico residents in Cañón down below.

Development Conflicts

During the past few years, there have been several struggles on the Hondo River. A couple of years back, residents of the Arroyo Hondo, Des Montes, and Valdez communities stopped a Taos Ski Valley expansion at the Hondo headwaters above them, on the grounds that their acequia waters would be seriously compromised by that expansion. And today the same people are fighting to halt a Taos Ski Valley expansion of its sewage system, on the grounds that the expansion would destroy what little water quality remains down below, and also open the way for increased population expansion above which one day threatens to either seriously cut off, or badly pollute, downstream water supplies.

Testimony of Wilfred Gutiérrez, Chairman, Las Nueve Acequias Steering Committee, Velarde

Democratic Institutions

Our acequias have been a form of democracy, where people with water use have elected their commission and *mayordomo* (ditch runner) through the free election process. This was done some three hundred years ago as it is done today. Consequently, the acequias during all these years have been the nucleus of the community. It is the common denominator of a way of life in the valley. . . . I feel with the majority of the people that, in order to preserve this unique way of life in the United States of America, we need first to preserve the acequias system in New Mexico.

Testimony of Phil Lovato, Mayor, Town of Taos

Value of Acequias

The region's residents have long depended on the water from the acequias for growing food, for income and social satisfactions. They are an integral part of the culture and heritage of the area. Their method of operation and use is very much the same today as when they were first established. The associations are relatively simple and this perhaps is their strongest point. They have served as a most useful tool in the development of irrigation in New Mexico. They have demonstrated a capability in resolving physical and human problems in a sympathetic and thoughtful way.

SIX

The Future of the Acequia Institution:

State Policies and Acequia
Action Strategies

Tensions in the Taos Valley did not end with the conclusion of the "Condo War" at Valdez in 1982. During the 1990s, acequia *parciantes* from the Valdez ditches continued to protest impacts caused by the development associated with the world-class ski resort near Taos. "The Taos Ski Lodge, with its thousands of day skiers at the peak of the season, acts as a magnet for explosive growth in the Valdez area, resulting in land values of up to $35,000–$40,000 per acre lots," reported David Arguello in the summer of 1996.[1] Addressing a team of researchers studying acequia-based family farms in southern Colorado and northern New Mexico, Arguello noted that environmental damage to the acequia infrastructure and intrusions on water quality in the ditch had been on the rise as a result of development in the area. Road runoff to the ditches had increased, he stated, contaminating the irrigation waters, which were then diverted into the fields and gardens downstream at Valdez. Sedimentation on ditches had increased as had the pollution of ditch waters. Heavy trucks, hauling cement, adobes, and other construction materials to land subdivision sites, crossed over ditch culverts that were not designed to support them, sometimes crushing the culverts and requiring their replacement.[2]

The sources of these impacts are subdivisions being built on what was once historic land-grant property. The road in question passes through the village proper. Historically, the road had served as a common road for use by the heirs of the upper Río Hondo Land Grant and other local villagers. In recent years, however, developers had bladed and widened the road to provide access to sixty or more condominium units built on the mountain slope overlooking Valdez. The owners of these dwellings claim they would be landlocked without their ability to use the land-grant road. During rainstorm events, the runoff carries sedimentation and other debris into the village acequia, causing it to malfunction. Also, during periods of additional construction, the builders and their subcontractors use the road to get to the project sites, thus increasing village traffic flow substantially. According to local residents, heavy trucks continue to haul construction materials to land subdivision sites for home building at a scale not suited to the village's infrastructure.[3]

Many questions and issues come to the attention of the acequia users at Valdez:

> Are the old land grant easements now public roads? Can the traditional community roads be fenced or gated to keep trespassers out? Hostilities are on the rise, as are tensions; newcomers and developers vs. natives; neighbors pitted against neighbors. What can be done?[4]

For the developers, millions of dollars are at stake in many of these housing subdivisions. Any and all obstacles, including the antiquated infrastructure of roads and ditch culverts, must be removed or improved to handle the growth. For the native locals, on the other hand, acequia water rights are at great risk since they can be sold at a high value and transferred to the new housing units. Each unit that goes up requires a domestic well on-site. Once these projects are approved, the forces of the market take over, leaving the traditional uses of water very vulnerable.[5]

The acequia irrigators can protest each time the county government reviews subdivision applications. But there is uneven preparation and unequal sophistication in terms of how to deal with these and other related planning issues. According to Arguello, the old-time *parciantes* of the Acequia de San Antonio need training and education around the many procedural, technical, and legal points concerned with land-use regulations, subdivision rules, and zoning enforcement:

> We need unity around commonalities in order to resist. We need technical help with land development issues, planning, and water laws. Some members are afraid to serve as commissioners anymore because they know they have to get bonded. They are afraid of potential lawsuits and costly litigation. There is also the threat of physical violence. Fences have been cut; [construction] trucks have broken them down. The locals retaliated by placing railroad ties to narrow

the road down to the original easement width. We need to inform members more and better, with greater depth; the legal issues and the financial stakes are high. There is a clash of cultures right before our very eyes, sometimes at very dizzying speeds.[6]

For the time being, the acequia irrigators from Valdez have begun to explore different avenues of response to curtail or mitigate the impact from development already approved by the Taos County government. Mindful of their historic powers to promulgate ditch rules that carry the force of law, in 1995 the members of the San Antonio Ditch amended their rules to require that culverts, bridges, and utility lines constructed within and across the ditch right-of-way meet minimum design standards. Written project plans for any repair or construction would have to be formally submitted to the ditch commissioners and the *mayordomo* for their review and ultimate approval. Reminiscent of the "Condo War" some fourteen years earlier, the *parciantes* of the Acequia de San Antonio posted a series of conspicuous signs with a stern warning leveled at potential trespassers:

NOTICE

THIS DITCH IS PROPERTY OF ACEQUIA DE SAN ANTONIO
IN VALDEZ, NEW MEXICO

WARNING!

SWIMMING, PLAYING, BOATING OR DISCHARGE OF
POLLUTANTS INTO THIS STREAM IS PROHIBITED.
ANYONE VIOLATING THIS ORDER WILL BE PROSECUTED
UNDER THE PROVISIONS OF THE ACEQUIA LAWS AND
SECTION FORBIDDING CRIMINAL TRESPASSING.

The sign went on to cite the new rules and regulations pertaining to the construction of culverts, bridges, or utility lines within or across any portion of the ditch. Apart from design specifications and a mandatory application procedure, the ditch rules and the posted sign gave notice that "no culvert, bridge or other construction shall diminish or obstruct the full flow of the ditch."[7] To ensure that all contractors and the entire public was dutifully informed, the text of the sign was also published in the Legal Notices section of the Taos newspaper during the month of June 1995.

In the years ahead, acequia associations likely will follow the example of the San Antonio Ditch at Valdez and assert their powers of rule making, probably with greater frequency and growing sophistication. Resistence at the local level, one case at a time, however, will not guarantee protection of the acequia culture as a whole. More broad-based policy and water-law reforms will be needed in order to integrate the goals of community sustainability with regional economic development in a manner responsive to traditional water users. If left to chance, the forces of the water markets will allocate water to the highest bidder in the short run, irrespective of historic uses or long-term sustainability.

Acequia Communities and State Economic Development

The public-policy challenge is to find a better way to account for the historic and cultural values of traditional water uses in the region. But how do state water officials and politicians evaluate the importance of community and other intangible values that cannot be accounted for in market-efficiency terms? Should water policymakers intervene by mitigating impacts that threaten social cohesion, family-support structures, or the ancestral farms of an endangered regional culture? Should the state and the county-government jurisdictions design and adopt a cornerstone rural growth management policy that steers intensive housing development away from the historic acequia farmlands?[8]

The case for preserving the old ways of acequia-irrigated agriculture in New Mexico often meets with skepticism, complete misunderstanding, or both. Some of the competing stakeholders perceive the acequia institution as antiquated and an obstacle to growth and development. To the critics, the acequia methods are wasteful of a scarce resource, producing only marginal economic returns of small-scale subsistence agriculture, at best.[9] But upon close examination, public-policy analysis can demonstrate that the protection of acequia customs and traditions is not particularly at odds with the economic goals of the state. The acequia communities already form part of the economic-development infrastructure of the upper Río Grande region in terms of the huge tourism industry that showcases the quaint village architecture, the farmers' markets in Santa Fe and other nearby cities, the greenbelts that define the landscapes of the river valleys, and very importantly, the cultural production renowned and marketed as "New Mexico village arts and crafts": the *santos, retablos,* wood furniture, and other hand-carved wood-crafts pieces; the folk art, tinworks, jewelry, hand-woven rugs, and other New Mexican products marketed worldwide.

Not often recognized, however, is the fact that these coveted objects cannot be replicated outside the cultural environment with which they are inextricably connected. Most of the skills and designs for these crafts have been passed on from generation to generation among families who depend on their products for cash sales and income, but who rely as much on the land base that has also been part of their inheritance. Waters from the family acequia sustain other aspects of their livelihood, season to season, year to year, for example, to irrigate pastures for small herds of cattle or flocks of sheep, or to irrigate the fruit orchards and family gardens. In turn, these rural landscapes and the amenities of the natural environment attract people to the region's urban centers, particularly when the state successfully lures an outside industry to relocate to or expand its plant operations in New Mexico, "The Land of Enchantment."

The crafts industries of the state and the region thrive in large part due to the setting in which objects and other handmade goods are produced by local artisans. Without water, these villages literally would dry up, as would the arts and crafts industry vital to the economic-development goals of the state of New Mexico. Policymakers should be mindful that acequia communities are a low-cost, renewable resource. Severing water rights from farmland for development purposes, on the other hand, eventually will erode the resource base that the acequia communities depend on. Because the tourism industry needs the rural and quaint village landscapes to sustain the attractions and amenities that visitors seek, elimination of acequia communities runs counter to tourism goals of the state.[10]

It is widely acknowledged that conventional approaches to economic development in the rural West, based on mineral extraction, industrial relocation, and capital-intensive tourism have met with dismal results. Jobs may be created, but the benefits are inequitably distributed; growth may or may not occur, but poverty and underdevelopment persist, and in the process, the community loses control of the resources it needs for long-term sustainable economic activity. Acequia-based agriculture, however, promotes cultural tourism while supporting social policy values of self-reliance, anti-poverty, and grassroots democracy at work. Contemporary principles of rural environmental planning confirm that local resources should form the basis for guiding economic development and growth that is sustainable and consistent with resource-base capacities: the natural, human, and cultural elements of development serve as the building blocks of any local economy. Such development is integrated with local institutions and conserves existing cultural resources.[11]

The Protection of Keystone Communities

Another policy challenge is to strengthen people's institutions that are already self-reliant. Should the state validate the importance of mutual-aid organizations by providing minimal levels of protection? Other public-policy values are better understood because they can be measured or quantified in economic terms, or because they can be regulated. But the cultural values and social aspects of water use are not as tidy. The acequia constituencies are fragmented. They lack a power base, the technical staffs, and, more often than not, sustained legal representation. The choice among competing values is not clear: instream flow to protect wildlife and to provide for urban recreational demands such as fishing and rafting? Acequias to preserve sustainable agriculture and a rural way of life? Or transfers of water to "higher values uses" for cities and high-tech industries?

These are difficult issues, but as concluded in a study of water-rights transfers in the western states by the National Research Council, New Mexico represents a compelling case for recognition of social and water-equity values:

> In the nineteenth century, Anglo property concepts were superimposed over the more communal traditions of the pueblos and Hispanic irrigation communities. Today New Mexico has a sophisticated water allocation system that basically treats water as a commodity to maximize the efficiency of use of the resource. But the clash of cultures makes northern New Mexico special; there are allocation tensions [here] that do not exist in other states. . . . If one wanted to make a case for protecting communities as entities, northern New Mexico would be the example to use.[12]

Some precedents to justify public-policy actions exist. Numerous times, governments at federal, state, and local levels have intervened in market arenas to preserve other natural resources and historic treasures: national forests, wildlife-refuge preserves, wetlands and other animal sancturies, land-trust territories, state open-space parks and trails, river-corridor *bosques*, historic main streets, town plazas, and buildings. In a parallel effort, acequia villages and towns should challenge the state to accept the proposition that their communities perpetuate a unique rural culture important to the region and the state economy as a whole. Acequia officials can argue that these rural enclaves are cultural resources as priceless as scenic or forested areas and should be protected from urban spillover effects, commercial exploitation, and the pressures of economic conversion as a unique and valued way of life.

At the federal level, acequia communities located within land-grant boundaries possibly could pursue claims to "federally reserved water rights" along with national parks, Indian reservations, and other federal reservations of land in the West.[13] If this designation was achieved, acequia water-rights priorities would be based no later than on the date the land grant was confirmed and the settlers allowed to take possession. As noted in Chapter 1, land-grant petitioners during the Spanish and Mexican periods sought and received parcels of land with access to irrigation water for the establishment and continuance of permanent colonies in the northern frontiers. Land grants for agricultural settlements could not be issued otherwise.

More widely, covering a much greater number of communities, acequias with pre-1848 water rights could pursue federal protection of their communal and customary water rights under the the Treaty of Guadalupe Hidalgo. Article VIII of this international treaty with Mexico guaranteed Mexicans who resided in the conquered territory the right to continue in residence and to retain their property rights: "property of every kind . . . shall be inviolably respected."[14] Though the treaty did not specifically mention water rights, lawyers and historians agree that property rights protected under the treaty most certainly encompassed water rights.[15] The Treaty of Guadalupe Hidalgo predates the New Mexico state constitution by more than sixty years and the water code by more than a half-century.

Without intervention by government, rapid economic and demographic change inevitably will hasten the displacement of an already endangered regional culture and the diversity of the rural landscape, which the acequia agroecosystem preserves. As decribed in more global terms by conservation biologist Reed Noss:

> The only success stories in real multiple-use conservation are a handful of indigenous peoples who have somehow been able to coexist with their environments for long periods without impoverishing them. Some indigenous cultures have even contributed to the biodiversity of their regions . . . suggesting that humans have the potential to act as a keystone species in the most positive sense.[16]

Following the criteria set by Noss, the acequia communities of the upper Río Grande region qualify as a keystone population. Research on acequia family farms by Devón Peña and his colleagues has demonstrated that
acequias create corridors of ecologic habitats that support plant and
wildlife biodiversity.[17] In many parts of New Mexico, these keystone communities also provide the cultural setting that makes possible the thriving
arts and crafts industry, which attracts tourists. Water transfers out of the
acequias over time could break links in the chain that holds the community together, as Sylvia Rodríguez warned after many years of intensive
ethnographic research in Taos County.[18] The land-grant and acequia
officials at Anton Chico protested the transfer of surface water rights from
one of their local ditches because of their fear that one water sale likely
would lead to others. A domino effect in Anton Chico, Taos or elsewhere
would then leave fewer *parciantes* to maintain the ditches, raise funds for
seasonal repairs, enforce and adminster the rules, and keep up with the
chores of organizational maintenance. A collapse of the acequia institution
would be catastrophic to the community and perhaps the surrounding
area.

State Policies and Local Strategies

In addition to broad-based policy supportive of the acequia regional culture, legislators in New Mexico may want to consider more direct interventions, including water-law reforms to protect acequia communities into
the twenty-first century. The summer of 1998 marked the four-hundredth
birthdate of Spanish-Mexican settlement on the upper Río Grande, an occasion that also commemorates the construction of the first Spanish acequias by Capitán General and Governor Juan de Oñate at San Juan de los
Caballeros and San Gabriel [now Chamita]. As a tribute to the *cuarto cen-
tenario*, New Mexico's legislators could amend existing water laws to allow
the designation of water-resources historic zones, declaring acequia communities as state historic treasures. Water transfers outside the zone or to
other uses would be prohibited or curtailed, similar to area-of-origin protections for small towns and rural communities afforded by statutes in
some of the western states.[19] In this case the public-policy objective would
be to insulate acequia water rights from the pressures of the water markets,
especially the forces of urban and industrial growth well outside the acequia localities. If enacted, state water law would recognize social, historic,
and cultural values in the allocation of water rights and water use, protect-

ing the rights of traditional water users to maintain the resource base that gave birth to their communities starting in 1598. Reference to the long history of protectionist legislation could help establish the framework for this proposed initiative: the Kearny Code in 1846, the first acequia laws in 1851–1852, the Water Code of 1907, and especially the laws of 1909, just before the adoption of the state constitution in 1912.[20]

As an implementation tool, the state could establish compensatory programs to purchase water rights from private individuals, including *parciantes*, who voluntarily transfer water rights to acequia associations. In cases of transfer to other uses or outside the designated zone, the state could levy an impact fee on transactions that transfer water from lower yields to more profitable uses. The fees, in turn, could capitalize a restoration fund. Taxing each of these and other agricultural water transfers seems to be an equitable remedy, providing the state with a fund to purchase water rights for reallocation to acequia zones most impacted by losses or most endangered by encroachment.[21]

Within the milieu of a supportive policy environment, there is also much that acequia irrigators can do for themselves. Already they have formed alliances that span the watersheds in the region. In the fall of 1988, a group of acequia officials from many New Mexico counties organized the First Annual Convention of Acequias. The delegates to the convention concluded their work by taking steps to establish an independent and statewide New Mexico Acequia Association (NMAA). The working organizational structure for the new association included a board of directors that was charged with developing action plans to guide the NMAA and the local acequias in critical areas of continuing need: assistance with the adjudication process in many of the streams, review of acequia laws and water rights, monitoring of government accountability for public funds appropriated to acequias, and the development of acequia input to the state and regional water-planning process underway at the time. Eventually NMAA expanded its purpose to include a program of technical assistance aimed at strengthening the capacity of the acequia associations to address the spectrum of issues facing the membership and to ensure the survival of the acequia democratic institution into the next century.[22]

During the middle 1990s, NMAA paid particular attention to the adjudication suits in the region and the growing threat of water transfers moving away from traditional uses. With the expansion of the mega Intel plant in Sandoval County, NMAA leaders were concerned that Intel and other high-tech corporations moving into the state's major cities could tilt state water policy toward urban and industrial growth at the expense of the tra-

ditional agricultural uses in the acequia communities.[23] As a statewide
association, NMAA prioritized the need to conduct seminars at the level of
local acequias in conjunction with the regional associations that were
emerging. Workshop topics ranged from sustainable agricultural practices
to the development of multimedia curricula on acequia affairs. By the summer of 1990 regional associations had been organized in the Taos Valley;
the lower Río Chama Valley; the Hondo Valley; the Mimbres River Valley; the Red River, the Pojoaque, Nambe, and Tesuque basins; and other
locations in New Mexico. Since then, regional associations have been organized in the Río Gallinas Valley and the Upper Río Pecos Valley, among
others.

The regional acequia associations have been very active in those issues
most critical to their respective watersheds. Participation in the adjudication process has been a common activity. In fact, some regional associations were created specifically to apply for adjudication-assistance grants
through the Acequia and Community Ditch Fund. The legislation that established this special fund in the laws of 1988 required that the ditches located within streams undergoing adjudication suits organize themselves
into a majority association in order to be eligible for funding as a group.
Once created, these regional associations become permanent coalitions
addressing a multitude of issues at the watershed level.

With these grant monies, the regional associations have conducted
baseline studies regarding community history, priority dates of ditch-
water use, acequia hydrology, and other essential topics. Once collected,
this data will serve the interests of the ditches well beyond the timeframe
of the adjudications in their streams. For example, the Río Gallinas Acequias Association, headquartered in Las Vegas, has been developing an acequia curriculum and database to support educational and other training
programs they will administer directly or in conjunction with the area
schools. Already the association has been training the rural youth and acequia *parciantes* on how to expand the acequia database and update the baseline information on a continuing basis. The participants not only gain
knowledge about acequia culture and history, but they also acquire skills
and research tools for future applications: training in historical and ethnographic research methods, legal-cases research, the design of field surveys, database and archival management, and community documentation
technologies.[24]

The area of field-based research holds great potential for the statewide,
regional, and local acequia associations. The possible areas for community-based research are almost without boundaries: documentation of lo-

cal architectural and cultural landscapes; acequia agriculture and pastoralism; management of common property resources; mutual-aid and self-governing institutions; conservation of land, water, and language rights; powers of acequia institutions; techniques for land banking, water leasing, and development of water trusts; patterns of land tenure, ownership and land-use practices; property rights, easements, and legal powers of acequias; methods for resource-planning assistance; alternative and sustainable agriculture models; the use of appropriate technologies; and countless other topics of wide interest to the acequia communities as they confront the challenges of the twenty-first century.

The databases and archives that result from an acequia-based research program, in turn, can help to design an equally large variety of training and planning-assistance programs.[25] Through a rural conservation program, for example, acequia irrigators can advocate the adoption of county-level regulations to control subdivision developments when they threaten to convert local farmland to other uses. While acequia institutions hold the status of political subdivisions, they do not have powers to regulate land use. The job of the acequia association would be to produce the resource inventories of land tenure depicting the acequia farmlands most susceptible to conversion and presenting this information to the county commissions. The county government could assess and collect impact fees in places where conversions are permitted and approved. These revenues, in turn, could be used to finance a farmland preservation program, to purchase development rights in the most critical locations, making up for any lost acreages.

Meanwhile, local ditch associations could form land and water trust banks to be able to acquire land and water rights either by purchase, voluntary transfers, or other innovative mechanisms. The best way to retain land and water rights in the community is for acequia communities to acquire them on a permanent basis. Since 1987, state water laws allow acequia associations, as opposed to just the individual *parciantes*, to acquire water rights, pool them, lease them, and transfer them to existing or new irrigators.[26] Establishment of water banks will allow the members to hold onto their water rights during periods of non-use while still earning income from the leasing of those rights. In 1991, the state statutes on forfeiture exempted acequia associations and other designated entities from water-rights forfeitures when these rights are acquired and placed in conservation programs of their design and operation.[27] As a side benefit, an internal water-banking or conservation program to retain water rights in the community will serve as direct evidence of the importance of water to the land base when acequia users protest applications that seek to transfer water rights to outside uses or destinations.

To retain ownership of their ancestral water rights, however, acequia *parciantes* are aware that the water rights must be put to beneficial use, perhaps by investing in permaculture and other alternative small-scale agricultural practices that will strengthen local production and raise incomes. Increasingly, the regional and local associations have begun to explore the potentials of crop diversification, organic farming, and speciality crop marketing. Some *parciantes* have experienced success with higher yield cash crops native to the region, such as: white corn for conversion into *chicos*, blue corn for *tortillas*, *capulín* (chokecherries) for jellies and specialty wines, *verdolagas* as a wild vegetable plant, and the banking of native seeds for future use and sale to other *parciante* families.[28] The Hispano Family Farms Project, scheduled for completion in 1998, intends to document some of these experiments and publish the results. (See note 17, p. 224.)

With the assistance of nearby colleges and universities, acequia associations may want to conduct inventories of cultural, natural, and historic resources in their communities. The results of these research projects can be used to nominate important sites and places to the national and state preservation registers.[29] For starters, each ditch watercourse, built at the time of initial settlement, should be identified, recorded by survey, and mapped for preservation as a historic communal property. Though many of the commons lands were partitioned, stolen, or misappropriated in some fashion, the *acequia de común* remains under self-governance and community control much as before. State water laws continue to recognize ownership rights in the physical ditchworks as separate from the water rights in the water passing through the ditch. According to an 1882 statute, which continues in effect, ownership of "all acequias, public or private," lies with the persons who "completed such acequias or ditches, and no person or persons who may desire to use the [acequia] waters . . . shall be allowed to do so without the consent of a majority of the owners of such acequias."[30] By all criteria, the ditch watercourse is a common property resource that the current irrigators should protect as a unique and extremely valuable community asset.

Along with other interested parties, acequia associations may want to participate in river and acequia corridor studies. Scientific field inventories will likely document the fact that acequia watercourses protect plant biodiversity, wildlife, and a host of other ecological values. In the process, acequia communities will gain new partners to advocate the common goal of sustainable development, a paradigm of development that can incor-

porate the historic and cultural values alongside environmental and economic dimensions. At a minimum, the extension of river-corridor inventories into the ditch watercourses will help to educate the public as to the
ecologic values of acequia-irrigation systems and practices, making possible the formation of extended partnerships and policy alliances.

Similarly, the headwaters sources for those acequias that share a common watershed should be documented and designated as critical natural
area zones.[31] These sensitive zones in the high *sierra* peaks should be protected from adverse development such as road clearings and timbering,
which can affect water quality and quantity at the acequia headgates, as has
been attempted in Colorado.[32] If not controlled or regulated, the clear-
cutting of forests at the higher altitudes can increase the amount of sedimentation, which eventually enters the community ditches downstream,
diminishing the value and productivity of acequia-irrigated fields. Also,
the vast amount of open space that results from excessive timber harvesting reduces the amount of forest canopy needed to retain and release winter snow in gradual amounts later in the spring and early summer, the
critical period for acequia-based irrigation and farming.[33]

Most of the peaks in the upper Río Grande region are already in the
public domain and should be recognized as watershed commons property
critical to sustaining the agropastoral economies downstream. It is important for acequia water users in each watershed to identify, map, and document the precise boundaries of their headwaters sources. As a second step,
they should work in partnerships with governmental agencies, not-for-
profit organizations, and preservation foundations to steer development
away from these and other valued natural areas. Strong enforcement tools
will likely be necessary to protect watersheds and tighten water-quality
standards in streams that are the most threatened by a continuing barrage
of projects to build condominiums, expand ski slopes, open new mines or,
clear-cut forests for timbering and logging purposes. Acequias should attempt to cultivate more broad-based support to protect the headwaters
sources vital not only to their own irrigation networks downstream, but
which appeal to other public values as well.[34]

Policy Alliances for the Future

During the 1980s and into the late 1990s, acequia associations experienced
many successes in organizing themselves into cohesive political forces at
the regional and state levels. The creation and financing of the Acequia

and Community Ditch Fund came about as a result of their own efforts, as have many other acequia support programs at the state and federal levels. These programs have already proven to be effective in bringing attention to the special role of the acequia as a watercourse and as a significant water-management institution. Approaching the turn of the century, however, acequia associations will need to span their base of support not just among themselves and their natural allies, but into other sectors and stakeholders: environmentalists, socially responsible corporations, Indian tribes, the scientific community, cultural and eco-tourism industries, local planning and zoning boards, and possibly others. The competition for scarce water resources will intensify. To acquire broad-based policy support, acequias will surely need an expanded network of advocates and partners.

The watercourse has always been a vital part of the acequia community ecosystem. New Mexico and Colorado policymakers need to look for ways to define, map, and protect the boundaries of the watercourse greenbelt, to include not just the river and adjacent *bosques*, but also the acequias traversing the foothills, the vegetated ditch banks, and the irrigated bottomlands. The watercourse is the most distinguishing feature of the typical acequia community and its relationship to the surrounding open and rural landscape: it shapes the edges of the varied terrain; it defines the natural and human-made boundaries; it sets the limits to growth; it allocates space for community development and the built environment; and it nourishes the plant and animal ecologic life within the corridor.

Comparatively, the upper Río Grande community acequias of southern Colorado and New Mexico stand apart from the fate of many other irrigation canals in the western United States and elsewhere. In Donald Worster's historical study, most irrigation systems in the American West have succumbed to the forces of the new hydrologic society, where water has been reduced to a simplified, abstracted resource, separated from the earth in a manipulative relationship with nature:

> The modern ditch is lined along its entire length with concrete to prevent the seepage of water into the soil; consequently, nothing green can take root along its banks, no trees, no sedges and reeds, no grassy meadows, no seeds or blossoms dropping lazily into a side-eddy. Nor can one find here an egret stalking frogs and salamanders, or a red-winged blackbird swaying on a stem, or a muskrat burrowing into the mud. Quite simply, the modern canal, unlike a river, is not an ecosystem.[35]

The earthen acequias of the upper Río Grande, on the other hand, still remain and function as common-property resource systems. The irrigators own the watercourses, regulate them, police them, and maintain them generation to generation. When compared with many other water-management regimes, the acequia of the upper Río Grande is a model institution. At the local level, it perpetuates cultural continuity, a sense of place, and a system of direct, participatory democracy, while providing for the management and stewardship of the most important life-sustaining resource. In turn, the network of acequia communities as a whole provides for spatial balance in the region. These keystone villages form a watershed-resource base for the benefit of other stakeholders, including the larger cities, the high-tech industries, and the vital tourism economy. The ribbonlike greenways and acequia fields act like a wetland system. The valley bottomlands and acequia watercourses are sponges that retain water, control soil erosion, recharge the aquifers, nurture the cottonwood forests and other native vegetation, and shelter the wildlife and fish habitats by maintaining instream flows, all the while preserving farmlands, open space, and historic cultures. The acequia institution of the upper Río Grande is a modern-day treasure with roots in the medieval Old World and an opportunity to contribute to global diversity in the twenty-first century and beyond.

DOCUMENTS

San Antonio Ditch Posted Sign, 1995

Some thirteen years after the "Condo War," the community of Valdez in Taos County again found itself on the defensive, faced with even more direct impacts of development, this time on the ditch infrastructure itself. During the spring of 1995, heavy trucks and other construction equipment hauling materials to nearby subdivision housing, not suited to local road conditions and ditch crossings, were damaging the culverts of the Acequia de San Antonio. The commercial road traffic was also causing environmental damage by way of runoff into the ditch-irrigation waters and increased sedimentation. In addition, some recreation enthusiasts from outside Valdez occasionally were utilizing the water flow in the acequia for boating adventures, such as kayaking downstream into and through the community. To control the situation, the ditch commissioners posted signs and published a legal notice prohibiting these uses and other polluting activities. The text of the sign was provided courtesy of the Acequia de San Antonio.

NOTICE
THIS DITCH IS PROPERTY OF ACEQUIA DE
SAN ANTONIO IN VALDEZ, NEW MEXICO.

WARNING!
SWIMMING, PLAYING, BOATING OR DISCHARGE OF POLLUTANTS
INTO THIS STREAM IS PROHIBITED. ANYONE VIOLATING THIS ORDER
WILL BE PROSECUTED UNDER THE PROVISIONS OF THE ACEQUIA
LAWS AND SECTION FORBIDDING CRIMINAL TRESPASSING.
LEGAL PUBLIC NOTICE

The Rules and Regulations of the Acequia de San Antonio in Valdez, New Mexico provide the following: No culvert, bridge, utility line or other construction may be placed within, or across the ditch, without prior written permission of the commission and *mayordomo*. Culverts shall have a minimum diameter of thirty six (36"). No culvert, bridge or other construction shall diminish or obstruct the full flow of the ditch. After May 15, 1995 new roadways constructed across the ditch shall be supported by bridges rather than culverts and any damaged roadway culvert shall be replaced by a bridge. Application for permission to construct, repair or improve a road or bridge across the ditch shall be made by submission of a written project plan to the commission and the *mayordomo*. The written plan shall include proof of legal title or easement, a sketch and profile of the bridge, an on-site and off-site drainage plan, proof of approval of the project by State Highway and Taos County Road Department, and such other information as the commission and *mayordomo* may require. (Article 4, Section 6: Rules and Regulations of the Acequia de San Antonio)

(N.B.: Published Legal Notice No. 2121 in the *Taos News* three consecutive weeks in June 1995.)

Notes

PREFACE

1. See Charles D. Kleymeyer, "Cultural Traditions and Community-Based Conservation," 20 *Grassroots Development: Journal of the Inter-American Foundation* 1 (1996), 27–35.

2. See Elinor Ostrom, *Governing the Commons: The Evolution of Institutions for Collective Action* (Cambridge, 1990); Michael Redclift and Colin Sage, *Strategies for Sustainable Development: Local Agendas for the Southern Hemisphere* (Chichester, 1994). Alan R. Emery notes that indigeneous peoples still occupy 20 percent of the world's land mass. "Their use of the land," he says, "is both for subsistence and as a part of their cultural roots and sense of identity." By contrast, Western societies view natural resources as wasted if not extracted and put to use. See Alan R. Emery, "The Participation of Indigenous Peoples and Their Knowledge in Environmental Assessment and Development Planning," a report from the Centre for Traditional Knowledge (December 1996), 2. For a related article on how to incorporate customary practices into modern legal systems, or perhaps vice versa, see Sanford D. Clark, "Tensions Between Water Legislation and Customary Rights," 30 *Natural Resources Journal* 3 (Summer 1990).

3. United Nations Conference on the Environment and Development, *The Río Declaration*, UNCED Doc. (June 1992).

4. Robert B. Hawkins, Jr., Foreword in Daniel W. Bromley, ed., *Making the Commons Work: Theory, Practice and Policy* (San Francisco, 1992), xii.

5. See especially Fikret Berkes, *Common Property Resources: Ecology and Community-Based Sustainable Development* (London, 1989), 3–5; and Kleymeyer, "Cultural Traditions and Community-Based Conservation."

6. Redclift and Sage, *Strategies for Sustainable Development*, 11.

7. Ibid., 188.

8. See Charles T. DuMars and Michele Minnis, "New Mexico Water Law: Determining Public Welfare Values in Water Rights Allocation," 31 *Ariz. Law Review*

4, 828–30; José A. Rivera, "Irrigation Communities of the Upper Río Grande Bio-region: Sustainable Resource Use in the Global Context," 36 *Natural Resources Journal* 4 (Fall 1996), 743–44.

9. See Ostrom, *Governing the Commons; Berkes, Common Property Resources*; Redclift and Sage, *Strategies for Sustainable Development*.

INTRODUCTION

1. For a cultural geography of the upper Río Grande region, see Alvar W. Carlson, *The Spanish-American Homeland: Four Centuries in New Mexico's Rio Arriba* (Baltimore, 1990).

2. Donald Worster, *Rivers of Empire: Water, Aridity and the Growth of the American West* (New York, 1985), 31.

3. Devón Peña, "Anatomy of the Disappeared," chapter 10 in *Gaia in Atzlan: Culture, Ecology and the Politics of Locality in the Upper Río Grande Watershed* (forthcoming, Tucson: University of Arizona Press), 32.

4. See José A. Rivera, "New Mexico Acequias and the Public Welfare," Research Report No. 008, Southwest Hispanic Research Institute, University of New Mexico (Spring 1996).

5. Daniel W. Bromley, "The Commons, Property, and Common-Property Regimes," in Bromley, *Making the Commons Work*, 11–12.

6. E. Walter Coward, Jr., "Planning Technical and Social Change in Irrigated Areas," in Michael M. Cernea, ed., *Putting People First: Sociological Variables in Rural Development* (New York, 1991), 52–53, 68–69.

7. Ibid., 53.

8. Projects and publications completed during the field-study period by the author and other collaborators included Research Report No. 003, "The Course of Upper Río Grande Waters: A Declaration of Concerns," Conference Proceedings of the Upper Río Grande Working Group, Southwest Hispanic Research Institute, University of New Mexico (December 1985), funded by the Ford Foundation; José A. Rivera and Anselmo Arellano, "*Acequias y Sangrías*: Guidebook to Photo Exhibit" (1986), funded by the New Mexico Humanities Council; Research Report No. 004, "Upper Río Grande Waters: Strategies," Conference Proceedings of the Upper Río Grande Working Group, Southwest Hispanic Research Institute, University of New Mexico (Fall 1987), funded by the Ford Foundation; José A. Rivera and Anselmo Arellano, "*Los Canales de Riego de las Comunidades de Nuevo México: Los Orígenes y la Situación Actual*," conference paper presented at *Tercero Congreso Internacional, Culturas Hispanas de los Estados Unidos de América*, Barcelona, Spain (June 1988); José A. Rivera, "The Acequia Sourcebook" (September 1990), funded by the New Mexico Engineering Research Institute, University of New Mexico; F. Lee Brown and José A. Rivera, "The Southwest: Global Issues in a Regional Setting," in *National Rural Studies Committee: A Proceedings* (Corvallis, Ore., May 14–16, 1992); José A. Rivera, "The Acequias of New Mexico and the Public Welfare,"

(Spring 1996), commissioned by the Northern New Mexico Legal Services; and Rivera, "Irrigation Communities of the Upper Río Grande Bioregion."

9. Most of the acequia papers and related documents were collected during the Acequias y Sangrías Project at the University of New Mexico Southwest Hispanic Research Institute from 1985 onward. The project investigators were José A. Rivera and Anselmo Arellano, who translated many of the documents.

10. For global collective action experiences in the area of irrigation, see Shui Yan Tang, *Institutions and Collective Action: Self-Governance in Irrigation* (San Francisco, 1992).

11. For an extended case study of decentralization in irrigation management, see El Operado Project described in Pieter van der Zaag, *Chicanery at the Canal: Changing Practice in Irrigation Management in Western Mexico* (Amsterdam, 1992).

12. See Elinor Ostrom, *Crafting Institutions for Self-Governing Irrigation Systems* (San Francisco, 1992), 13–14.

13. Yan Tang, *Institutions and Collective Action*, 129.

14. Ibid., 130.

15. Yan Tang, *Institutions for Collective Action*; Ostrom, *Crafting Institutions*; Bromley, *Making the Commons Work*; Coward, "Planning Technical and Social Change." Also see Benjamin U. Bagadion and Frances F. Korten, "Developing Irrigators' Organizations: A Learning Process Approach," and David M. Freeman and Max L. Lowermilk, "Middle-level Farmer Organizations as Links between Farms and Central Irrigation Systems," in Cernea, *Putting People First*.

16. Cernea, "Editor's Note," *Putting People First*, 43.

17. Bagadion and Korten, "Developing Irrigators' Organizations," 74–75.

18. Ibid., 93–97.

CHAPTER I

1. Linda S. Cordell, *Prehistory of the Southwest* (Orlando, 1984), 222–23.

2. Ibid., 190.

3. See Kurt F. Anschuetz, "Two Sides of a Coin: Early Pueblo Indian Farming Practices in the Río Arriba and the Río Abajo of the Northern Río Grande Region," paper presented at the 60th Annual Meeting of the Society for American Archaeology (May 3–7, 1995), Minneapolis, 2, 5–8, 11; W. H. Wills, Thomas A. Baker, and Lee A. Baker, "Aerial Perspectives on Prehistoric Agricultural Fields of the Middle Río Grande Valley, New Mexico," in *Clues to the Past: Papers in Honor of William M. Sundt*, Archaeological Society of New Mexico, 16 (1990), 315, 317, and 328. For a more contemporary account of Pueblo Indian irrigation practices, see Richard I. Ford, "The Technology of Irrigation in a New Mexico Pueblo," in Heather Lechtman and Robert S. Merrill, eds., *Material Culture: Styles, Organization and Dynamics of Technology* (St. Paul, 1977), 139–54.

4. See Ralph Emerson Twitchell, *Old Santa Fe: The Story of New Mexico's Ancient Capital* (Santa Fe, 1925), 20–21; Malcolm Ebright, "Report on Santa Fe Water Priorities," unpublished paper (1981), 2. Twitchell describes archaeological evidence

that a large population of Pueblo Indians had occupied portions of Santa Fe near the main plaza as well as "along the slopes to the Río Santa Fe to the east and to the west." From this, Ebright infers that the Spanish possibly constructed their acequias where vestiges of Indian ditches may have been located.

5. Laws of the Indies extracted from chapters 3 and 4 of Frederic Hall, *The Laws of Mexico* (1985), as cited in appendix C of Charles T. DuMars, Marilyn O'Leary, and Albert E. Utton, *Pueblo Indian Water Rights: Struggle for a Precious Resource* (Tucson, 1984), 138–39.

6. Marc Simmons, "Spanish Irrigation Practices in New Mexico," 47 *New Mexico Historical Review* 2 (April 1972), 138. Simmons speculates that the Villa de San Gabriel, the new capital of the province after its relocation from San Juan de los Caballeros, was itself moved to a more distant site at Santa Fe in 1610 because of its encroachment on Tewa Indian lands.

7. This description of the acequia construction process is derived in part from Rivera and Arellano, *"Acequias y Sangrías."*

8. Simmons, "Spanish Irrigation Practices," 138; and Marc Simmons, *The Last Conquistador* (Norman, 1991), 114, 148–49. Also see George P. Hammond and Agapito Rey, eds., *Don Juan de Oñate, Colonizer of New Mexico, 1595–1628*, 2 vols. (Albuquerque, 1953), 1:17, 320–23, 346; and Wells A. Hutchins, "The Community Acequia: Its Origin and Development," 31 *Southwestern Historical Quarterly* (July 1927–April 1928), 275. The acequia that was dug out for eventual use in the planned townsite of San Francisco appears to have been the first Spanish ditch. However, there is no historical record as to its ultimate fate. Was it ever completed or put into use by Oñate? Was it abandoned after Oñate moved the site for his capital to San Gabriel (now Chamita) on the opposite bank of the Río Grande to the west? Or, perhaps, should the Acequia de Chamita, diverted from the Río Chama for the San Gabriel settlement, be recognized as the first Spanish ditch? To cloud the issue even further, Simmons, in *Last Conquistador*, raises the possibility that the San Francisco site could have been planned for the *west* side of the Río Grande, placing it above or below San Gabriel (114). The completion and actual use of the Acequia de Chamita, however, is well documented and readily accepted by the scholars as an historic ditch. For evidence, they cite a report by the Franciscan historian, Juan de Torquemada, where he says he observed the practice of irrigated agriculture at San Gabriel by 1612–13: "San Gabriel . . . is situated [between] two rivers, one of which has less water than the other. This small one [the Río Chama] irrigates all the varieties of wheat, barley, corn, in irrigated fields, and other things that are planted in gardens." Fray Juan de Torquemada, *Monarquía Indiana*, 3 vols., Tercera Edición, (México, D.F.: Editorial Salvador Chávez Hayhoe, 1943), 1:678.

9. Simmons, "Spanish Irrigation Practices," 138. Also see John O. Baxter, *Dividing New Mexico's Waters, 1700–1912* (Albuquerque, 1997), 1–2.

10. Simmons, "Spanish Irrigation Practices," 138–39. Twitchell, *Old Santa Fe*, 21, agrees with others that the Santa Fe site provided a more strategic location for the frontier capital city, especially from the perspective of military control and secu-

rity against possible assaults undertaken by "warlike tribes" from the mountains and the plains. Other factors he includes as possible reasons for the relocation are the water supply, agricultural potential, timber resources, and the climate. After the Pueblo Revolt, when Governor Diego de Vargas laid out plans to recolonize New Mexico, he chose a valley further to the north of Santa Fe, with plentiful water, as the site for an additional town. According to Baxter, in *Dividing New Mexico's Waters*, De Vargas had been concerned that the Santa Fe environs did not provide sufficient irrigation water to support the large population already congregated there by the late seventeenth century. Thus, de Vargas's municipality would be located twenty miles north of Santa Fe, where the fertile valley land there could be easily irrigated, as he proclaimed directly on April 19, 1695, when he founded "La Villa Nueva de Santa Cruz de la Cañada." See Baxter, *Dividing New Mexico's Waters*, 5–6.

11. See Simmons, "Spanish Irrigation Practices," 135–36; Ira G. Clark, *Water in New Mexico: A History of Its Management and Use* (Albuquerque, 1987), 9–10. Clark notes that the Moorish influence on Spanish water law was especially fundamental, owing to the aridity of North Africa and the Islamic law of thirst, which granted free access to water for all living things to satisfy their needs. This moral obligation to offer help in times of need or to share water during conditions of drought is a deeply held tradition of the acequia irrigators of the upper Río Grande. As illustrations of this conviction, see the discussion of "*auxilio*" (emergency mutual aid) and "*aguas sobrantes*" (surplus waters) in Chapter 5 of this text. Also, note that many of the terms in the acequia glossary are of arabic origin; for example, *acequia, atarque, tarea, noria*.

12. Both ordinances are translated in Dora P. Crouch, Daniel J. Garr, and Axel I. Mundigo, *Spanish City Planning in North America* (Cambridge, 1982), 8–9.

13. For the complete set of instructions, see *El Plan de Pitic de 1789 y las Nuevas Poblaciones Proyectadas en las Provincias Internas de la Nueva España*, trans. and ed. Joseph P. Sánchez, 2 *Colonial Latin American Historical Review* 4 (Fall 1993), 449–67.

14. Letter of Coronado to Mendoza, Aug. 3, 1540, in George P. Hammond and Agapito Rey, eds., *Narratives of the Coronado Expedition 1540–1542* (Albuquerque, 1940), 2:175.

15. Translated and edited in George P. Hammond and Agapito Rey, eds., *The Rediscovery of New Mexico, 1580–1594* (Albuquerque, 1966), 224.

16. Ibid., 182.

17. Though outside the upper Río Grande region, the initial steps taken to prepare La Villa de San Fernando de Béxar (later San Antonio, Texas) as a strategic location for permanent Spanish occupation were strikingly similar to those in Santa Fe and Albuquerque. The Presidio and five missions, built along both banks of the Río de San Antonio, were supported by seven acequias, necessary from inception and through various stages of population growth to irrigate cultivated crops and fields organized into *labores* and *suertes*. Without the network of dams, acequias, and an aqueduct, the settlement process and the formation of a cohesive

community in this otherwise borderland frontier would not have progressed as rapidly as it did. See Jesús F. de la Teja, *San Antonio de Béxar: A Community on New Spain's Northern Frontier* (Albuquerque, 1995), 31–48.

18. Translated and edited in Lansing B. Bloom, "Alburquerque and Galisteo Certificate of Their Founding, 1706," 10 *New Mexico Historical Review* 1 (January 1935), 48–49. Bloom states: "The document was found in the Archivo General de la Nación (México), sección de las Provincias Internas, tomo 36, ramo 5."

19. Ibid.

20. Eleanor B. Adams and Fray Angelico Chavez, *The Missions of New Mexico, 1776: A Description by Fray Francisco Atanasio Domínguez with Other Contemporary Documents* (Albuquerque, 1956), 83.

21. Laws of the Indies, Book Four, Title Twelve, cited in W. A. Keleher, "Law of the New Mexico Land Grant," 4 *New Mexico Historical Review* 4 (October 1929), 352.

22. Clark S. Knowlton, "Land Loss as a Cause of Unrest among the Rural Spanish American Village Population of Northern New Mexico," 2 *Agriculture and Human Values* 3 (Summer 1985), 27. Also, see Baxter, *Dividing New Mexico's Waters*, 12.

23. John O. Baxter, *Spanish Irrigation in Taos Valley, New Mexico*, State Engineer Office (Santa Fe, September 1990), 17. Also, see Ben Tafoya, "Water and Land Development in Cañón de Fernández and Northern New Mexico: The Banking of Water Rights" (master's thesis, Antioch University, 1986), 24–25.

24. *Merced de Agua*, cited and translated in Tafoya, "Water and Land Development," 24–25. Baxter identifies the *alcalde*'s document as "Records of the Surveyor General of New Mexico (SG), no. 125, Don Fernando de Taos Grant, State Records Center and Archives, (SRCA) Santa Fe, N.M." See Baxter, *Dividing New Mexico's Waters*, 17–18 and 113.

25. Hutchins, "Community Acequia," 278.

26. See Mora Case Study, in Rivera and Arellano, "*Acequias y Sangrías*"; also, see Robert D. Shadow and María Rodríguez-Shadow, "From *Repartición* to Partition: A History of the Mora Land Grant, 1835–1916," 70 *New Mexico Historical Review* 3 (July 1995), 257–98.

27. Rivera and Arellano, "*Acequias y Sangrías*."

CHAPTER 2

1. José A. Rivera y Anselmo Arellano, "*Los Canales de Riego de las Comunidades de Nuevo México: Los Orígines y la Situación Actual*," in María Jesús Buxó Rey y Tomás Calvo Buezas, eds., *Culturas Hispanas de los Estados Unidos de América* (Madrid, 1990), 91–94.

2. Thomas F. Glick, *Irrigation and Society in Medieval Valencia* (Cambridge, 1970).

3. Ibid., 35–37.

4. Ibid., 40.

5. Document appears in Malcolm Ebright, "Report on Santa Fe Water Priorities," Exhibit E Spanish Document, trans. Ebright. The document is at SANM II, Reel 6, frames 30–32.

6. Ebright, "Report on Santa Fe Water Priorities," 7.

7. Glick, *Irrigation and Society in Medieval Valencia*, 31.

8. Ibid., 34.

9. Baxter, *Spanish Irrigation in Taos Valley*, 16. In a more recent work, Baxter describes an earlier case, this time involving land-grant encroachment on Indian water resources. In brief, he describes how Governor Tomás Velez Cachupín was petitioned for a land grant at Tesuque, north of Santa Fe, in 1752. Following his normal procedures, the governor dispatched an *alcalde* to confer with Tesuque Pueblo leaders and other parties located in the vicinity as to possible adverse claims. The owner of a *rancho* downstream from the proposed land grant protested immediately. Eventually, the petitioner organized a cooperative effort for the construction of a storage *tanque* (reservoir pond) to retain a sufficient amount of irrigation water for use by the entire community. Baxter, *Dividing New Mexico's Waters*, 21.

10. Juan Estevan Arellano, "*La Querencia: La Raza* Bioregionalism," 72 *New Mexico Historical Review* 1 (Jan. 1997), 31–37.

11. Title Five, Book Four, Laws of the Indies, trans. and cited in Arellano, "*La Querencia*," 32–33.

12. Title Seven, Book Four, trans. and cited in Arellano, "*La Querencia*," 34–35.

13. Glick, *Irrigation and Society in Medieval Valencia*, 54–55.

14. Malcolm Ebright, *Land Grants and Lawsuits in Northern New Mexico* (Albuquerque, 1994), 90.

15. Provincial Statutes, trans. Lynn I. Perrigo, "Notes and Documents," 27 *New Mexico Historical Review* 1 (January 1952), 66–72.

16. Sections 13 and 24, Act of 7 January 1852, *N.M. Revised Statutes and Laws* (Studley 1865).

17. Laws of 1868 and 1872, cited by Clark, *Water in New Mexico*, 30–31.

18. Laws of 1880, 1897 and 1899, cited by Clark, *Water in New Mexico*, 31.

19. See 1895 Agreement in appendix to *Acequia Madre del Cerro* v. *Pete Mertian et al.*, Final Judgement, No. 4208, District Court, County of Taos, Oct. 31, 1946.

20. Attributed by Estevan Arellano to the former ditch *mayordomo* at San Cristóbal, in Taos County, the widely respected Cleofas Vigil, *Water Platica Series*, University of New Mexico Community and Regional Planning Program, Nov. 21, 1996.

21. Corrales Ditch Rules, 1928. For ditch rules and other acequia documents, consult the acequia materials archive. José A. Rivera Collection, *Papers 1982–94, No. MSS 587 BC*, Center for Southwest Research, Zimmerman Library, University of New Mexico, Albuquerque.

22. Margarita Ditch Rules, 1911.

23. Jacona Ditch Rules, c. 1950s.

24. See Devón Peña and Rubén Martínez, co-principal investigators, "Upper

Río Grande Hispano Farms Study," research project supported by a grant from the National Endowment for the Humanities, Interpretative and Collaborative Research Projects Division, Grant No. RO 22707–94, Colorado College, 1994–1998.

25. Ibid.

26. See Rivera, "Irrigation Communities of the Upper Río Grande Bioregion, 758."

27. Ebright, *Land Grants and Lawsuits*, 62–63.

28. Ibid., 79, 83. Also, see Baxter, *Dividing New Mexico's Waters*, 38–39.

29. Baxter, *Dividing New Mexico's Waters*, 17–30. Baxter provides a number of dispute cases illustrating these types of complaints and how they were resolved by colonial authorities.

30. See Ebright, "Report on Santa Fe Water Priorities."

31. Ibid.

32. Ibid.

33. *Margarita de Luna* v. *Zalasares*, Abiquiu, 1770, SANM II, Reel 10, frames 619–623, trans. Anselmo Arellano.

34. Ibid.

35. Document appears in Marc Simmons, ed. and trans., "An Alcalde's Proclamation: A Rare New Mexico Document," 75 *El Palacio* 2 (Summer 1968), 5–9.

36. Ibid.

37. Ibid.

38. Ibid.

39. Provincial Statutes, trans. Perrigo, "Notes and Documents," 66–72.

40. The formalizing of acequia-irrigation laws coincides with the early Mexican period not only in the Nuevo México jurisdiction, but elsewhere as well. According to Glick, beginning in the 1820s the San Antonio, Texas, town council "began to make explicit, in its ordinances and deliberations, many procedures and precepts which may not have been previously recorded or formalized. Similarly, beginning in the Mexican period one can describe a process of codification, whereby customary irrigation law, as it had developed in the course of the eighteenth century, was written down, both in San Antonio and throughout the state of Coahuila-Texas." Thomas F. Glick, *The Old World Background of the Irrigation System of San Antonio, Texas* (El Paso, 1972), 55.

41. Provincial Statutes, trans. Perrigo, "Notes and Documents," 69.

42. Daniel Tyler testimony in Adjudication Hearing on Custom and Tradition, *State of New Mexico* v. *Eduardo Abeyta and Celso Arellano et al.*, United States District Court for the District of New Mexico, Transcript, May 20, 1991, 22, 31, 34, 72.

43. Ibid., 23, 31, 71–72.

44. Ebright, *Land Grants and Lawsuits*, 27.

45. Ibid., 72–83.

46. Ibid., 73.

47. Governor Abreu, cited by Ebright, *Land Grants and Lawsuits*, 81.

48. Zebulon Montgomery Pike, in Milo Milton Quaife, ed., *The Southwestern Expedition of Zebulon M. Pike* (Chicago, 1925), 152–53.

49. Josiah Gregg, *Commerce of the Prairies* (1844; Norman, 1954), 107.

50. Ibid., 108.

51. Ibid., 107–8.

52. Ibid., 108.

CHAPTER 3

1. Kearny Code, 1846, *Organic Law for the Territory of New Mexico*, Compiled under the Directions of General Kearny, in *Occupation of Mexican Territory*, Senate Doc. No. 896, 62d Congress, 2d Session, Washington Government Printing Office, 1912.

2. Laws of 1851, sections 2, 5, 6, and 8, *N.M. Revised Statutes and Laws* (Studley 1865).

3. Laws of 1852, sections 10, 11, 13, 14, and 17, *N.M. Revised Statutes and Laws* (Studley 1865).

4. Ibid., section 21. This is the official translation as published in 1852.

5. Wells A. Hutchins, "Community Acequias or Ditches in New Mexico," *Eighth Biennial Report of the State Engineer of New Mexico, 1926–1928* (Santa Fe, 1926–28), 229.

6. Vernon L. Sullivan, "Irrigation in New Mexico," USDA Office of Experiment Stations, *Bulletin 215* (June 25, 1909), 33.

7. "Report of Commission of Irrigation and Water Rights, Territory of New Mexico" (Dec. 15, 1898), 12.

8. See Clark, *Water in New Mexico*; Phil Lovato, *Las Acequias del Norte*, Technical Report No. 1 (Taos, 1974); Michael C. Meyer, *Water in the Hispanic Southwest* (Tucson, 1984); Charlotte Benson Crossland, "Acequia Rights in Law and Tradition," 32 *Journal of the Southwest* 3 (Autumn 1990).

9. Fred J. Waltz, "Powers of Acequias," in Conference Proceedings of the Upper Río Grande Working Group, *Upper Río Grande Waters: Strategies*, Southwest Hispanic Research Institute, Research Report No. 004 (Fall 1987), 61.

10. Laws of 1897, section 9, *Compiled Laws of the Territory of New Mexico of 1897*.

11. Hutchins, "Community Acequias or Ditches in New Mexico," 236.

12. Michael C. Meyer, "New Mexico's Hispanic Water Regimen, 1540–1912, with Special Reference to the Taos Valley," unpublished report (1997), 78–79.

13. Laws of 1851, section 5.

14. Laws of 1852, section 27. This is the official translation as published in 1852.

15. Meyer, "New Mexico's Hispanic Water Regimen," 78–79.

16. Ibid.

17. A variant of "*acequias de común*" appears in the 1932 minutes of the Acequia de Corrales in the opening paragraph: "*Los oficiales de la asequia mancomún del presinto número 2 de Corrales por el año de 1932 son los siguientes.*" [The officers of the community ditch in Corrales precinct number 2 for 1932 are the following.] Per

Meyer's intrepretation, the verb *mancomunicar* can be defined as the joining together of persons for a given purpose. Hence, his translation of *mancomunidades* as
voluntarily formed associations. See Meyers, "New Mexico's Hispanic Water Regimen," 41.

18. Marc Simmons, "Settlement Patterns and Village Plans in Colonial New
Mexico," 8 *Journal of the West* 1 (January 1969), 12.

19. Ibid., 13, 17.

20. Marc Simmons, *Coronado's Land: Essays on Daily Life in Colonial New Mexico*
(Albuquerque, 1991), 118–19.

21. Daniel Tyler, *The Mythical Pueblo Rights Doctrine: Water Administration in
Hispanic New Mexico* (El Paso, 1990), 12–13.

22. Ibid., 20. Also, see Marc Simmons, *Spanish Government in New Mexico* (Albuquerque, 1968), 176.

23. See, among others, Arthur L. Campa, *Hispanic Culture in the Southwest* (Norman, 1979); Simmons, "Spanish Irrigation Practices in New Mexico"; Meyer,
Water in the Hispanic Southwest.

24. France V. Scholes, "Civil Government and Society in New Mexico in the
Seventeenth Century," 10 *New Mexico Historical Review* 2 (April 1935), 76. Also, Sim-
mons, "Spanish Irrigation Practices," 141, and Simmons, *Spanish Government in
New Mexico,* 54–55.

25. Tyler, *Mythical Pueblo Rights Doctrine,* 22–23.

26. Simmons, "Spanish Irrigation Practices," 141.

27. Meyer, "New Mexico's Hispanic Water Regimen," n. 120. Meyer notes that
the term *mayordomo* is generic to any type of supervisor, such as the resident boss
in charge of the workforce on a Mexican hacienda. (Similarly, in New Mexico,
mayordomo is commonly applied to ranch foremen, church custodians from the
community, and, of course, ditch superintendents.)

28. See Provincial Statutes, trans. Perrigo, "Notes and Documents," 72.

29. Laws of 1852, section 13.

30. Ibid., section 15.

31. Laws of 1864, section 40, *N.M. Revised Statutes and Laws* (Studley 1865).

32. Laws of 1867, section 2, *Laws of the Territory of New Mexico* (Manderfield and
Tucker 1867).

33. Laws of 1880, section 2, *Acts of the N.M. Legislative Assembly* (Webb 1880).

34. Laws of 1863, section 34, and Laws of 1865, sections 2–3, *Colección de Leyes
del Territorio de Nuevo México* (Ronquillo 1881).

35. Laws of 1895, section 1 and 2, *Acts of the N.M. Legislative Assembly* (N.M.
Printing Co., 1895).

36. Ibid., section 4.

37. Ibid., section 2.

38. See Laws of 1903, chapter 44, section 1, March 12, cited and interpreted by
Clark, *Water in New Mexico,* 101–2.

39. For an account of when and why each of these new water institutions were

authorized, see Clark, *Water in New Mexico,* 100–14. Much of the historical background presented here is based on this source. Baxter points out that the 1887 law authorizing the formation of private irrigation companies safeguarded acequias by stipulating that water companies could not take water during the acequia irrigation season without unanimous approval of ditch landowners. He cites this provision as an example of the superimposition beginning to take place in order to accommodate the old with the new, bridging acequia traditions with the more recent innovative irrigation technology. However, Baxter concludes, this process created a "dualistic authority," which "sometimes led to conflicts when the two systems came together." Baxter, *Dividing New Mexico's Waters,* 83.

40. From among the new water institutions, scholars agree that conservancy districts proved to have the greatest adverse impacts on acequias watercourses and on the system of self-government. In the decades prior to their formation, community acequias still irrigated a significant proportion of total irrigated lands in New Mexico. During the period 1909–1910, 480 acequias accounted for almost half of all irrigated acreages. See Hutchins, "Community Acequias or Ditches in New Mexico," 230. The largest conservancy districts on the Río Grande, Elephant Butte and the Middle Río Grande, were established in areas where irrigation had been practiced for centuries by means of community acequias. Embracing some 110,000 acres in the Mesilla and Rincon valleys, the Elephant Butte project, built between c. 1908 and 1918, eliminated most of the community ditches by incorporating them into the jurisdiction of the Reclamation Service (now the Bureau of Reclamation) or by causing delinquencies, foreclosures, and land losses. The scale of the project favored commercial agricultural interests at the expense of the smaller family farms, such those owned by acequia irrigators. In his dissertation study of social organization in Doña Ana County some twenty years later, Sigurd Johansen found that "[m]any small Spanish-American farm owners lost their land. Instead of being farm owners, they either became farm tenants or laborers, usually farm laborers." Sigurd Johansen, *Rural Social Organization in a Spanish-American Culture Area* (Albuquerque, 1948), 26.

The Middle Río Grande project was located between White Rock Canyon, some forty-five miles north of Albuquerque, and San Marcial, about fifteen miles south of Socorro. For the project to succeed, acequia water users would have to relinquish control of their irrigation canals and submit to a conservancy district with vast administrative and taxation powers. Prior to the formation of the district in 1928, approximately seventy-two community ditches had been irrigating much of the valley's bottomlands. By 1936, the district had completed the bulk of the construction projects of diversion dams, canals, and siphons. Some lateral canals were new, but almost half of them, 214 miles of laterals, were incorporated from the acequia systems in the valley. Management of these community systems shifted to district officials in Albuquerque. Power struggles ensued in some areas when acequia officials challenged the supervisory authority of the district. But, as happened at Elephant Butte, hundreds of traditional farmers with small tracts eventually lost their lands due to delinquencies when it came to pay the assessments. See Clark, *Water in New Mexico;* Hugh Calkins, *Reconnaissance Survey of Human Dependency on Resources in the Río Grande Watershed* (Albuquerque, 1936); Stanley Phillippi, "Middle Río Grande Conservancy District," WPA Records—Conservation, Mining, Timber, Irrigation, Folder 130, SANM, 1937.

41. New Mexico Water Code, Laws of 1907, sections 58 and 59, 75–8–1. Baxter seems to disagree with most scholars concerning the impact of the code on acequias. Most historians and legal scholars credit the water code as safeguarding the rights of acequia senior rights that predated the code. Baxter, on the other hand, remains skeptical. In his interpretation, the Water Code of 1907 centralized water administration for the benefit of interests promoting growth and development, but at the expense of "Hispanos accustomed to traditional ways." As for the safeguards, he concludes that they were nothing more than dutiful "lip service," which "left large loopholes that were easily exploited by sharp operators." Baxter, *Dividing New Mexico's Waters*, 104.

42. See Robert E. Clark, "Water Rights Problems in the Upper Río Grande Watershed and Adjoining Areas," 11 *Natural Resources Journal* 1 (January 1971), 60–61. The 1909 law, N.M. Stat. Ann. 72–5–29, reads: "To the end that the waters of several stream systems of the state may be conserved and utilized so as to prevent erosion, waste and damage caused by torrential floods, and in order that the benefits of the use of such water may be distributed among the inhabitants and landowners of the country along said streams as equitably as possible without interfering with vested rights, the natural right of the people living in the upper valleys of the several stream systems to impound and utilize a reasonable share of the waters which are precipitated upon and have their source in such valleys and superadjacent mountains is hereby recognized, the exercise of such right, however, to be subject to the provisions of this article."

CHAPTER 4

1. See *Candelaria* v. *Vallejos*, c 1905; *Snow* v. *Abalos*, 1914; Attorney General Opinions No. 3432 and 63–112, February 21, 1940, and August 28, 1963, respectively. All are cited or excerpted in *Report of the Attorney General of New Mexico*, 2 vols. (Santa Fe, 1963–64), 1:247–52.

2. Laws of 1903, section 3, chapter 32, March 11.

3. Simmons, "Spanish Irrigation Practices," 141.

4. Hutchins, "Community Acequias or Ditches in New Mexico," 233.

5. Ibid., 233.

6. Simmons, "Spanish Irrigation Practices," 141 and 148 n. 36. Simmons describes this rare document: *Lista de los Dueños de Terreno Bajo el Regadío de la Asequia Nueva del Chamisal y Sus Medidos*, ca. 1845, Misc. Papers, Archives of the Archdiocese of Santa Fe.

7. Consult the acequia materials archive, José A. Rivera Collection, *Papers*

1982–1994, No. MSS 587BC, and companion photoarchive No. 000-587, Center for Southwest Research, Zimmerman Library, University of New Mexico, Albuquerque. Also, see the Belen Ditch Papers, Río Grande Historial Collection/Hobson-Huntsinger University Archives, New Mexico State University, Las Cruces, and the Phil Lovato Papers, Kit Carson Memorial Foundation, Taos.

8. See "Notes and Documents," 34 *New Mexico Historical Review* 4 (October 1959), 307.

9. The minutes of February 27, 1922, for the Corrales Ditch show an actual enforcement of this rule. In this case, four prominent irrigators had failed to clean out the *enfrentes* or ditch frontages on their properties, per a complaint filed with the commissioners by the *mayordomo*. The commissioners ruled that the transgressors would not be permitted to irrigate their fields without the permission of the *mayordomo*, presumably after they dutifully cleaned out their *enfrentes*.

10. Glick, *Irrigation and Society in Medieval Valencia*, 48–51.

11. Ruth Behar, *Santa María del Monte: The Presence of the Past in a Spanish Village* (Princeton, 1986), 168–69.

12. See Phil Lovato, *Las Acequias del Norte*, Technical Report No. 1, Four Corners Regional Commission (Taos, 1974); and Luis Torres, *The Acequia Bylaws Handbook*, Southwest Research and Information Center (Albuquerque, April 1986).

13. See Yan Tang, *Institutions and Collective Action;* Daniel W. Bromley, "The Commons, Property, and Common-Property Regimes," in Bromley, *Making the Commons Work.*

14. David Kammer, "National Register of Historic Places Inventory – Nomination Form," Office of Cultural Affairs, New Mexico Historic Preservation Division (Santa Fe, 1986).

15. Consult the Río Grande Historical Collection/Hobson-Huntsinger University Archives, New Mexico State University Library, Las Cruces, N.M. Also, consult the records office of the Middle Río Grande Conservancy District, Albuquerque, N.M.

16. Herbert W. Yeo, "Report on Irrigation Water Supply of the Río Grande and Its Tributaries in New Mexico" (Santa Fe, 1910).

17. The written agreement between the Los Lentes and Belen ditches is on file at the Middle Río Grande Conservancy District (hereafter cited as MRGCD), Albuquerque, as well as agreements with MRGCD itself from 1935 to the early 1950s.

CHAPTER 5

1. *Snow v. Abalos*, 18 N.M. 681, 140 Pac. 1044 (1914), cited and excerpted in *Report of the Attorney General of New Mexico* (1963–64), 248–49.

2. *Candelaria v. Vallejos*, 13 N.M. 146, 81 Pac. 589 (1905), cited and excerpted in *Report of the Attorney General of New Mexico* (1963–64), 250–51.

3. New Mexico Constitution, Article VIII, Sec. 3, cited in *Report of the Attorney General of New Mexico* (1963–64), 250.

4. See Attorney General Opinions No. 63–112, August 28, 1963, and 3432, February 21, 1940, excerpted in *Report of the Attorney General of New Mexico* (1963–64), 247–52.

5. Ibid., 249.

6. Laws of 1965, chapter 145, 73-2-28.

7. Laws of 1965, chapter 183, 73-2-22.

8. Water Resources Development Act of 1986, PL 99–662, 99th Congress, Section 1113.

9. Ibid.

10. Executive Order No. 88–06, January 1988.

11. See *1996 Annual Report*, State Engineer Office/Interstate Stream Commission, July 1, 1995–June 30, 1996, 47.

12. The Laws of 1993 provided the Acequia Commission with permanent status, retaining in statute its initial advisory duties, and requiring it to meet "not less than quarterly and not more than once a month." See 73-2-65, chapter 293.

13. The mainstay program for ditch rehabilitation and soil conservation since 1961 has been the USDA Agricultural Stabilization and Conservation Program (ASCS Cost-Share), supplemented with design and engineering assistance provided by the Soil Conservation Service, now the USDA Natural Resources Conservation Service. Also, see the various grants-in-aid, low-interest loans and contracts financed through the Irrigation Works Construction Fund and other sources administered by the Interstate Stream Commission jointly with the Office of the State Engineer. These state sources most often are used to match the USDA program, along with the cost share provided by the local ditch associations. From 1964 to 1991, the ASCS program assisted about seven hundred acequia projects at a cost of approximately 15 million dollars. See *Acequias*, New Mexico State Engineer Office, June 1991, 17–19.

14. In his review of acequia bylaws in 1974, Phil Lovato reported that acequias were still being managed according to local customs, and even their adopted by-laws, when they became required by the state, were developed to reflect local needs and conditions. In his experience and according to sources he consulted for his study, Lovato indicated that "when the law does not state to the contrary, local customs and traditions prevail and will usually have the force of law." This interpretation is still prevalent among the acequia irrigators themselves, allowing them to operate with a fair amount of autonomy, as Lovato observed in 1974. See Lovato, *Las Acequias del Norte*, 40.

15. Sylvia Rodríguez, "Acequias, Resource Domains, and the Economic Future of the Río Arriba," paper presented at the Annual Meeting of National Association of Chicano Studies, El Paso (Apr. 11, 1986), 9.

16. Figures cited by Geoff Bryce, panelist at "The Role of the Acequias and Legal Issues Facing Them: A Roundtable," Annual Conference of the Western Social Sciences Association, Albuquerque (Apr. 23–26, 1997).

17. The El Llano Unit case history follows the accounts of two individuals who

were on site during most of the events described. Rosemary Horvath was the reporter from the *Rio Grande Sun* assigned to cover the project and its many controversies for a period of almost two years. Sue-Ellen Jacobs, on the other hand, was contracted by the Bureau of Reclamation to conduct a preliminary social-impact study of the project while it was in the late planning stages, the period of local opposition. Both observers ultimately published their accounts of the case. See Rosemary Horvath, "Velarde and the Llano Canal: A Case Study of Community Action," 1 *La Confluencia* 1 (1976); Sue-Ellen Jacobs, "Top-Down Planning: Analysis of Obstacles to Community Development in an Economically Poor Region of the Southwestern United States," 37 *Human Organization* 3 (Fall 1978).

18. Horvath, "Velarde and the Llano Canal," 13–14; Jacobs, "Top-Down Planning," 251.

19. Horvath, "Velarde and the Llano Canal," 15; Jacobs, "Top-Down Planning," 251.

20. Horvath, "Velarde and the Llano Canal," 14; Jacobs, "Top-Down Planning," 249.

21. Jacobs, "Top-Down Planning," 252.

22. Horvath, "Velarde and the Llano Canal," 14.

23. Jacobs, "Top-Down Planning," 252–53.

24. Ibid., 250.

25. Horvath, "Velarde and the Llano Canal," 16.

26. See ibid., 16–17.

27. The Indian Camp Dam case history is based on the accounts described by diverse sources, some of whom were eyewitnesses or participants, while others analyzed the events later on: Tres Ríos Association, "Conservancy District Position Paper" (Taos, 1976); John Nichols, *If Mountains Die: A New Mexico Memoir* (New York, 1979); Andrés Martínez, Testimony, "Record of Hearing on New Mexico Acequias by United States Senator Pete V. Domenici" (Santa Fe, NM, Jan. 7, 1980); C. Lynn Reynolds, "Economic Decision-Making: The Influence of Traditional Hispanic Land Use Attitudes on Acceptance of Innovation," 13 *Social Science Journal* 3 (October 1976); and Sylvia Rodríguez, "Land, Water, and Ethnic Identity in Taos," in Charles L. Briggs and John R. Van Ness, *Land, Water, and Culture: New Perspectives on Hispanic Land Grants* (Albuquerque, 1987), 313–403.

28. Nichols, *If Mountains Die*, attributing remarks to the Bureau of Reclamation and the Office of the State Engineer, 121.

29. Ibid.

30. Reynolds, "Economic Decision-Making," 25.

31. Ibid., 26; Nichols, *If Mountains Die*, 121.

32. Reynolds, "Economic Decision-Making," 25–27; Tres Ríos Association, "Conservancy District Position Paper," 11–12.

33. Andrés Martínez, Testimony, in *Record of Hearing on New Mexico Acequias by United States Senator Pete V. Domenici*, Santa Fe (Jan. 7, 1980), 1.

34. Tres Ríos Association, "Conservancy District Position Paper," 1.

35. Ibid.

36. Nichols, *If Mountains Die*, 129.

37. Rodríguez, "Land, Water and Ethnic Identity in Taos," 353–54. Some observers, including Rodríguez, attribute the emergence of acequia coalition organizations directly to the protests mobilized against the El Llano Unit, Indian Camp Dam, and the barrage of other condominium, resort, and ski-lodge projects that would appear in different parts of the upper Río Grande through the rest of the twentieth century. Per Rodríguez, each local acequia delineates "a bounded, self-identified resource domain coextensive with the village or community it serves." As such, acequias empower rural Hispanos to protest real estate developments and other threats to cultural survival and community self-determination. See Sylvia Rodríguez, "The Hispano Homeland Debate Revisited," 3 *Perspectives in Mexican-American Studies* (University of Arizona, 1992), 95–114.

38. For a full account of the Valdez "Condo War," see Rodríguez, "Land, Water and Ethnic Identity in Taos," 362–81. Only a summation is presented here.

39. Ibid., 367–68.

40. Ibid., 356.

41. Ibid., 368–69.

42. Ibid., 370–71.

43. Ibid., 379.

44. See DuMars and Minnis, "New Mexico Water Law," 824–26; F. Lee Brown and José A. Rivera, "The Southwest: Global Issues in a Regional Setting," in *National Rural Studies Committee: A Proceedings*, Las Vegas, N.M., (May 14–16, 1992), 33–34.

45. Judge Art Encinias, Division V/First Judicial District, *In the Matter of Howard Sleeper et al.*, Rio Arriba County Cause No. RA 84–53 (C), Apr. 16, 1985.

46. N.M. Stat Ann. 72–5–23 (Michie 1978, Repl. Pamp. 1985 and Cum. Supp. 1996) (Appropriation and Use of Surface Water).

47. For a review of how the public-welfare criterion developed in western United States water law and how such a requirement could be defined more explicitly by the State Engineer's Office in New Mexico, see Consuelo Bokum's proposed public-welfare regulation outlined in her article, "Implementing the Public Welfare Requirement in New Mexico's Water Code," 36 *Natural Resources Journal* 4 (Fall 1996). Also, see related issues in Charles T. DuMars, "Changing Interpretations of New Mexico's Constitutional Provisions Allocating Water Resources: Integrating Private Property Rights and Public Values," 26 *New Mexico Law Review* (Summer 1996).

48. For a more complete account of the Pecos River water-transfer case, see José A. Rivera, "The Acequias of New Mexico and the Public Welfare," Research Report No. 008, Southwest Hispanic Research Institute (Spring 1996); and Rivera, "Irrigation Communities of the Upper Río Grande Bioregion."

49. José A. Rivera, Field Notes, Interview of Ditch and Land Grant Officials (La Loma Community Center, July 23, 1994).

50. *The New Mexican*, Aug. 31, 1994, B3.

51. See "Status of Adjudications," 1995–96 Annual Report, State Engineer Office/Interstate Stream Commission (July 1, 1995–June 30, 1996), 21–26.

52. Acequia and Community Ditch Fund Act, Sec. 73–2A–1 to 73–2A–3, NMSA 1978, Laws of 1988, chapter 157, sections 1–5.

53. For a review of the adjudication process and the use of anthropological and ethnohistorical evidence to support traditional water rights, see Frances Levine, "Dividing the Water: The Impact of Water Rights Adjudication on New Mexican Communities," 32 *Journal of the Southwest* 3 (Autumn 1990), and Levine, "Making a Place for Tradition in Land and Water Use Conflicts," paper presented at the Annual Conference of the Western Social Science Association, Albuquerque (Apr. 23–26, 1997).

54. Report of the Special Master, Frank B. Zinn, to the Honorable Santiago E. Campos, United States District Judge, July 23, 1993, in the matter of the State of New Mexico vs. Eduardo Abeyta, et. al., and Celso Arellano, et. al., CV. No. 7896 SC, Río Pueblo de Taos, and CV No. 7939 SC, Río Hondo, United States District Court for the District of New Mexico.

55. Affidavit in the United States District Court for the District of New Mexico, Exhibit 1, "Motion to Adjudicate Local or Community Customs of Water Division or Allocation Between and Among Acequias on the Río Lucero and Arroyo Seco," No. CIV-7896 SC and No. CIV-7939 SC, filed March 18, 1991.

56. Acequia Laws, 1851, and Kearny Code, 1848.

57. Affidavit in the United States District Court for the District of New Mexico, Exhibit 1.

58. *State of New Mexico* v. *Eduardo Abeyta and Celso Arellano et al.*, testimony of Expert Witness, Daniel Tyler, transcript, May 20, 1991, 18–102.

59. Ibid., 38–39, in reference to Tyler's report, "The Role of Hispanic Custom in Defining New Mexican Land and Water Rights" (May 1991), Defendant's Exhibit, Acequias No. 3. Also, see Daniel Tyler, "The Spanish Colonial Legacy and the Role of Hispanic Custom in Defining New Mexico Land and Water Rights," 4 *Colonial Latin American Historical Review* 2 (Spring 1995, 149–65).

60. Ibid., testimony of Candido Valerio, transcript, May 20, 1991, 109.

61. Ibid., testimony of Juan I. Valerio, transcript, May 20, 1991, 119–20.

62. Ibid., testimony of Esequiel Trujillo, transcript, May 20, 1991, 233.

63. Ibid., testimony of Palemón Martínez, transcript, May 21, 1991, 25.

64. Ibid., testimony of Expert Witness, Carlos Miera, transcript, May 21, 1991, 96–98.

65. These latter points were raised in an unpublished paper by David Benavides, "Problem Outline Regarding Water Distribution Customs," Public Administration 551, University of New Mexico, Jan. 10, 1991.

66. *State of New Mexico* v. *Eduardo Abeyta and Celso Arellano et al.*, testimony of Elías Espinosa, transcript, June 11, 1991, 26–27.

67. Report of the Special Master, Frank B. Zinn, July 23, 1993, 23. The 72–9–2

NMSA 1978 statute reads: "In all cases where local or community customs, rules and regulations have been adopted and are in force . . . and are not detrimental to the public welfare, . . . such rules and regulations shall govern the distribution of water from such ditches . . . and such customs, rules and regulations shall not be molested or changed . . . if they do not impair the authority of the state to regulate the distribution of water."

68. Stipulations on behalf of the State of New Mexico, Charlotte Benson Crossland, transcript, May 20, 1991, 15–17.

69. See Stipulations Between New Mexico and Certain Community Ditches Regarding Declarations of Customary Allocations of Water Between and Among Acequias, Nov. 22, 1993; Joint Motion, Nov. 22, 1993; and Order Adopting Stipulation, Dec. 3, 1993.

70. Fred J. Waltz, personal communication, October 17, 1997.

71. See, for example, an acequia report by José A. Rivera that addresses the theme of resource and community sustainability: "Acequias of New Mexico and the Public Welfare (Spring 1996)." The next section of the text highlights some of the points contained in this report.

72. See, in particular, John R. Van Ness, "Hispanic Land Grants: Ecology and Subsistence in the Uplands of Northern New Mexico and Southern Colorado," in Briggs and Van Ness, *Land, Water and Culture*; and Carlson, *Spanish-American Homeland: Four Centuries in New Mexico's Rio Arriba*.

73. For the Great Depression and the New Deal era, see Suzanne Forest, *The Preservation of the Village: New Mexico's Hispanics and the New Deal* (Albuquerque, 1989).

CHAPTER 6

1. David F. Arguello, "*Sobreviviendo los Cambios*," remarks at the Third Annual Retreat, NEH Upper Río Grande Hispano Farms Study, August 1996, Colorado College at the Baca Ranch.

2. Ibid.

3. David F. Arguello, Geoff Bryce, Elías Espinoza, and Charlie López, "The Role of the Acequias and Legal Issues Facing Them: A Roundtable," Annual Conference of the Western Social Sciences Association, Albuquerque (April 23–26, 1997).

4. Arguello, "*Sobreviviendo los Cambios*."

5. Ibid.

6. Ibid.

7. Posted sign authorized by the commissioners of the Acequia de San Antonio, Valdez, N.M. See pp. 202–3 for full text of sign.

8. See Rivera, "Irrigation Communities of the Upper Río Grande Bioregion." The presentation here as well as the section on keystone communities is based on this source.

9. The bias against acequias is not coincident only to the modern period when

competition for a depleting quantity of water has pitted stakeholder against stakeholder. During the territorial period, prominent politicians, farmer-stockmen, irrigation engineers, and promoters who presented testimony to a U.S. Senate committee on irrigation in 1890 all agreed that the community acequia still dominated the Río Grande, but that it had changed little over many generations while perpetuating primitive and wasteful methods. Reported in Clark, *Water in New Mexico*, 67–68. Later, a WPA report, prepared by a MRGCD engineer, described the formation of the Middle Rio Grande Conservancy District. This 1937 document opined that the community ditches absorbed by the district pretty much deserved the termination fate they received: "The irrigation of the valley was carried through about 72 independent community ditches, many of them built by the Indians prior to the coming of the Spaniards, and many of the others were built as community ditches in a hit and miss fashion in the centuries following, each operating independently of all others, with no person or one authority to control the distribution of waters of the river, each ditch taking what it could or wanted, resulting not only in woeful waste but much trouble." Stanley Phillippi, "WPA Records – Conservation, Mining, Timber, Irrigation," Folder 130, State Records Center and Archives, Santa Fe, N.M.

10. In an impact assessment commissioned by the New Mexico Office of Cultural Affairs, a private marketing firm and other consultants found that "New Mexico cultural resources as a whole represent a major industry in the State," accounting for direct expenditures of 292 million dollars and total economic impacts of 1.6 billion dollars annually. Among the top ten reasons respondents gave for their visits to New Mexico, scenic beauty, Indian culture, historic sites, and Hispanic culture ranked first, second, third, and sixth, respectively. *See New Mexico Cultural Resources Impact Assessment*, State of New Mexico Office of Cultural Affairs (Santa Fe, 1995), 8, 33.

11. Frederic O. Sargent, Paul Lusk, José A. Rivera, and María Varela, *Rural Environmental Planning for Sustainable Communities* (Washington, 1991), 63, 181–83.

12. National Research Council, *Water Transfers in the West: Efficiency, Equity, and the Environment* (Washington, D.C., 1992), 162, 175.

13. This suggestion is based on the United States Supreme Court ruling that federal reservations of land are entitled to water-supply quantities sufficient to fulfill the purposes for which the reservations were initially established. The priority date for each of these "federally reserved rights," as they are called, is the date of the reservation. See *Winters v. United States*, 207 U.S. 564, 577 (1908).

14. Article VIII, Treaty of Guadalupe Hidalgo, Treaty of Peace, Friendship, Limits and Settlement with the Republic of Mexico, Feb. 2, 1848, 9 STAT, 922 (1848).

15. DuMars opined that "[in] 1848, in the Treaty of Guadalupe Hidalgo, the United States pledged itself to protect the property rights, including water rights, of Mexican citizens." Charles T. DuMars, "New Mexico Water Law: An Overview and Discussion of Current Issues," 22 *Natural Resources Journal* 4 (October 1982),

1060. In a special report addressing the scope of the treaty, historian Michael Meyer concluded that it is "abundantly clear" that water rights "were protected prior to, at the time of and following the Mexican cession." Since water rights were property rights under Spanish colonial and Mexican law, he argues, the water rights of acequia communities, among other entitled users, enjoy full protection under the terms of the treaty. Meyer, "New Mexico's Hispanic Water Regimen." During the custom and tradition hearings held in 1991, the state of New Mexico conceded that "Article 8 of the Treaty of Guadalupe Hidalgo protects water rights which were valid under the prior sovereigns of Spain and Mexico as of 1846." See p. 170 of this book.

16. Reed F. Noss, "A Sustainable Forest Is a Diverse and Natural Forest," in Bill DeVall, ed., *Clearcut: The Tragedy of Industrial Forestry* (San Francisco, 1994), 37.

17. Devón Peña and Rubén Martínez, co-principal investigators, "Upper Río Grande Hispano Farms Study", research project supported by a grant from the National Endowment for the Humanities, Interpretative and Collaborative Research Projects Division, Grant No. RO–22707–94, Colorado College, 1994–1998.

18. Rodríguez, "Land, Water, and Ethnic Identity in Taos," 356.

19. Some western states have enacted statutory area-of-origin protections aimed at curbing the transfer of water rights from rural communities to urban centers. The premise behind these provisions is that the transfer of water rights to the larger municipalities can trigger costly social and economic impacts in the areas of origin from where the water is taken. Moreover, out-of-area transfers will deprive these impacted communities from conserving or recapturing water for their own future growth, expansion, and economic development. For a review of these laws, see Susanne Hoffman-Dooley, "Preventing Urban Thirst from Wilting Rural Economies: Area of Origin Protection in the Western United States," unpublished paper, University of New Mexico, Advanced Water Law, Spring 1996. From the published literature she cites, among other sources, Lawrence J. MacDonnell and Teresa A. Rice, "Moving Agricultural Water to Cities: The Search for Smarter Approaches," 2 Hastings W-N.W., *Environmental Law and Policy* 27 (1994).

20. See discussion of these codes and laws in Chapter 3 of this text. Hoffman-Dooley views the 1909 law as an early type of "area-of-origin" statute in New Mexico water law that has relevance to contemporary conditions in the uplands region of the state: "The statute recognizes a right of the people living in the upper valleys of stream systems to impound and utilize water which has its origin in these valleys." Her interpretation is that the intent of the legislation in 1909 was to alleviate any fear that "increasing downstream uses of water would impair the rights of Spanish land grantees and their heirs" in the future. She acknowledges, however, that there is no reported case law to test the ability of this provision to protect area-of-origin water transfers. Hoffman-Dooley, "Preventing Urban Thirst from Wilting Rural Economies," 42–44.

21. Rivera, "Acequias of New Mexico and the Public Welfare" (Spring 1996), 57. For an application of the restoration-fund model, see Gregory A. Thomas, "Con-

serving Aquatic Biodiversity: A Critical Comparison of Legal Tools for Augment-ing Stream Flows in California," 15 *Stanford Environmental Law Journal* 1 (January 1996), 45–52. According to this source, the federal government levies fees on trans-actions that transfer Central Valley Project water in California from agricultural to urban uses, thus creating a restoration fund which the Secretary of Interior can then use to augment California's aquatic biodiversity.

22. See the NMAA membership brochure and the newsletter, *!Acequia!*, New Mexico Acequia Association, Vol. 1, No. 1, February 1997.

23. Nacasio Romero, President, New Mexico Acequia Association, remarks at the Water *Plática* Series, Nov. 21, 1996, School of Architecture and Planning, Uni-versity of New Mexico. Also, see "Intel Water Purchase Plan Sparks Widespread Opposition," SWOP *Community Update*, Southwest Organizing Project, (Spring 1997), 1.

24. Río de las Gallinas Acequias Association, Acequia Curriculum Project, pro-posal to Center for Regional Studies, University of New Mexico, March 28, 1996.

25. See Rivera, "Irrigation Communities of the Upper Río Grande Bioregion," 750–60, for a range of possible action strategies that local, regional, and state as-sociations may want to consider. The presentation here includes some of these ini-tiatives and is based on this source.

26. Laws of 1987, 73–2–22.1, chapter 352, section 1.

27. Laws of 1991, chapter 102.

28. Estevan Arellano, remarks at the Water *Plática* Series, Nov. 21, 1996. In ad-dition, Arellano participated as one of the family farms in the Hispano Family Farms Project cited earlier. His farm at Embudo serves as a demonstration farm for permaculture and organic-farmimg techniques suitable to acequia irrigation and the cultivation of traditional crops for specialized market niches.

29. For suggested approaches, see Neal W. Ackerly, *A Review of the Historic Significance of and Management Recommendations for Preserving New Mexico's Acequia Systems*, New Mexico State Historic Preservation Division (Santa Fe, 1996), 138–68.

30. N.M. Statutes Annotated 1953, 75–14–7. The ownership of the ditches was first established in the territorial period; see Laws of 1882, ch. 30, sec. 1 or C.L. 1884, sec. 15.

31. For techniques to preserve critical natural areas and other valued sites, see Samuel N. Stokes et. al., for the National Trust for Historic Preservation, *Saving America's Countryside: A Guide to Rural Conservation* (Baltimore, 1989).

32. Since 1995, the Costilla County Board of Commissioners has been consid-ering a draft resolution intended to safeguard watersheds above eight-thousand-foot elevations against adverse land use impacts from development that might threaten the forest canopies. Though the proposal has been controversial, the com-missioners continue to hold public hearings and are hopeful of its eventual passage and the subsequent revisions to the county's land-use code. See draft resolution no. 95–100 published in *La Sierra* newspaper, San Luis, Colorado, June 23, 1995.

33. Devón Peña, "Cultural Landscapes and Biodiversity: The Ethnoecology of an Upper Río Grande Watershed Commons," paper presented at Conference on Ethnoecology, Ethnoecology and Biodiversity Laboratory, University of Georgia, April 7–8, 1995, 3. Other impacts of industrial logging and road building include habitat loss, fragmentation of the forest ecosystem, and diminished water quality. See Robert Curry, Michael Soulé, Devón Peña, and Michael McGowan, "Critical Analysis of Montana Best Management Practices and Sustainable Alternatives," consultant's report submitted to the Costilla County Land Use Planning Commission (Oct. 31, 1996), 3–6. The report claims that extractive industrial uses of forest resources generate fewer jobs in the long run when compared to forest-management alternatives such as recreational, educational, agricultural, and scientific uses (26–27). Also, see appendix 1 of the report, "Proposed Revisions to Article 111, Division 2 of the Costilla County Land Use Code: Integrating Environmental and Economic Values for Watershed Protection," 19–5.

34. In 1997, for example, Representative Gary King of Moriarty, N.M., sponsored a bill to designate "unique stream waters" in the state with "exceptional recreational or ecological significance" or to be home to threatened and endangered species. If enacted, state water-quality scientists would develop more stringent rules against projects that would increase the load of sediments or other pollutants in any of the ten proposed unique water streams from the upper Río Grande to the headwaters of the Santa Fe River and the West Fork of the Gila River. See "Rules Posed for 'Unique Waters,'" *Albuquerque Journal North*, Feb. 27, 1997, 1 and 3.

35. Worster, *Rivers of Empire*, 5.

Acequia Glossary

NOTE: The glossary terms span three or more periods of usage in the upper Río Grande region of northern New Mexico and southern Colorado. Not all acequia terms or shades of meaning were included; priority was given to terms and definitions that assist the reader with the understanding of the terms as they appear in this book by historical period and in context. Thus, the glossary definitions were derived from the many sources, primary and secondary, that were consulted, including the acequia organizationl papers and documents. When useful, the terms are qualified to identify the historical period in question or simply to distinguish them from the definitions now in use during the contemporary period. For the most part, the terms are defined broadly for the general reading audience and are not meant to be taken as conclusive, legal descriptions applicable to all cases or situations. Also, some meanings can vary not only across historical periods but also by locality according to community practices and the customs of each acequia.

ACEQUIA   A ditch or community irrigation canal. Can also refer to the ditch association in a community. Locally, the term is often pronounced as *"cequia,"* as was the spelling in medieval Valencia, Spain, where the irrigation manager was called the *"cequier"* and the mother canal the *"cequia mare."*

ACEQUIA MADRE   Literally means "Mother Ditch." The *acequia madre* is the main irrigation canal cut at one end of a community to carry water downstream along the foothills or slope enclosing the fields until it empties back into the river source at the lower end of the community.

ACEQUIA MANCOMÚN   A common property ditch or *"acequia de común"* made up of all land owners irrigating from a single canal.

ADJUDICACIÓN DE AGUAS   The contemporary adjudication of water rights through a formal court proceeding that determines priority dates and the ownership of legal water rights in a stream and other related matters.

AGUAS SOBRANTES   Surplus, excess, or leftover water.

ANCÓN   A terrace to irrigate small parcels of land with slopes, such as those along the banks of a stream.

ARRENDAMIENTO DE DERECHOS DE AGUA   The leasing of water rights. *Arrendatarios de tierras* are farmers holding leases on irrigated lands.

ASIGNACIÓN   Assignment or allocation of labor requirements to clean and maintain a ditch.

ATARQUE   A temporary dam built across a river to divert water into the *acequia madre*. Traditionally, they are built of juniper brush, rocks, logs, and other local materials and resemble large beaver dams.

AUXILIO   The custom of one ditch allowing some of its own share of stream waters to be diverted and used by a nearby ditch during periods of drought or specific emergency need.

BORDO   A mound of earth along a furrow to contain irrigation water within a section of a field. Also refers to the earthen embankment on each side of an acequia.

CAÑO   An enclosed tubular cylinder used in the same manner as a *canoa*. This type of flume is usually made of metal or wood planks tied together.

CANOA   A hand-hewn flume cut out of a large log designed to carry acequia water across an arroyo.

COMISIÓN   The commission or governing body of an acequia association. Made up of three members — president, treasurer, and secretary — *comisionados* convene meetings, establish rules and policies, determine fees and fines, resolve disputes among the irrigators, and generally conduct the business affairs of the acequia. They are elected biennially by the irrigators. Prior to 1987, they were elected on an annual basis.

COMPUERTA   The headgate used to release and regulate water flow from the stream into the *acequia madre*. The main headgate also marks the point of diversion where water is taken from the stream source, described in historical documents as the "*toma de agua*," meaning the mouth of the ditch at the point of intake, or the "*saca de acequia*."

CONCILIACIÓN   A customary process used widely during the Mexican period to settle ditch disputes informally rather than going to a formal trial. Also see *hombre buenos*.

CONTRA ACEQUIA   A "counter" ditch cut from a larger irrigation canal to divert water to a pasture or another plot of land.

CUBO   A small gate or valve used to turn irrigation water onto the fields.

CUOTAS   The water fees, dues, or taxes assessed of each irrigator to remain in good standing and enjoy the benefits of the ditch system. Funds collected by way of these taxes are used to pay for maintenance, repairs, and other operating expenses. Also called *impuestos*.

DELINCUENCIA   A fine imposed on an irrigator who fails to show up at the annual ditch cleanings enabling the *mayordomo* to hire *peones* who will substitute for the *parciante*.

DERECHOS DE AGUA   The water rights owned by the irrigator.

DESAGÜE   A small channel or outlet used to drain *aguas sobrantes* or surplus waters. Also refers to excess waters that flow back into the river at the lower end of the ditch.

ENFRENTE   Frontage sides of the *acequia madre*.

ENTRAMPE   A blockage inside the ditch that needs to be cleared and removed.

ESCREPA   A mule-drawn scoop used in the construction or cleaning of irrigation ditches; also called a *fresno*, especially when used for field leveling. Comes from the English "scraper."

ESCURRIDURAS   Excess water running off a field, usually due to a slope or natural drainage; often, adjacent fields are irrigated in the process.

ESTANQUE   A small earthen tank of water used to retain irrigation water, as in a stock tank or reservoir pond. Sometimes shortened to "*tanque*."

FAENA or FAINA   From "work" or "labor," a work assignment received by a member during the cleaning of the ditch.

FATIGA   Ditch work or fatigue labor, especially during the spring cleaning.

FIANZA   A bond issued by a mutual insurance company to indemnify a ditch association against the loss of money or property through any misconduct on the part of the officers. New Mexico law requires the bonding of the officials who receive and administer ditch funds, the treasurer and the *mayordomo*.

HOMBRES BUENOS   Literally, "good and honest men" who assisted the *alcalde* in arriving at a fair settlement when two irrigators had a dispute of one kind or another. Each disputant usually named an *hombre bueno* to represent his interests in the matter at hand.

HOMBRES PERITOS   "Expert men" or sages who helped the *juez de pruebas* (probate judge) and other officials evaluate and resolve local acequia disputes.

JARDÍN   A family garden usually located adjacent to or near the home. Traditionally, ditch waters were reserved for the watering of *jardines* once a week, usually on Sundays.

MANCOMUNIDAD   A loose, voluntary association formed by the irrigators who constructed and then shared a common ditch in the early stages of community settlement. *Mancomunidades* were the forerunners of the acequia associations recognized and empowered later during the territorial period as corporate bodies.

MAYORDOMO   The ditch boss or superintendent elected by the acequia irrigators to manage the day-to-day affairs of the ditch system, from overseeing the spring cleaning to allocating waters throughout the irrigation season according to the established set of rules, customs, and acequia laws.

MOLINO   A grist mill along a river or ditch used for grinding corn, wheat, and other grains. They were very common during earlier periods of acequia history.

NORIA   A well dug to appropriate underground water, whether for domestic use or irrigation.

OJO   A natural spring. Some acequias are fed by way of natural springs in whole or in part.

PARCIANTE   A member of the acequia association. This contemporary term derives from the partitioning of land and water rights. In the acequia records of New Mexico, ditch users are self-described as: *porciantes, propietarios, parcionistas, parcioneros, regadores, usadores de agua, dueños de propiedad regable, vecinos,* or simply *asociados.*

PEÓN   A substitute worker sent to fill in for an absent *parciante* during the annual ditch cleaning in order to avoid paying the *delincuencia* or fine. *Piones* refers to shares of irrigation ditch water.

PRESA   A dam built on the stream in order to divert waters into the *acequia madre*. A *presa* is larger and usually more permanent than an *atarque*, although the terms are used interchangeably.

PROPIETARIOS   Landowners who are entitled to water rights on the acequia system. They form the general membership and own the acequia watercourse in common, hence the phrase "*acequia de común.*"

RAYADOR   From r*ayar*, to draw a line. The *rayador* is the individual who marks off the sections of a ditch into *tareas* or *tequios* during the annual cleaning.

REGADÍO   From the Spanish verb, "*regar*," to irrigate. *Regadío* is a section of farmland that is irrigated.

REGLAS   The rules or regulations of a ditch association that govern all matters pertaining to the ditch system. Ditch rules spell out the common benefits and obligations of the irrigators and are essential to the system of direct democracy and self-government.

REPARTIMIENTO DE AGUA   The partitioning or dividing of waters between ditches that share the same stream or among the *parciantes* within a single acequia. A *reparto* is the local process of dividing the waters, usually quantified into fractions or percentages of total available water. Other ditches divide the use of water according to weekly schedules of designated turns and cycles of rotation.

SACAR LA ACEQUIA   To clean out the ditch in the spring, just before the start of the irrigation season. Sometimes described as "*la limpia de la acequia*," "*el día de la saca*," or "*la saca de la acequia.*" The phrase, "*sacar la acequia*," was also used in historical documents to describe the initial digging or construction of a ditch starting at the point of diversion from the stream source. See also *compuerta* and *toma de agua*.

SANGRÍA   A lateral ditch cut perpendicular from the *acequia madre* to irrigate individual plots of land. *Sangría* is usually translated into English as "bleeding" or "bloodletting"; thus, the many *sangrías* cut from the main ditch resemble a bloodletting when they are flowing with waters.

SOBRANTES   See *aguas sobrantes*.

SUERTES   A tract of land allocated to each petitioner in a community land grant for agricultural uses during the Spanish colonial and Mexican periods. Also, see *"tira."* In addition, petitioners received *solares* for their house lots.

SURCO   A *surco de agua* is a measurement of water used in irrigation. The measurement was determined by the amount of water that would flow through the hub of a Mexican cartwheel placed at the mouth of a ditch, roughly calculated to be about fifty-one gallons per minute.

TAPANCO   A small and temporary dam built on the spot, with a shovel, across a *sangria* or lateral ditch to flood a portion of the agricultural field by channeling it into the desired section.

TAREA   The work assignment or section of the ditch marked off by the *rayador* with a *vara* (staff) for each *parciante* to clean out. The sections are marked and cleaned in a rotation manner, usually in a downstream movement, until the entire ditch is cleaned out. Also, see *tequio.*

TASO or TASA   "Measure" or "rule," as in the measurement of water a *parciante* can use at a given time. Also, an assessment or tax levied, based on the number of acres irrigated by each *parciante* and usually expressed in costs per each day of *taso.*

TEQUIO   A long, premeasured stick used to mark off the sections of the ditch to be cleaned out by individual *parciantes.* Thus, a *tequio* can also mean a particular work section. See also *tarea.* In Spain, *tequio* is a general term for a public task performed by citizens, such as the repair of a road.

TIRA   A strip or long lot field measured in *varas.* This term has replaced the historic term *suertes* for the individual parcels assigned to land-grant petitioners.

VARA   The linear measurement roughly equivalent to the English yard, but contains thirty-three rather than thirty-six inches. Historically, the *vara* was the unit by which the width of individual long lots were measured when an *alcalde* conveyed a community grant to the petitioners and proceeded to divide the land into *suertes* or parcels.

VECINOS or VESINOS   A local term referring to all water users sharing the same ditch system. Also conveys the general meaning of neighbors or community citizens.

VEEDOR   An overseer, judge, or inspector usually appointed by an *alcalde mayor* during the colonial period to inspect agricultural fields and distribute water to the users when levels of stream waters were low.

VEGA   A meadow or pasture. Historically, the term referred to the common pasturelands included in a community grant, for use by all settlers for grazing their livestock.

VENAS   Meaning "blood veins," but referring to lateral ditches cut from the *acequia madre* to transport water to the irrigated fields. See also *sangrías.*

VUELTA LA OLLA   Literally, "turn the pot over," a signal to start a new section or tarea during ditch cleaning, much like the chain-gang method and process.

ZANJA   Generally a small ditch, trench, or drain. In California and other places, *zanjero* is the official in charge of ditch maintenance, similar to the role and responsibilities of the *mayordomo*. In the Philippines, a *zanjera* is at once the irrigation ditch and the organization, comparable to an acequia as a physical canal and as a water management institution.

SOURCES FOR GLOSSARY TERMS:

José A. Rivera and Anselmo Arellano, "Guidebook to Photo Exhibit: *Acequias y Sangrías*—The Course of New Mexico Waters," Southwest Hispanic Research Institute, University of New Mexico (1986)

Thomas F. Glick, *Irrigation and Society in Medieval Valencia* (Harvard Univerity Press, 1970)

Michael C. Meyer, *Water in the Hispanic Southwest: A Social and Legal History, 1550–1850* (University of Arizona Press, 1984)

David Kammer, *Report on the Historic Acequia Systems of the Upper Río Mora*, New Mexico Historic Preservation Division (1992)

John O. Baxter, *Dividing New Mexico's Waters, 1700–1912*, (University of New Mexico Press, 1997)

Malcolm Ebright, *Land Grants & Lawsuits in Northern New Mexico* (University of New Mexico Press, 1994)

Daniel Tyler, *The Mythical Pueblo Rights Doctrine: Water Administration in Hispanic New Mexico* (Texas Western Press, University of Texas at El Paso, 1990)

Selected Readings

The sources cited in the chapters of this book appear in the Notes section. Below is a listing of the more useful background works pertaining to acequia history and culture. The bibliography is not exhaustive and instead represents the acequia and closely related literature that is published and accessible to most readers. Published works devoted entirely to acequias are few, but the selected readings below feature acequias and the interdependence of water, land and community.

BOOKS

Baxter, John O. *Dividing New Mexico's Waters, 1700–1912*. Albuquerque: University of New Mexico Press, 1997.

Briggs, Charles L. and John R. Van Ness, eds. *Land, Water and Culture: New Perspectives on Hispanic Land Grants*. Albuquerque: University of New Mexico Press, 1987.

Brown, F. Lee, and Helen M. Ingram. *Water and Poverty in the Southwest*. Tucson: University of Arizona Press, 1987.

Carlson, Alvar W. *The Spanish-American Homeland: Four Centuries in New Mexico's Río Arriba*. Baltimore: Johns Hopkins University Press, 1990.

Clark, Ira G. *Water in New Mexico: A History of Its Management and Use*. Albuquerque: University of New Mexico Press, 1987.

Crawford, Stanley. *Mayordomo: Chronicle of an Acequia in Northern New Mexico*. Albuquerque: University of New Mexico Press, 1988.

deBuys, William, *Enchantment and Exploitation: The Life and Hard Times of a New Mexico Mountain Range*. Albuquerque: University of New Mexico Press, 1985.

DuMars, Charles T., and Marilyn O'Leary and Albert E. Utton. *Pueblo Indian Water Rights: Struggle for a Precious Resource.* Tucson: University of Arizona Press, 1984.

Ebright, Malcolm. *Land Grants and Lawsuits in Northern New Mexico.* Albuquerque: University of New Mexico Press, 1994.

LaFarge, Oliver. *The Mother Ditch: La Acequia Madre.* Santa Fe: Sunstone Press, 1983.

Meyer, Michael C. *Water in the Hispanic Southwest: A Social and Legal History, 1550–1850.* Tucson: University of Arizona Press, 1984.

MONOGRAPHS AND REPORTS

Ackerly, Neal W. *A Review of the Historic Significance of and Management Recommendations for Preserving New Mexico's Acequia Systems.* Santa Fe: New Mexico Historic Preservation Division, 1996.

Baxter, John O. *Spanish Irrigation in the Pojoaque and Tesuque Valleys During the Eighteenth and Early Nineteenth Centuries.* A Study Prepared for the New Mexico State Engineer Office. Santa Fe, 1984.

Baxter, John O. *Spanish Irrigation in Taos Valley.* A Study Prepared for the New Mexico State Engineer Office. Santa Fe, 1990.

Glick, Thomas F. *The Old World Background of the Irrigation System of San Antonio, Texas.* El Paso: University of Texas, Texas Western Press, Southwestern Studies Series No. 35, 1972.

Lovato, Phil. *Las Acequias del Norte.* Technical Report No. 1, Four Corners Regional Commission, 1974. (Reprinted by the State Engineer Office, Santa Fe, NM)

Tyler, Daniel. *The Mythical Pueblo Rights Doctrine: Water Administration in Hispanic New Mexico.* El Paso: University of Texas, Texas Western Press, Southwestern Studies Series, No. 91, 1990.

Upper Río Grande Working Group. *The Course of Upper Río Grande Waters: A Declaration of Concerns,* December 1985. (Conference report reprinted by the Southwest Hispanic Research Institute, University of New Mexico, Albuquerque, NM)

Upper Río Grande Working Group. *Upper Río Grande Waters: Strategies/A Conference on Traditional Water Use,* Fall 1987. (Conference report reprinted by the Southwest Hispanic Research Institute, University of New Mexico, Albuquerque, NM)

Wilson, Chris and David Kammer. *Community and Continuity: The History, Architecture and Cultural Landscape of La Tierra Amarilla.* Santa Fe: New Mexico Historic Preservation Division, 1989.

ARTICLES AND BOOK CHAPTERS

Arellano, Juan Estevan. "*La Querencia: La Raza* Bioregionalism." 72 *New Mexico Historical Review* 1 (Jan. 1997), 31–37.

Crossland, Charlotte Benson, "Acequia Rights in Law and Tradition." 32 *Journal of the Southwest* 3 (Autumn 1990), 278–87.

Ford, Richard I. "The Technology of Irrigation in a New Mexico Pueblo." In Heather Lechtman and Robert S. Merrill, eds., *Material Culture: Styles, Organization and Dynamics of Technology*. St. Paul: West Publishing Co., 1977.

Hutchins, Wells. "The Community Acequia: Its Origins and Development." 31 *Southwestern Historical Quarterly* (July 1927–April 1928), 261–84.

Jacobs, Sue-Ellen. "Top-Down Planning: Analysis of Obstacles to Community Development in an Economically Poor Region of the Southwestern United States." 37 *Human Organization* 3 (Fall 1978), 246–56.

Levine, Frances. "Dividing the Water: The Impact of Water Rights Adjudication on New Mexican Communities." 32 *Journal of the Southwest* 3 (Autumn 1990), 268–77.

Meyer, Michael C. "The Legal Relationship of Land to Water in Northern Mexico and the Hispanic Southwest." 60 *New Mexico Historical Review* 1 (Jan. 1985), 61–79.

Peña, Devón. "Cultural Landscapes and Biodiversity: The Ethnoecology of a Watershed Commons." In Vincent Cabeza de Baca, ed., *Hispanic Life and History*. Denver: Colorado Historical Society, 1997.

Rivera, José A. "Irrigation Communities of the Upper Río Grande Bioregion: Sustainable Resource Use in the Global Context." 36 *Natural Resources Journal* 4 (Fall 1996), 731–60.

Rodríguez, Sylvia. "Land, Water, and Ethnic Identity in Taos." In Charles L. Briggs and John R. Van Ness, eds., *Land, Water and Culture: New Perspectives on Hispanic Land Grants*. Albuquerque: University of New Mexico Press, 1987.

Simmons, Marc. "Settlement Patterns and Village Plans in Colonial New Mexico." 8 *Journal of the West* 1 (Jan. 1969), 7–21.

Simmons, Marc. "Spanish Irrigation Practices in New Mexico." 47 *New Mexico Historical Review* 2 (April 1972), 135–50.

Tyler, Daniel. "Dating the Caño Ditch: Detective Work in the Pojoaque Valley." 61 *New Mexico Historical Review* 1 (Jan. 1986), 15–25.

Tyler, Daniel. "The Spanish Colonial Legacy and the Role of Hispanic Custom in Defining New Mexico Land and Water Rights." 4 *Colonial Latin American Historical Review* 2 (Spring 1995), 149–65.

Van Ness, John R. "Hispanic Land Grants: Ecology and Subsistence in the Uplands of Northern New Mexico and Southern Colorado." In Charles L. Briggs and John R. Van Ness, eds., *Land, Water, and Culture: New Perspectives on Hispanic Land Grants*. Albuquerque: University of New Mexico Press, 1987

Index